A HANDBOOK OF THE ORDINARY DIALECT OF THE TAMIL LANGUAGE

A HANDBOOK OF THE ORDINARY DIALECT OF THE TAMIL LANGUAGE

BY THE

REV. G. U. POPE, M.A. D.D.

BALLIOL COLLEGE, OXFORD

'Difficulties will vanish as you learn on.'—Prov.

SEVENTH EDITION

GYAN

Published by

GYAN

Gyan Publishing House
5, Ansari Road
Daryaganj, New Delhi-110002
Phone: 011-47034999, 9811692060
E-mail: books@gyanbooks.com

Distribution Network
gyanbooks.com
India, USA, Canada, UK, Australia, France

ISBN : 978-81-212-4413-8 (PB)
First Published, 1911

2nd Impression 2020

Printed at: Gyan Press, Delhi.

A Handbook of the Ordinary Dialect of the Tamil Language
Author: G. U. Pope

A HANDBOOK OF THE
ORDINARY DIALECT OF
THE TAMIL LANGUAGE

BY THE

REV. G. U. POPE, M.A., D.D.

BALLIOL COLLEGE, OXFORD

கற்கக் கற்கக் கசடறும்

'Difficulties will vanish as you learn on.'—PROV.

SEVENTH EDITION

OXFORD UNIVERSITY PRESS

LONDON : HUMPHREY MILFORD

PREFACE TO THE FIRST EDITION

No apology is necessary for offering to the Tamil student a book which has long been wanted. In regard to the imperfections which detract from its value, the writer can only say, he has done what he could. He has tried to state the FACTS of this noble language succinctly and clearly. The examples, with few exceptions, have been selected from books in universal use in the Tamil country. Should a second edition be published, these examples will be considerably increased in number.

No work can remove from the elements of a language like Tamil all that may embarrass the learner. There are difficulties in it which must be met bravely; but there are, certainly, none which a very moderate degree of attention will not enable any one, however unpractised in such studies, to overcome.

The following hints may be of use to those who use this book:—

1. Do not proceed too quickly. An entirely new language requires great accuracy in the mastering of its elements.

2. Write down everything from the very beginning. Read always with pen, or pencil, in hand.

3. Read aloud all the exercises with a Tamil teacher; and be very careful in ascertaining the correctness of what you have written.

4. At first, whenever you meet with a new word, look for it in the Vocabulary, and decline or conjugate it in full.

5. Begin to talk—though with stammering lips—as soon as possible—the very first day. Never speak English to a native if you can help it. Why say 'salt,' when you can say 'உப்பு'? Do not be afraid of making mistakes.

6. Be very careful in noting down differences in idiom, between Tamil and your own language. If you hean much Christian or Cutcherry Tamil, beware of thinking all you near to be really Tamil. Try to cultivate a Tamil ear, so as to detect an unidiomatic expression as you would a false note in music. You should *understand* all you hear: you need not *use* any expression that is not *good Tamil.*

This little work has been written with a deep feeling of the vast importance of the acquisition by ALL who sojourn in the land, of the language of the people among whom they dwell. Two hours a day for a year will enable most people to converse freely on ordinary topics with those around them.

It is proposed in due time to publish a second part[1] in which the poetry of the language will be illustrated.

[1] See *Tamil Poetical Anthology* and *Third Grammar.*

The author would scarcely have ventured to publish, in this country, a book requiring such peculiar attention to accuracy in type and arrangement, had he not been zealously seconded by Mr. P. R. Hunt, the able superintendent of the American Mission Press, to whose efforts to improve Tamil typography all who use the language are indebted.

The earnest wish and prayer of the writer is that his efforts may tend, in however small a degree, to facilitate free intercourse between Hindūs and their brethren from the West, and so aid in the impartation to the former, of all that God has bestowed upon the latter.

TANJORE MISSION HOUSE,
October 5th, 1855.

PREFACE TO THE SEVENTH EDITION

THIS work, originally published in 1855, has been reprinted many times, and in various forms, during the half-century of its existence. The author has had the opportunity of consulting with very many who have used it both as teachers and as scholars. In October, 1885, the author was appointed University Teacher of Tamil and Telugu in Oxford, and as the *Handbook* is the text-book prescribed for the young civilians appointed to Madras, he has had peculiarly favourable opportunities of testing its usefulness and ascertaining its deficiencies. The result of nearly twenty years' teaching is embodied in this final edition. It is hoped that nothing of importance has been overlooked. The advice given in the Preface to the first edition is precisely what requires to be urged now upon every student of Tamil. Here, as elsewhere, *Festina lente*, is a good motto.

The author is under especial obligations to many kind friends who have rendered assistance in the preparation of this edition.

Especial thanks are due to the Secretary of State for India for assistance towards the publication.

Mr. Pembrey, as on former occasions, has with great patience and skill helped to issue what it is believed will prove to be, in regard to typography, one of the correctest works in a foreign character ever issued from the English Press.

G. U. POPE.

OXFORD,
January, 1904.

A TAMIL HANDBOOK

INTRODUCTION.

§ I. The Tamil Language in General.

1. The Tamil (தமிழ், Skt. *Draviḍa*) is the vernacular speech of about thirteen millions of people, inhabiting the great plain of the Carnatic. The limits within which it prevails are thus defined in the *Naṉṉūl* (a standard native grammar): 'The eastern boundary is the eastern sea (the Bay of Bengal), the southern boundary is Cape Comorin, the western boundary is the west sea, the northern boundary is Vengaḍam (or Tripety, a town about eighty miles north-west of Madras, nearly on the same parallel with Pulicat).' Here the western boundary from Comorin [குமரி] to Trivandrum [திருவனந்தபுரம்] is correctly stated, but from Trivandrum northward the Tamil country is confined to the eastern side of the Ghāts. The Tamil region thus includes a portion of South Travancore, the entire Zillahs of Tinevelly, Madura (including the dominions of the Tondiman Rāja), Trichinopoly, Coimbatore, a great part of Salem and of North Arcot, with the whole of South Arcot and Chingleput. North Ceylon also is a Tamil Colony. Tamil communities are to be found in most of the British cantonments in the Dekkan, and in various colonies of the Empire.

2. The principal languages cognate to Tamil are the Telugu, the Kanarese or Kannaḍī, and the Malayāḷam.

The Telugu is bounded on the north by the Uriya (beginning with the district of Ganjam), on the north-west by the Marāṭhī, on the south-west by the Kanarese, and on the south by the Tamil. It differs from the Tamil more widely than do the other cognate dialects.

The Kanarese is the language of the table-land of Mysore, of part of the Nizam's territory, and of a part of Kanara.

The Malayāḷam is spoken on the western side of the Malaya mountains from Mangalore to Trivandrum.

Minor cognate dialects are (1) the Tuluva, which is a dialect spoken in the neighbourhood of Mangalore, and is nearly allied to the Kanarese.

(2) The various dialects spoken by the rude inhabitants of the Nīlagiris, of which the Tuḍa is more allied to Tamil, and the Kōta [GŌHATA] to the Kanarese. The Burgher [BAḌAGA] is simply old Kanarese, much corrupted.

(3) The Gond and Ku, in Gondwāna and the adjoining hills. The rude languages of some other mountain tribes in Central and North-western India such as Brahūi possess more or less resemblance to Tamil in idiom and structure.

To this family of languages the epithet 'Drāviḍian' has been applied. This is hardly correct, as that term must include Marāṭhī. They have also been styled 'Tamilian,' from Tamil, their chief member.

3. The origin and affinities of the South Indian group of languages have been much discussed.

On the one hand, the more deeply they are studied the more close will their affinity to Sanskrit be seen to be, and the more evident will it appear that they possess a primitive and very near relationship to the languages of the Indo-European group.

Yet they are certainly not mere Prākrits, or corruptions of Sanskrit. Some have supposed that their place is among the members of the last-mentioned family, and that they are probably *disjecta membra* of a language coeval with Sanskrit, and having the same origin with it.

They certainly contain many traces of a close connexion with the Greek, the Gothic, the Persian, and other languages of the same family, in points even where Sanskrit presents no parallel.

On the other hand, Professor Rask, Mr. Norris, and more recently Dr. Caldwell, have striven to show that the original language of the nomadic tribes from whom the races of South India have sprung was probably what they term 'Scythian,' that is, a member of that group of tongues in which are included the 'Finnish, Turkish, Mongolian, and Tungūsian families.'

4. Grammars of the Tamil may be divided into two classes: those composed by native scholars, and those written by Europeans to facilitate the acquisition of the language by foreigners.

(1) In the first class it is only necessary to mention the following:—

(*a*) *Agastya's Sūtras.* It seems very doubtful whether the book which now goes under the name of பேர் அகத்தியம் is really an ancient composition. As a whole this work is not extant, but fragments of it have been published.

(*b*) *The Tolkāppiyam*, written by திரணதூமாக்கினி of the town of தொல்காப்பியக்குடி, south of Madura. This has been edited by S. V. Dāmōdaram Piḷḷai.

(*c*) The நன்னூல் (நல் = *good*, நூல் = *scientific treatise*), composed by Pavaṇanti of the town of சனகை. Of this very able work many editions have been published, and a copious commentary has been added by சங்கர நமச்சிவாயர் of Tinevelly. The whole of the *Naṉṉūl*, with a plain prose commentary, vocabulary, and summaries in English, has been published as the second part of my Third Grammar. I would recommend the learner, who may wish to carry his studies beyond the present work, to read over this Third Grammar, as introductory to the *Naṉṉūl*. I venture to hope he will find after mastering that work, that the writings of the Tamil Grammarians will present scarcely any difficulties.

(*d*) The தொன்னூல் (தொல் = *ancient*), compiled under the direction of the learned Jesuit, C. J. Beschius. This is a very comprehensive work; but its author imitates the native writers not in their excellencies only. It can hardly be considered an original work, though the chapters on Composition and Prosody are more so than the former part.

(2) (*a*) The earliest Grammars published by Europeans were those of the Rev. C. J. Beschius, of which there are two, one of the common dialect (கொடுந்தமிழ்) and the other of the poetical (செந்தமிழ்). They were written in Latin.

A translation of the common Tamil Grammar was published by Mr. Horst, and subsequently with corrections by the Rev. G. W. Mahon. It has been superseded in a great measure by later publications, yet is deserving of an attentive perusal by the Tamil student.

The 'Shen' Tamil Grammar was translated and published by Mr. Babington. This is a correct and scholarlike edition of a masterly work. An edition of the original was issued under the supervision of Dr. Burnell.

(*b*) The early Missionaries of Tranquebar published a Tamil Grammar, copies of which are in the British Museum [1].

(*c*) A Grammar was published in Europe by Mr. Anderson, of the Madras Civil Service. This is an able work, but its usefulness is lessened by its strict imitation of the native grammars.

(*d*) The next was by the Rev. C. T. E. Rhenius, of Palamcottah. This is a very clear and useful work, and was founded upon that of Beschius. It has gone through three editions, and though not a scientific grammar, is a plain, useful manual. The Syntax

[1] The following are two of these publications: (1) Ziegenbalg's *Grammatica Damulica*, Halae, 1716; (2) Walther's *Observationes Grammaticae*, &c., Trangambariae, 1739.

is deficient, and the examples were mostly made for the grammar, and not taken from standard Tamil authors.

(*e*) Dr. Graul, late director of the Leipzig Lutheran Mission, published a small manual, which, while it contains little new, is an elegant and scholarlike compendium.

(*f*) Since the publication of the first edition of this work a Comparative Grammar of the Drāviḍian Languages has been published by Dr. Caldwell, which throws great light upon every part of the subject.

5. The native Tamil literature, though inferior in extent to the Sanskrit, contains many works which will amply repay the careful student. The names of a few of these, in the order of their difficulty, I subjoin. I venture to mention the 'Poetical Anthology,' as containing the choicest bits of Tamil poetry, with the necessary apparatus. (See my *Nālaḍiyār*, pp. xxxvi–xlvii.)

(1) The writings of Auvai (Lesson 97).

When the student is able to read plain prose Tamil with ease he will find the little works of this far-famed poetess the best introduction to the study of the poetical Tamil. They consist of,

(*a*) The Ātti-çūḍi (ஆத்திசூடி),

(*b*) The Konṟai-vēynthan (கொன்றை வேய்ந்தன்), and

(*c*) The Mūthurai (மூதுரை).

The two former of these consist of Ethical and Miscellaneous Maxims, arranged in alphabetical order. The last work is not altogether a genuine production of the authoress; but the greater number of the verses are of considerable antiquity and of undeniable merit.

They have been published by the Rev. P. Percival, under the title of 'Minor Poets,' in a beautiful little volume.

(2) The Kurraḷ of Tiruvaḷḷuvar.

This unique work was intended by its author to be a compendium of all wisdom, and to stand in the place of the Vedas to the Tamil people[1].

(3) The Rāmāyaṇam of Kamban.

Nothing can exceed the sweetness and harmony of the versification of this real poet.

The first portion, or பாலகாண்டம் (the canto which relates to the youth of Rāma, the hero; Skt. BĀLA, *a youth*, KĀṆḌAM, *a chapter*), is deserving of careful study.

[1] See *The Sacred Kurraḷ of Tiruvaḷḷuva-Nāyanār*, with introduction, grammar, translation, &c. By the Rev. Dr. G. U. Pope, London, 1886, 8vo.

(4) The Nāladi-nānūru (நால், *four*, அடி, *line*, நானூறு, *four hundred* (§ 172) = the four hundred quatrains).

This work consists of forty chapters on the same subjects as the Kurraḷ. The Tamil is pure, and many of the verses are of singular beauty[1].

(5) The Naiṣadham, a poetical version, by King Aḍivīrarāma-pāṇḍiyan, of the History of Nala. Of this work it is proverbially said, 'The Naishadam is the nectar of poets.'

(6) The Jīvaga Çintāmaṇi, an Epic founded on the history of King Jīvagan. This is a difficult work, but without doubt the finest Tamil composition extant.

(7) The Tēmbāvaṇi (தேம்பா, *unfading*, அணி, *a garland*) of Beschius must not be omitted in this enumeration.

This work contains a kind of summary of the Bible, mingled with legends. It is a close imitation of the Çintāmaṇi, from which much of its poetical diction and most of its figures are borrowed. Some verses are brilliantly poetical.

There are many prose works in Tamil, which are translations or adaptations from the Sanskrit. All of these are, more or less, unsafe models of style, being full of foreign idioms and pedantic expressions. The following are much read, and will be useful to the discriminating student:—

(*a*) கதாமஞ்சரி (கதா, *fable*, மஞ்சரி, *cluster*).

(*b*) கதாசிந்தாமணி (Skt. chintāmaṇi, *a gem supposed to yield whatever its possessors wish for*).

(*c*) பஞ்சதந்திரக்கதை (பஞ்ச, *five*, தந்திரம், *method of acting*), translated from the Sanskrit.

6. There is a large and rapidly increasing translated literature in Tamil. These works had better be studied sparingly by the learner, until his progress in the language shall enable him to detect unidiomatic forms and expressions.

[1] See *The Nālaḍiyār*, with introduction, translation, and notes. By the Rev. Dr. G. U. Pope, Oxford, 1893, 8vo.

§ II. The Alphabet.

[The following pages are intended to assist the student who reads with a teacher. Throughout the work all matter included in brackets, or printed in small type, may be left by the learner to the second or third perusal.]

i. The Tamil primary letters (எழுத்து) are 30 in number: 12 vowels and 18 consonants.

☞ [The characters by which these are represented are evidently derived from the Grantham, which is itself derived from an ancient cave character, the earlier form of the Devanāgarī.]

ii. The vowels are—

1. *Short* (குறில்).	2. *Long* (நெடில்).	3. *Diphthongs.*
1. அ *a*	6. ஆ *ā* (ா added)	
2. இ *i*	7. ஈ or ஈ *ī*	
3. உ *u*	8. ஊ *ū*	
4. எ *e*	9. ஏ *ē*	11. ஐ *ai*
5. ஒ *o*	10. ஓ *ō*	12. ஔ *au*

[A vowel is called உயிர் எழுத்து = *life-letter.*]

To pronounce

அ, merely open the mouth, and produce an unmodified short *ă*. Example: *America.*

ஆ is the same sound lengthened. Example: *Father.*

இ is *i*, as in *pin.*

ஈ is the same lengthened, as in *machine.*

உ is to be pronounced nearly like *oo* in *cook*. The Italian *u.*

ஊ, like *u* in *rule*, or *oo* in *school.*

எ and ஏ, like the *e* and *a* in *enable*, respectively.

ஒ and ஓ, like *o* in *opinion* and in *opium*, respectively.

ஐ, as *ai* in *aisle*, and sometimes as *ai* in *maid* := *āi* or *ăi.*

ஔ, like *ow* in *fowl.*

☞ The vowels are remarkably pure and simple. The most careful attention is necessary in order to catch the sounds.

Much of importance in regard to Tamil vowels will be found in Pope's Grammar, 2–6.

They are sometimes used as Demonstratives (comp. Lesson 6) and sometimes as Interrogatives (comp. Lesson 13).

iii. The consonants are—

No.	*Class* (இனம்).		*Pronunciation.*	*Class.*	*Trans-literated by*
1	1	க்	As *k* and *g* in *king, gone*	Guttural	*k, g*
2		ங்	As *ng* in *long* . .	,,	*ṅ*
3	2	ச்	Pronounced as nearly as possible as a dental	Palatal	*ç*
4		ஞ்	The Spanish *ñ* . .	,,	*ñ*
5	3	ட்	When doubled ட்ட் = *ṭṭ*. The sharp sound of ட்	Lingual	*ḍ, ṭṭ*
6		ண்	. . . .	,,	*ṇ*
7	4	த்	(*d*, in Sanskrit derivatives only)	Dental	*t, th*
8		ந்	. . . .	,,	*n*
9	5	ப்	. . . .	Labial	*p, b*
10		ம்	. . . .	,,	*m*
11	6	ய்	. . . .	Palatal	*y*
12		ர்	Very soft—as nearly dental as possible		*r*
13		ல்			*l*
14		வ்	. . . .	Labial	*v*
15	7	ழ்	Something like the Welsh *ll*	Cerebral or Lingual	*ṛ*
16		ள்	. . . .		*ḷ*
17	8	ற்	When doubled ற்ற் = *ṯṯ* .	Palatal	*ṟ, ṯṯ*
18		ன்	The English sound .	,,	*ṉ*

[A consonant is called மெய் எழுத்து = *body-letter.*]

☞ [The more advanced student will find it useful to study the following arrangement of the consonants. (Comp. Pope's Grammar, 8, 9, 10.)]

Tamil grammarians divide the consonants into—

1. Strong, வல்லினம், வல்லெழுத்து [வல்=*strong*, இனம்=*class*], which includes க், ச், ட், த், ப், ற் [கசடதபற].

☞ These cannot end a word.

2. Weak, மெல்லினம், மெல்லெழுத்து [மெல்=*soft*], which includes ங், ஞ், ண், ந், ம், ன் [ஙஞணநமன]. These are *nasals*.

Here each letter is the corresponding nasal to the one above.

☞ Of these ஞ், ந், ம் only are initial. All except ங் may be final.

3. Middle, இடையினம், இடையெழுத்து [இடை=*middle*], which includes ய், ர், ல், வ், ழ், ள் [யரலவழள]. These are *semi-vowels*.

☞ [Of these ய் and வ் only are initial: all may be final.]

In euphonic combinations, whenever a nasal precedes a 'strong' letter, the former is always changed to the nasal of the same class as the latter.

(*a*) A circle or dot (புள்ளி), ° or ·, above a consonant makes it mute: க் *k*, ச் *ç*. Remove the dot and it is sounded with short *a*: க *ka*, ச *ça*. To indicate that a letter is not mute, a horizontal line is sometimes put over it: க̄, ச̄; but this is unnecessary, and is seldom used.

(*b*) Some of these letters when used to express a Sanskrit or other foreign word may vary in sound. For such cases no general rules can be laid down.

(*c*) க், த், ப் are pronounced *sharp* or *hard* (1) in the beginning of a word, (2) when they have the mute mark, and (3) when they are doubled; but *soft* or *flat* in all other cases. *These letters are therefore (surd or) hard at the beginning of a word, and when doubled; but (sonant or) soft when they occur singly, in the middle of a word.*

Examples—

1. கண் (*kaṇ*), eye.
   பக்கம் (*pakkam*), side.
2. தவம் (*tavam*), penance.
   தபம் (*tabam*), penance.
   [ப is pronounced like *b*, with a slight aspiration.]
   சத்தம் (*çattam*), sound.

மகன் (*magan̠*), a son (as in German *Tag*).

மதம் (*matham*), arrogance (as *th* in *this*).

பாதி (*pāthi*), half.

3. பணம் (*paṇam*), money.
அப்பம் (*appam*), rice-cake, bread.
[Cp. the Hebrew use of the Dagesh.]
என்பான் (*eṉbāṉ*), he will say.
பாம்பு (*pāmbu*), a snake.

(*d*) ச் = ç is not a sibilant, but a very soft palatal: e.g. மாசு (*māçu*), a blemish.

But (1) ச்ச = *çça* (ç being pronounced as *ch* in *church*): e.g. அச்சம் (*aççam*), fear.

(2) ச் after ட் or ற் = ç: e.g. ஆட்சி (*āḍçi*), possession; முயற்சி (*muyaṟçi*), effort.

(3) ச் after ஞ் = *j*: e.g. அஞ்சு (*añju*), fear thou; five.

(*e*) The first five classes in the table (iii) consist of a guttural (க்), a palatal (almost a dental) (ச்), a lingual (ட்), a dental (த்), and a labial (ப்). Each of these has its nasal (ங், ஞ், ண், ந், ம்), by which it is often accompanied: அங்கே, *there*; பஞ்சு, *cotton*; கண்டான், *he saw*; இந்த, *this*; அம்பு, *an arrow*.

(*f*) There are three *r* sounds: ர், ற், ழ்.

ர் (as nearly a dental as may be): Bring the tip of the tongue to the insertion of the upper teeth, and pronounce a gentle *r* [மரம், *a tree*; மலர், *a flower*].

ற் (palatal): Apply the tip of the tongue to the ridge of the palate, and pronounce a rough, vibrating *r* [மறம், *vice*; பாறை, *a crag*].

ழ் (cerebral): Apply the tip of the tongue, as far back as you can, to the palate, and pronounce a rough *rrr*, in which a *z* sound will mingle: மழை, *rain*. In the South, unable to articulate this letter, they use a strong *ḷ* (ள்) instead. In the North in the same way they use ய் for ழ். (Comp. § 123.)

☞ These are never initial. The ர் and ழ் are never doubled.

(*g*) There are three *n* sounds: ந், ன், ண்.

ந் (dental): Bring the tip of the tongue to the lower edge of the upper teeth, and pronounce a soft *n* [நகம், *nail*; வந்தான், *he came*].

ன் (palatal): Apply the tip of the tongue to the ridge of the palate, and pronounce a distinct *n* (மனம், *mind*; பலன், *fruit*].

ண் (lingual): Turn the tip of the tongue as far back as you can, and pronounce a strong *n* [மணம், *perfume*; அரண், *beauty, defence*].

☞ ந் is seldom (or never) final; ன் and ண் never initial.

(*h*) There are three *t* sounds: த், ற்ற், ட்ட்.

த் (dental): Tongue to the lower edge of the upper teeth [தான், *self*; முத்தம், *pearl*].

ற்ற் (palatal): Tongue to the ridge of the palate [முற்றம், *courtyard*].

This use of ற்ற் to represent a palatal *ṯ* is an orthographical device. There is no Tamil sign for a palatal *ṯ*, so a double ற் is used. [In transliteration a line drawn under is the sign of a palatal, when needful.]

ட்ட் (cerebral): Tongue curled round as far back as possible [மூட்டம், *a covered fire*]. This use of ட்ட் is also a mere orthographical device.

☞ த் is never final.

[த் single, in the middle of a word, is sounded like *th* in *this*, not like *th* in *thin*, and not like *d*: which is a very common mistake.]

(*i*) There are two *l* sounds: ல், ள்.

ல் (palatal): Tongue to the ridge of the palate, and pronounce a soft *l* [கல், *a stone*].

ள் (cerebral): Tongue curled round as far back as possible [கள், *toddy*].

☞ These are never properly initial.

(*j*) ன்ற் is pronounced *ndr*, i.e. a *d* sound is introduced for the sake of euphony. என்றான் (*eṉḏṟāṉ*), he said.

iv. When a vowel follows a consonant it is attached to that consonant, and forms with it what is called a *Vowel-consonant* [உயிர்மெய்=a living body].

(*a*) Remove the sign (° or ˙) and அ is inherent in the consonant, க *ka*, ச *ça*, த *ta*, &c. (As in Hebrew, Sanskrit, &c.)

(*b*) ஆ, when it follows a consonant, is changed into ா or ூ (அ+ூ=ஆ).

(These two forms are the same really. The intermediate form is found in Malayāḷam, &c.) கா *kā*, சா *çā*, தா *tā*, &c. The latter form is only used in these three cases:—

ண்+ஆ=ணா. ன்+ஆ=னா. ற்+ஆ=றா.

(*c*) When இ is added to a consonant, only the ി is joined to the upper part of the consonant.

க்+இ=கி. ச்+இ=சி. ட்+இ=டி.

VOWEL-CONSONANTS.

—	அ a	ஆ ā	இ i	ஈ ī	உ u	ஊ ū	எ e	ஏ ē	ஐ ai	ஒ o	ஓ ō	ஔ au
க் k	க ka	கா kā	கி ki	கீ kī	கு ku	கூ kū	கெ ke	கே kē	கை kai	கொ ko	கோ kō	கௌ kau
ங் ṅ	ங ṅa	ஙா ṅā	ஙி ṅi	ஙீ ṅī	ஙு ṅu	ஙூ ṅū	ஙெ ṅe	ஙே ṅē	ஙை ṅai	ஙொ ṅo	ஙோ ṅō	ஙௌ ṅau
ச் ç	ச ça	சா çā	சி çi	சீ çī	சு çu	சூ çū	செ çe	சே çē	சை çai	சொ ço	சோ çō	சௌ çau
ஞ் ñ	ஞ ña	ஞா ñā	ஞி ñi	ஞீ ñī	ஞு ñu	ஞூ ñū	ஞெ ñe	ஞே ñē	ஞை ñai	ஞொ ño	ஞோ ñō	ஞௌ ñau
ட் ḍ	ட ḍa	டா ḍā	டி ḍi	டீ ḍī	டு ḍu	டூ ḍū	டெ ḍe	டே ḍē	டை ḍai	டொ ḍo	டோ ḍō	டௌ ḍau
ண் ṇ	ண ṇa	ணா ṇā	ணி ṇi	ணீ ṇī	ணு ṇu	ணூ ṇū	ணெ ṇe	ணே ṇē	ணை ṇai	ணொ ṇo	ணோ ṇō	ணௌ ṇau
த் t	த ta	தா tā	தி ti	தீ tī	து tu	தூ tū	தெ te	தே tē	தை tai	தொ to	தோ tō	தௌ tau
ந் n	ந na	நா nā	நி ni	நீ nī	நு nu	நூ nū	நெ ne	நே nē	நை nai	நொ no	நோ nō	நௌ nau
ப் p	ப pa	பா pā	பி pi	பீ pī	பு pu	பூ pū	பெ pe	பே pē	பை pai	பொ po	போ pō	பௌ pau
ம் m	ம ma	மா mā	மி mi	மீ mī	மு mu	மூ mū	மெ me	மே mē	மை mai	மொ mo	மோ mō	மௌ mau
ய் y	ய ya	யா yā	யி yi	யீ yī	யு yu	யூ yū	யெ ye	யே yē	யை yai	யொ yo	யோ yō	யௌ yau
ர் r	ர ra	ரா rā	ரி ri	ரீ rī	ரு ru	ரூ rū	ரெ re	ரே rē	ரை rai	ரொ ro	ரோ rō	ரௌ rau
ல் l	ல la	லா lā	லி li	லீ lī	லு lu	லூ lū	லெ le	லே lē	லை lai	லொ lo	லோ lō	லௌ lau
வ் v	வ va	வா vā	வி vi	வீ vī	வு vu	வூ vū	வெ ve	வே vē	வை vai	வொ vo	வோ vō	வௌ vau
ழ் ṛ	ழ ṛa	ழா ṛā	ழி ṛi	ழீ ṛī	ழு ṛu	ழூ ṛū	ழெ ṛe	ழே ṛē	ழை ṛai	ழொ ṛo	ழோ ṛō	ழௌ ṛau
ள் ḷ	ள ḷa	ளா ḷā	ளி ḷi	ளீ ḷī	ளு ḷu	ளூ ḷū	ளெ ḷe	ளே ḷē	ளை ḷai	ளொ ḷo	ளோ ḷō	ளௌ ḷau
ற் ṟ	ற ṟa	றா ṟā	றி ṟi	றீ ṟī	று ṟu	றூ ṟū	றெ ṟe	றே ṟē	றை ṟai	றொ ṟo	றோ ṟō	றௌ ṟau
ன் ṉ	ன ṉa	னா ṉā	னி ṉi	னீ ṉī	னு ṉu	னூ ṉū	னெ ṉe	னே ṉē	னை ṉai	னொ ṉo	னோ ṉō	னௌ ṉau

[To face p. 11.

(*d*) உ is changed into ு joined to the under part of the consonant, or / singly added, or with a loop ூ.

க்+உ=கு. ச்+உ=சு. ட்+உ=டு. ண்+உ=ணு. ம்+உ=மு, &c.

(*e*) ஊ is the preceding, with an additional stroke or loop to denote length.

க்+ஊ=கூ (irregular). ச்+ஊ=சூ. ட்+ஊ=டூ. ண்+ஊ=ணூ, &c.

(*f*) எ and ஏ are changed into ெ and ே respectively, and prefixed to the consonant.

[They were formerly joined; thus, க்+எ=கெ, and there was no difference in form between the long and the short. The same may be said of ஒ and ஓ.]

க்+எ=கெ. க்+ஏ=கே.

(*g*) ஐ becomes ை and precedes the consonant.

[This also was formerly joined; thus, ழ்+ஐ=ழை.]

க்+ஐ=கை, *a hand*. To all those letters which begin with a loop it is still joined; thus, ணை, &c.

(*h*) ஒ, ஓ become ெ-ா and ே-ா respectively, the consonant standing between.

க்+ஒ=கொ } (In old alphabets கொ is [old form] and கோ is [old form].
க்+ஓ=கோ } Compare the English *k*.)

(*i*) ஔ become ெ-ள:

க்+ஔ=கௌ. (These combinations are rarely used.)

(*j*) The number of these vowel-consonants is 18×12=216. These are shown in the table of vowel-consonants.

(*k*) In pronouncing the letters in Tamil schools they lengthen a short vowel and add *na*; thus,

க is pronounced *kā-na*, கி *kī-na*.

To a long vowel they add *vena* or *yena*; *v* or *y* being inserted for euphony.

கா is pronounced *kā-vena*, கை *kai-yena*, &c.

☞ The sooner this is got rid of the better. Children should be taught to pronounce *ka*, *kā*, &c.

(*l*) But கரம் is sometimes added to a short letter, and காரம் to a long one.

அ is then *a-garam*, ஆ *ā-gāram*, க *ka-garam*, கா *kā-gāram*, &c.

[Here the letter க is transliterated *g*, being no longer initial; comp. iii. *c*, p. 8.]

v. (*a*) If the consonants are properly pronounced, the vowels preceding some of them will be *necessarily modified*, in a manner analogous to the German 'umlaut.'

Examples.

அவன், he, *aven* (not *avan*). அவர், he (politely), *aver* (not *avar*).
வீடு, house (*viidu*). பெண், female (*pöṇ*).

இடம், *a place.*	பிறன், *a neighbour.*	வேளை, *an opportunity.*
தேள், *a scorpion.*	செயல், *a doing.*	வேறு, *another.*
கீழ், *under.*	பேறு, *an acquisition.*	விடு, *leave.*

☞ The learner must take care to vary the sound of the vowel only just so much as is necessary to the proper pronunciation of the following consonant.

[அ before the final ன், ண், ர், ழ், ல், or ள் of all but monosyllables takes very nearly the sound of எ. In the words இரண்டு, *two*, and இரத்தினம், *a gem*, the அ of the vowel-consonant ர is pronounced very short, and vulgarly as எ. So also in Sanskrit words, as கந்தகம், *sulphur.*]

(*b*) Initial இ, ஈ, எ, ஏ (chiefly when followed by a cerebral or palatal) are often pronounced as if preceded by ய் (as the English initial *u* is often sounded *yu*, as in *union*).

எல்லாம், *all.*	எது, *which.*	ஏனம், *a vessel, dish.*
ஈடு, *an equivalent.*	இனம், *kindred.*	எவன், *which man?*

☞ This *y* sound is sometimes written, both in Tamil and in its kindred dialects.

(*c*) ஐ seldom has its full sound, except in the first syllable of a word. In other cases it is often sounded *ēy*, only differing from ஏ in the slight *y* sound in which it ends.

AISLE and MAID give the two sounds very nearly.

Compare from your teacher's lips the different sounds of—

கை, *a hand*, and பருக்கை, *a pebble.*
பை, *a bag*, and அவனை, *him.*
மை, *ink*, and சபை, *a congregation.*
வை, *put!* and மேசை, *a table.*
} (Here it is எ + இ.)

In the middle of a word it is often sounded almost like அ: அனைவரும், *all.* The rule given in the *Naṉṉūl* (95) is, that ஐ *has its full quantity only when it is used to express its own name.*

[In Telugu and Malayāḷam *a* is often used where Tamil uses ஐ; and எ answers to it often in Kanarese. Thus: Tel. VELA=

விலை, *price.* Mal. AVA=அவை, *those things.* Kan. HALAGE=பலகை, *a board.*]

(*d*) உ final is always pronounced very slightly, and by the common people is often turned into இ. It is almost always added to facilitate the enunciation of the final consonant. (G. 15.)

[The Telugu and Kanarese also use உ in a similar manner.]

மாடு, an animal of the genus Bos=almost to மாட். படிக்கு, *in order to,* is often pronounced படிக்கி. Initial உ is sometimes pronounced vulgarly as ஒ: thus உன், *thy,* becomes ஒன். உடனே=ஒடனே, *immediately.*

(*e*) ஔ is often written அவ் or அவு. Thus மௌனம், *silence,* is written மவுனம். This letter *does not really belong to the language,* and was introduced, apparently, under Sanskrit influences.

ஔவை, *a certain poetess.* (p. 4)=அவ்வை.

(*f*) Commonly, ஆ and ஓ before க் are pronounced as if followed by ய்:—

ஆக்கி, *having made,* becomes ஆய்க்கி.
நோக்கி, *having looked at,* is pronounced as if written நோய்க்கி.
பாக்கியம், *bliss,* becomes பாய்க்கியம்.

vi. A letter called *āytham* (G. 12), and written thus, ஃ or (= the Greek χ), is used in poetry only. It may be an imitation of the Sanskrit visarga.

vii. From the old Grantham alphabet[1] are borrowed the following letters, to assist in the expression of foreign words:—

ஷ SH	ஸ S	ஹ H
(Cerebral; generally ட்)	the English *s*	(generally க்)
ஜ *j*	க்ஷ *ksh*	ஂ *m*
(generally ச் or ய்)	(ட்ச்)	(sometimes in the end of a word in MSS.)

With these the vowels may be joined.

முனிஷி, *a teacher.* ஸ்திரீ, *a woman.* ஹானி, *loss.*
நஷ்டம், நட்டம், } *loss.* கஜம், கசம், } *an elephant.* மோட்சம், மோக்ஷம், } *heaven.*
ஜாதி=சாதி [Skt. jāti], *race.*

The question of the strict scientific expression of Sanskrit words in Tamil characters is discussed in an especial section of the *Nannūl* [வடமொழியாக்கம்], 146, 7. It is much to be desired that these rules should be strictly obeyed wherever possible; and the analogy of these rules should be followed in the introduction into Tamil of other foreign words. Much of the Tamil in popular use wears a very barbarous appearance through their neglect.

[1] See Bühler's *Indische Palaeographie*, pp. 68 et seq.

viii. The following abbreviations and signs are in use :—

நன்செய்	புன்செய்	வேலி	நாளது
wet cultivation	*dry cultivation*	*a land measure*	*current*
ந	பு	லி	ந
மாசம்	தேதி	வருஷம்	நிலம்
month	*day*	*year*	*ground*
௴	௳	௵ or ௵	நீ
நிலுவை	பற்று	வரவு	வசம்
balance	*received*	*receipts*	*charge*
நீ	பு	வ	வு
மேற்படி	பணம்	காசு	வராகன்
aforesaid	*money*	*cash*	*a pagoda*
௸	பு	கா	வ
ரூபாய்	பொன்	கஜம்	வரைக்கும்
rupee	10 *fanams*	*a yard*	*until*
௹ or ரூ	பொ	க	வ or ரு
குழி	ஆக	அணா	பைசா
a square yard	*total*	*an anna*	*a pie*
கு	ஆ	அ	டபை
வகையறா	சில்வானம்	நெல்லு	கலம்
belonging to	*more or less*	*paddy*	*a measure*
வ	சி	நெ	க

சிரஞ்சீவி	இராச இராசஸ்திரி	வும்	யும்
a polite title for a junior	*most honourable, a title*	வு	யு
சி	ஸ்ரீ—ஸ்ரீ		
	(for *rāja-çrī*)		

ix. The following lists, given for the sake of practice, contain none but useful, ordinary words. It will be well to commit them to memory. The pronunciation must be practised with a competent teacher. The notes may be useful to the student hereafter.

(1) Words containing க.

நகம், *a finger-nail.*	நுகம், *a yoke.*	கூடு, *a cage.*
நாகம், *a large snake.*	கிணறு, *a well.*	காடு, *a jungle.*
கொலை, *murder.*	லோகம், *the world.*	கேடு, *loss.*
கோல், *a stick.*	லோகம், } *a metal,*	கீறல், *a scratch.*
கோலம், *pomp.*	லோஹம், } [lōham.]	சிக்கு, *an entanglement.*
குளம், *a tank.*	கூளம், *chaff, stalks, &c.*	கிறிஸ்து, *Christ.*

a. க represents the Sanskrit *k*, *kh*, *g*, *gh* and *h*, and is consequently *surd* or *sonant* according to its position. The Greek γ, κ, χ.

b. க is often doubled, but only when it follows a vowel. It is never transmuted or elided.

c. The use of க for the Sanskrit *h* arises from the fact that *the Tamil possesses no aspirate whatsoever.*

d. The sound of க in the middle of words is very soft, like the final *g* in some German words.

(2) Words with ங.

தங்கம், *pure gold.*	தேங்காய், *a cocoanut.*	பங்கு, *a share.*
சங்கம், *an assembly.*	எங்கே, *where?*	கங்கை, *the Ganges.*
பொங்கு, *boil up.*	சிங்கம், *a lion.*	காங்கை, *heat.*

a. ங never occurs at the beginning or end of a word.

b. ம் followed by க becomes ங். (Comp. iii. *e*, p. 9.)

(3) Words containing ண், ன் or ந்.

ஆண், *a male.*	ஆந்தை, *an owl.*	அண்டம், *a world.*
அணி, *an ornament.*	ஏணி, *a ladder.*	அந்தம், *an end.*
ஆணி, *a nail.*	ஏன், *why.*	அன்னம், *food, boiled rice.*
அணை, *a dam.*	பிணி, *disease.*	பண்ணு, *make.*
பானை, *a pot.*	ஏந்து, *lift in the arms.*	மனம், மநம், *mind.*
ஆணை, *an oath.*	சிந்து, *spill.*	அந்த, *that.*
ஆநந்தம், ஆனந்தம், *bliss.*	பூனை, *cat.*	அண்டை, *near.*
அணு, *an atom.*		இன்று, *to-day.*

a. ன and ண are never found at the beginning of a word.

b. ந is not found at the end of a word, and only of a syllable when followed by த.

c. ந and ன are interchanged occasionally. In poetry ந after ன often disappears.

d. ம before த becomes ந. (Comp. iii. *e*, p. 9.)

e. ன is sometimes changed into ற் before a hard letter. (ல் suffers the same change.)

f. ண sometimes becomes ட் before a hard letter.

(4) Words with ஞ.

ஞாபகம், *memory, memorial.*	அஞ்சு (vulg.), *five.*	பஞ்சு, *cotton.*
ஞானம், *wisdom.*	கஞ்சி, *rice-water.*	மஞ்சள், *saffron.*
ஞாயிறு, *the sun, Sunday.*	வஞ்சனை, *deceit.*	நஞ்சு, *poison.*

a. ஞ is never found at the end of a word.

b. It is, in high Tamil, used for ந, and *vice versa.*

c. When ம comes before ச it may be changed into ஞ. (Comp. iii. *e*, p. 9.)

d. In common Tamil ந்து are often changed into ஞ்சு. For காய்ந்தது, *it has grown hot*, is used காய்ஞ்சது.

(5) Words with ட்ட், த்த், ற்ற்.

கூற்றம், *death.*
கூட்டம், *an assembly.*
கூத்து, *a dance.*
மட்டு, *limit.*
மாட்டு, *hook it!*
மற்று, *other.*
மாற்று, *change it!*
மாத்திரம், *only.*

குற்றத்தை, *a fault* (obj. case).
கூட்டத்தை, *an assembly* (obj. case).
அற்ற, *less.*
குற்றம் அற்ற, *faultless.*
புத்தகம், } *a book.*
புஸ்தகம், }

காத்தான், *he preserved.*
கற்று, *having learned.*
காற்று, *wind.*
கட்டு, *tie!*
காட்டு, *show!*
சிஷ்டிகர், } *a creator.*
சிட்டிகர், }

a. ட்ட is often written for ஷ்ட in Sanskrit words.

b. த்த is often written for ஸ்த in Sanskrit words.

c. த்த or ற்ற is interchangeable with ச்ச.

(6) Words with த், ட் (*t* and *ḍ*) [*th* flat as in the English *there*, never sharp as in *thin*. *Not* d, *unless in Sanskrit words!*].

தேவன், *a god* (Sanskrit *d*).
தேன், *honey.*
பாதம், *a foot.*
பாடம், *a lesson.*
நாதம், *sound.*

காது, *an ear.*
காடு, *a jungle.*
காற்று, *wind.*
வாதி, *complainant.*
மாடு, *an animal of the genus Bos.*

மாது, *a woman.*
மாட்டேன், *I cannot.*
பாதை, *a path.*
நாடான், *a landowner.*
நாற்றம், *a stench.*

a. த் becomes ட் occasionally when it follows a cerebral.

b. It becomes ற் sometimes after a palatal.

c. த் represents Sanskrit *t, th, d, dh.*

d. ட் represents Sanskrit *ṭ, ṭh, ḍ, ḍh.*

(7) Words with ச், ச்ச்.

சாதி, *species* (*s* or *j*).
செபம், *prayer* (*s* or *j*).
சனம், *people* (*s* or *j*).
சோதி, *light* (*s* or *j*).
யோசனை, *counsel.*
கூச்சம், *shame.*

யோஜனை, } *about* 13 *miles.*
யோசனை, }
மாசம், } *a month.*
மாதம், }
முயற்சி, *effort.*
காட்சி, *sight, vision.*

சாட்சி, *witness.*
மனசு, } *the mind.*
மனது, }
இராசன், } *a king.*
இராயன், }

a. ச் represents the Sanskrit *c, ch, j, jh, ç, ṣ.*

b. The Sanskrit *s* is sometimes represented by த் and ய்.

c. The Tamil possesses no pure sibilants; but in common use ச்=ç. The vulgar constantly pronounce செய் *chey.*

d. ச் and ய் are often interchanged; thus உயிர், *life*, is often pronounced உசுரு.

(8) Words with ப், வ், ம்.

இன்பம், *pleasure.*	பானை, *a pot.*	வானம், } *heaven*
துன்பம், *affliction.*	வீணை, *a lute.*	மானம், } (vulg.).
பாவம், } *sin.*	அற்புதம், *a miracle.*	வழி, *a way.*
பாபம், }	பூமி, *the earth.*	பழி, *vengeance.*
தவசு, } *penance.*		மழை, *rain.*
தபசு, }		

a. In Sanskrit words ப் and வ் are often interchanged.

b. In vulgar talk ம் is often used for வ்.

c. க் is sometimes written for வ்.

d. In Kanarese *h* is often used for ப்.

e. ப is sometimes used for the Skt. *bh* [பூமி = BHŪMI].

(9) Words with ர், ற், ழ்.

மரம், *a tree.*	மறி, *a foal.*	பழம், } *fruit.*
மறம், *violence, sin.*	கழி, *a stick.*	பலம், }
மழலை, *childish prattle.*	சரி, *right.*	கோழி, *a fowl.*

a. ழ் is pronounced like ள் in Tinevelly, and like ய் in Madras.

b. ர் and ற் are often confounded by the common people.

c. ற் at the end of the former member of a compound is always a transmutation of ல் or ள் (p. 22).

(10) Words with ல் or ள்.

கல்(லு), *a stone.*	பல்(லு), *a tooth.*	புள்ளி, *a cipher or dot.*
கள்(ளு), *toddy.*	நெல் (நெல்லு), *unhusked rice.*	புளி, *tamarind.*
கொல்(லு), *kill!*	பள்ளம், *a hollow.*	புலி, *a tiger.*
கொள்(ளு), *buy, take.*	புல்(லு), *grass.*	எலி, *a rat.*
சொல்(லு), *say.*	பிள்ளை, *a child.*	
செலவு, *expenditure.*		

a. ல் and ள் are changed into ன் and ண் sometimes before ம் (p. 22); *b.* and into ற் and ட் before a hard letter.

(11) Words with ய்.

யானை, ஆனை, } *an elephant.*	ஆயி, ஆய், } *having become.*	ஐயா! } *sir!*
இயானை, }	ஆகி, }	அய்யா! }
மாயம், *deceit.*	நாய், *a dog.*	நியாயம், *equity.*

a. When a word begins with ய், இ may be put before it.

b. When a word ends in யி, இ may be omitted, or யி changed to கி.

c. அய் is sometimes written for ஐ.

(12) Sanskrit words in Tamil.

சூக்ஷமம், }	பட்சி, }	சந்தோஷம், *joy.*
சூட்சமம், } *subtility,*	பக்ஷி, } *a bird.*	சந்தோஷித்தாள், *she rejoiced.*
சூட்டுமம், } *refinement.*	பக்கி, }	
சூக்குமம், }		

பக்ஷம், பட்சம், பக்கம்,	*a side.*	இராஜா, இராசா, அரசன், இராயன், இராசன்,	all forms of Skt. rājan, *a king.*
நிஜம், நிசம்,	*certainty.*	லோகம், உலோகம், உலகம், உலகு,	forms of Skt. lōka, *world.*
லாபம், இலாபம்,	*profit.*		
மவுனம், மௌனம்,	*silence.*		

a. When a word begins with *r*, *l*, or *y* in Sanskrit, it will in Tamil generally take இ, உ, அ before the initial consonant; since those letters cannot begin a word, according to strict Tamil rules.

b. *au* of the Sanskrit may be expressed by ஔ or அவ்; the latter being the real Tamil method.

x. The following are a few of the double letters used in MSS. :—

க, கி, கு, கே, கை, த, தி, ட.
க்க, க்கி, க்கு, க்கே, க்கை, த்த, த்தி, ட்ட.

xi. The following hints regarding pronunciation may be of use:—

1. As a general rule it may be stated that *Tamil scarcely admits of accent upon individual syllables.* Sometimes particles added to a word are emphasized; but, it is safe to *aim at pronouncing all syllables alike,* with due regard to quantity. The root syllable will, however, be distinguished by something akin to accent.

2. In reading be very careful to avoid the English emphasis and tone. An *even, distinct* articulation is all that is required.

3. Tamil should be read rather faster than English.

4. Be very careful in pronouncing all double letters. புளி is *tamarind*, but புள்ளி is *a dot!*

5. It need scarcely be said that the pupil must use very great pains in accustoming himself to pronounce each consonant accurately by stopping it at the right place—lips, palate, throat, or base of the brain. Unless this be done, the Tamil letter is not produced, but merely something analogous to it. This will require at first some exaggeration, but will tone

down in a little while. The consonants are very seldom the English consonants!

6. If each consonant be stopped at its proper place, this will occasion, by a mechanical necessity, a certain modification (or *umlaut*) of the vowel preceding. This must only be allowed as far as is *mechanically* necessary. When the consonant is right, the preceding vowel will come right naturally.

7. NO SYLLABLE AFTER THE FIRST CAN IN TAMIL BEGIN WITH A VOWEL. This is of exceeding importance. It follows that when to a short syllable another beginning with a vowel is added, a consonant will often have to be doubled. Thus கல் becomes கல்லை, and this doubled consonant must be sounded with the second syllable, or the meaning is lost. This is at the root of the whole system of doubling consonants.

8. There are in Tamil four kinds of syllables:—

(1) Short open: க.
(2) Short closed: கல்.
(3) Long open: கா.
(4) Long closed: கால்.

It is easy to divide the syllables, and so pronounce correctly, if the learner keep in mind the rule: ALL BUT INITIAL SYLLABLES BEGIN WITH A CONSONANT.

9. In reading Tamil it is to be remembered that many English stops and pauses are out of place. The genius of the Tamil language requires that there should be a short pause after the principal members in every sentence; but that all words which are adjuncts, enlargements, adjectival appendages, or adverbial extensions, should be read *with the words to which they belong*, without any intervening pause. The complete enlarged noun, with all its enlargements, forms a single compound word, to be pronounced flowingly without any break. Pauses may be made where you pass from subject to predicate, and in general where there is the introduction of a new idea. This requires a good deal of practice. The Englishman generally introduces far too many pauses.

xii. Synopsis of the combinations and changes of letters.

[Compare and study well the table of vowel-consonants; also G. 19–42, for a complete view of the subject.]

It may be useful to the student to have before him the principal changes of letters in Tamil composition, though these rules are not strictly observed in all cases. It is desirable to write, as far as possible, as well-educated people speak, not using unnecessary changes; but retaining those which are euphonic and natural.

All that is essential is included under the following six heads:—

I. *Combination without Change:* இயல்புப் புணர்ச்சி.

The final consonant of a word often combines simply with the initial vowel of the following.

நிலம் + இருக்கிறது = நிலமிருக்கிறது, *there is ground.*

☞ It is in general better, however, to separate the words.

When words combine there may be changes: விகாரப் புணர்ச்சி. These are three: Insertion, Transmutation, Omission.

II. *Insertion of Letters:* தோன்றல்.

[This is called தோன்றல் = *appearing*, since a new letter appears.]

Fundamental principles:—

a. TWO VOWELS CANNOT COME TOGETHER.

b. க், ச், த், ப் ARE DOUBLED AFTER A VOWEL, WHEN THE LATTER WORD GOVERNS THE FORMER; BUT NOT WHEN THE PRECEDING WORD SIMPLY QUALIFIES THE LATTER, OR WHEN THERE IS AN ELLIPSIS.

Rules.

(1) The final consonant of a monosyllable whose vowel is short, is doubled before a vowel in the beginning of the following word (p. 19).

மண் + அரிது = மண்ணரிது, *the earth is rare.*

பொன் + அருமை = பொன்னருமை, *the preciousness of gold.*

(2) When a vowel at the end of a word meets a vowel in the beginning of a following word, ய் or வ் is inserted, to avoid the hiatus. (§ 18.)

[The same letters are used in all the cognate languages. Telugu also uses *n*.]

a. இ, ஈ, and ஐ take ய் (as most homogeneous).

b. ஏ takes either ய் or வ்.

c. The other vowels take வ் only.

இனி + உண்டு = இனியுண்டு, *there is yet.*
தீ + எரியும் = தீயெரியும், *the fire will burn.*
கை + ஐ = கையை, *a hand* (obj.).
இது + ஏ = இதுவே, *that indeed.*
அரசனே + அவன் = அரசனேயவன், *he is indeed a king.*

(3) When அ, இ, உ or எ, demonstrative or interrogative, are prefixed to words, the following consonant is doubled.

அ + மனிதன் = அம்மனிதன், *that man.*
இ + வீடு = இவ்வீடு, *this house.*
எ + வகை = எவ்வகை, *what way?*

(4) After a vowel, initial க், ச், த், ப் are doubled, the sonant being thus changed into a surd.

மற்ற + காரியம் = மற்றக் காரியம், *the other affair.*
இந்த + சத்தம் = இந்தச் சத்தம், *this sound.*

To this there are regular classes of exceptions.

a. அவனு கொடுத்தான், *did he give?* (after an interrogative or emphatic particle or letter.)

b. அண்ணு கொடும், *O elder brother, give!* (after a vocative case.)

c. செய்தை தம்பி, *thou didst, O younger brother!* (after a finite verb.)

d. ஓடின குதிரை, *a horse that ran* (after a relative participle).

e. ஆடு கால், *the post of a picota* (after a verbal root used as an adj.).

f. அது பெரிது, *that is great* (after a pronoun).

g. அவனோடு போ, *go with him* }
எனது தலை, *my head* } (after a case of a noun).

☞ There are many anomalies here, especially when one (or both) of the words is Sanskrit. In general, whenever the latter in any way governs the former, and there is no ellipsis, the க், ச், த், ப் must be doubled, thus throwing the force of the compound on the governing word.

(5) After ய், ர், ழ் a following க், ச், த் or ப் will, for the most part, be doubled.

பொய் + செல்வம் = பொய்ச் செல்வம், *false prosperity.*
நீர் + குமிழி = நீர்க்குமிழி, *a bubble on the water.*

(6) ஞ், ம், ந் are often doubled after ய் or ஐ at the end of monosyllables.

மெய் + ஞானம் = மெய்ஞ்ஞானம், *true wisdom.*

III. *Transmutation of Letters.*

[This is called திரிதல் = *turning*.]

Fundamental principle :—

CONSONANTS WHICH MEET MUST BE OF THE SAME CLASS AND ORGAN. This is assimilation.

Rules.

(1) Final ம் is changed into ங் before க்.

எம் + கள் = எங்கள் (§ 37), *our.*

Final ம் is changed into ஞ் before ச்.

பாவம் + செய்தேன் = பாவஞ்செய்தேன், *I have sinned.*

Final ம் is changed into ந் before த்.

பணம் + தந்தான் = பணந்தந்தான், *he gave money.*

That is, ம் is changed into the nasal of the class to which the following consonant belongs (pp. 8, 9).

(2) ண் and ள் before க், ச், த், and ப் are often changed into ட்.

உள் + பிரவேசித்தான் = உட்பிரவேசித்தான், *he entered in.*

நாள் + தோறும் = நாடோறும், *every day.*

[Here the த் of the following word is lost.]

(3) ன் and ல் before க், ச், த், and ப் are often changed into ற்.

பொன் + சாடி = பொற்சாடி, *a golden vessel.*

பொன் + தகடு = பொற்றகடு, *a golden plate.*

[Here த் is also changed.]

கல் + கூடம் = கற்கூடம், *a stone building.*

கடல் + திரை = கடற்றிரை, *a wave of the sea.*

[Here the த் is also changed into ற்.]

In high Tamil a letter called *āytham* and written ஃ is also found here. It is equivalent to the Greek χ, and is used for ற் in certain transmutations. Thus we often meet with அஃது for அது. [G. 12.]

(4) ல் and ள் before ந் are changed into ன் and ண் respectively, and ந் itself is changed into the same letters, or disappears altogether.

நல் + நூல் = நன்னூல், *a good composition.*

அருள் + நாதன் = அருணாதன், *Lord of grace.*

(5) ல் and ள் before ம் are changed into ன் and ண் respectively.

கல் + மலை = கன்மலை, *a mountain of stone.*

முள் + முடி = முண்முடி, *a crown of thorns.*

(6) ந after ண் and ன் is sometimes changed into those letters respectively.

கண் + நீர் = கண்ணீர், *tears.*

தன் + நலம் = தன்னலம், *his good.*

[And sometimes one of the double letters is omitted.]

IV. *Omission of Letters.*

[This is called கெடுதல் = *destruction.*]

Fundamental principle :—

TAMIL SENTENCES MUST GLIDE ON GENTLY WITHOUT INTERRUPTION.

Rules.

(1) A final உ (in all words except dissyllables whose first vowel is short) is called குற்றியல் உகரம் (*short-nature-*உ), and is lost before a following vowel.

மாடு + உண்டு = மாடுண்டு [G. 15], *a bullock is there.*

But பசு + உண்டு = பசுவுண்டு, *there is a cow.*

Yet இது + என்ன = இதென்ன, *what is this?*

(2) Final ம் is often dropped before ம or ந.

காலம் + மாறும் = காலமாறும், *the time will change.*

நாமம் + நல்லது = நாமநல்லது [POET.], *the name is good.*

V. *Sanskrit Compounds.*

The following are the most common Sanskrit changes :—

(1) அ + அ = ஆ. சர + அசர = சராசர, *movable and immovable.*

அ + ஆ = ஆ. தேவ + ஆலயம் = தேவாலயம், *a temple of God.*

(2) அ + உ or ஊ = ஓ. ஞான + உபதேசம் = ஞானோபதேசம், *spiritual instruction.*

(3) அ + இ or ஈ = ஏ. சர்வ + ஈஸ்வரன் = சர்வேஸ்வரன், *Lord of all.* யத + இஷ்டம் = யதேஷ்டம், *according to one's desire.*

VI. *Miscellaneous Changes.*

(1) There are certain anomalous changes which words undergo when compounded : thus—

பனை + காடு = பனங்காடு, *a palmyra forest.*

(2) Letters are omitted : thus—

திருவுள்ளம் is written திருவுளம்.

இல்லாதவன் is written இல்லான் or இலான்.

[This takes place chiefly in poetry.]

FIRST LESSONS IN TAMIL

[1. In the first few lessons letters inserted for the sake of euphony are put in brackets.

2. None but common words are used.

3. The exercises should be written and committed to memory, after being corrected. Let the learner frame more exercises for himself, and repeat each sentence, *again and again*, after the teacher, imitating his tone and accent. A little trouble and perseverance at first will save time in the end.

4. The figures in brackets refer to paragraphs.

5. Every word in each Vocabulary should be looked out in Part III, and the synonyms carefully learnt.

6. A key to the exercises is given in Part II. This should be used with judgement.]

LESSON 1.

§ 1. **Vocabulary.**

மனிதன், *a man.* குமாரன், *a son.*
தேவன், *a god.*
கணக்கன், *an accountant*, from
கணக்கு, *an account.*
வர்த்தகன், *a merchant.*
அவன், *he.*
ஒரு, *one* (*a* or *an*).
உம், *and.*

நல்லவன், *a good man* (§ 184).
கண்டேன், *I saw.*
வந்தான், (*he*) *came.*
செய்தான், (*he*) *did.*
பண்ணினான், (*he*) *made.*
தொட்டான், (*he*) *touched.*
(These are irregular past tenses. Comp. §§ 58–70.)

§ 2. Nouns in ன் are generally masculine. Names of irrational animals and of things without life are neuter. [G. 52, 53.]

§ 3. The sign of the accusative (or second case)—case of the direct object—is the vowel ஐ (p. 12. *c*), which is added to nouns in ன், thus: மனிதன் + ஐ = மனிதனை. குமாரன் + ஐ = குமாரனை.

This case, which *follows the verb* in English, *comes immediately before it* in Tamil, thus: வர்த்தகனை[க்] கண்டேன், (*I*) *saw the merchant.* [G. 58.]

§ 4. After the sign of the second case any one of the letters க், ச், த் or ப் MUST be doubled, thus: அவனை[த்] தொட்டான், (*he*) *touched him.* [G. 27.]

§ 5. The subject-pronoun is often omitted in Tamil (after the manner of the classical languages) where the English requires its insertion, thus: வந்தான், (*he*) *came* (not அவன் வந்தான்).

§ 6. The verb *to be* is often *omitted* in Tamil: அவன் தேவன், *he* [is] *a god.*

§ 7. When two words would be joined in English by putting *and* between them, உம் must be added to BOTH, thus: கணக்கனும் வர்த்தகனும், (*an*) *accountant and* (*a*) *merchant.* [G. 113.]

A single உம் would signify *even, also, too,* according to the context, thus: குமாரனும் வந்தான், (*the*) *son also came*, or *even* (*the*) *son came*, or (*the*) *son too came.*

§ 8. Tamil has no article; but ஒரு (§ 172), which means *one*, may sometimes be used for *a* or *an.* There is no precise equivalent for *the.* [But comp. § 25 and Less. 48.]

Exercise 1.

(To be rendered into English.)

§ 9. 1 கணக்கன் வந்தான். 2 ஒரு மனிதனை[க்] கண்டேன். 3 அவன் மனிதன். 4 குமாரன் பண்ணினான். 5 வர்த்தகன் செய்தான். 6 அவனும் குமாரனும். 7 கணக்கனை[த்] தொட்டான். 8 வர்த்தகனை[க்] கண்டான். 9 வர்த்தகன் மனிதனை[த்] தொட்டான். 10 ஒரு தேவனும். 11 வர்த்தகன் நல்லவன். 12 குமாரன் செய்தான்.

(To be rendered into Tamil.)

1 The accountant did. 2 The merchant made. 3 (He) touched the man. 4 I saw the man. 5 He [is] (a) merchant. 6 The man and the merchant. 7 A man and a merchant. 8 The accountant also came. 9 Even the son touched him. 10 He did. 11 The son [is] good. 12 The son saw.

LESSON 2.

§ 10. PRONOUNS. [LESS. 10. G. 71–73.]

NOM. or 1st case, SING.	நான், *I*	நீ, *thou* நீர், *you*	அவன், *he* அவர், *he* (politely)	அவள், *she*	அது, *it*
ACC. or 2nd case, SING.	என்னை, *me*	உன்னை, *thee* உம்மை, *you*	அவனை, *him* (regular)	அவளை, *her* (regular)	அதை, *it*

NOM. PLUR.	நாம், நாங்கள், *we*	நீங்கள், *you*	அவர்கள், *they* (m. or f.)	அவை, அவைகள், *they* (n.)
ACC. PLUR.	நம்மை, எங்களை, *us*	உங்களை, *you*	அவர்களை, *them* (m. or f.)	அவைகளை or அவற்றை, *them* (n.)

§ **11.** (*a*) In Tamil, as in most languages, the pronouns are irregular; those of the 3rd person, however, present the fewest anomalies.

(*b*) நீர் is what is called an *honorific* or polite form; and is used as the English *you*. [G. 138.]

The plurals of all the pronouns may be used in this way for the singular.

(*c*) The difference between நாம் and நாங்கள் is, that நாம் *includes those that are spoken to*, நாங்கள் *excludes them.* The only exception to this is when a superior speaks of himself honorifically in the plural. Thus kings say *We*. In this case நாம் does not include those spoken to.

[நாம் may thus be considered as a dual form. The language affords no other traces of the dual, in this agreeing with both Pāli and Prākrit.]

§ **12.** Adjectives (or words so used) are undeclined, and set BEFORE the nouns they qualify, as in English. [Less. 43. G. 118–121.]

§ **13.** **Vocabulary.**

தாய், *a mother.*
நாய், *a dog.*
செய், *do* (the root and also the imperative).
மரம், *a tree.*
மகன், *a son.*
மகள், *a daughter.*
நல்ல, *good.*
கெட்ட, *bad.*
பெரிய, *great.*
சின்ன, *little.*
புது or புதிய, *new.*
பழைய, *old.*
பையன், *a boy.*
கூப்பிட்டான், *he called.*
வைத்தியன், *a physician.*

☞ He saw me, என்னை[க்] கண்டான், (*me* [he] *saw*). [G. 130.]

Exercise 2.

§ **14.** 1 பெரிய மனிதன். 2 அவள் நல்ல தாய். 3 கெட்ட நாய். 4 சின்ன மகள். 5 நல்ல பையனை[க்] கண்டேன். 6 பெரிய வர்த்தகன் வந்தான். 7 பழைய மரம். 8 அதை[ச்] செய். 9 எங்களை[த்] தொட்டான். 10 நீ சின்ன[ப்] பையன். 11 நீர் பெரிய வர்த்தகன். 12 என்னையும், உன்னையும், அவனையும் கூப்பிட்டான். [ய் inserted to prevent hiatus, p. 20.]

[1] A little dog. [2] A new accountant. [3] A good daughter. [4] She [is] a little daughter. [5] He [is] a big boy. [6] The little boy touched the mother. [7] He called the great merchant. [8] The new physician called them. [9] He saw a boy and a little dog. [10] Do that. [11] He touched us and them. [12] He called me and thee. [13] That great physician is good.

LESSON 3.

THE VERB. (வினைச் சொல் = *action-word.*) [G. 75–81.]

§ **15.** There are some things relating to the conjugation of Tamil verbs that, at first sight, appear difficult; but, in reality, the whole system is very easy; and, once mastered, will be seen to be exceedingly simple.

(*a*) Tamil verbs have only three simple tenses; viz. the present, the past, and the future. [G. 78.]

(*b*) These forms, when analysed, are found to consist of the root (பகுதி), the middle particle denoting time (இடை நிலை), and the terminations which distinguish person and number (விகுதி); thus,

படிக்கிறேன் is the 1st person singular present tense, *I read.*

படித்தேன் is the 1st person sing. past tense, *I read.*

படிப்பேன் is the 1st person sing. future tense, *I shall read.*

These three forms have the *same root*, படி, signifying *read* or *learn.* They have also the same termination, ஏன், signifying *I*, the sign of the first person singular. They differ only in the middle particle, which being added to the root, distinguishes the tense or time.

(*c*) The middle particle, or sign, of the present is கிறு (கிற்) or க்கிறு. [G. 80.]

(*d*) The middle particle, or sign, of the past is த் (or த்த் or ந்த்) or இன்[1]. [G. 79.]

(*e*) The middle particle, or sign, of the future is ப் (ப்ப் or வ்). [G. 81.]

In conjugating any verb, then, the learner must ascertain (first) the ROOT, and (secondly) the particular MIDDLE PARTICLES which it receives.

(*f*) As a general rule verbs which are active-transitive in their signification take க்கிறு in the present, த்த் in the past, and ப்ப் in the future, while other verbs take கிறு in the present, ந்த் in

[1] ன் is an euphonic insertion.

the past, and ப் in the future [G. 82]:—thus, படி, *learn*, being transitive, makes

Present.	*Past.*	*Future.*
படி-க்கிறு (கிற்)	படி-த்த்	படி-ப்ப்

[The final உ in று will be lost before a vowel.]

From these, by adding the termination என் for the 1st pers. sing., ஆன் for the 3rd pers. sing. masc., ஆள் for the 3rd pers. sing. fem., and அது for the 3rd pers. sing. neut., we shall obtain :—

	Present.	*Past.*	*Future.*
The 1st pers. sing.	படி-க்கிறேன் *I learn or read, or am learning*	படி-த்தேன் *I learned*	படி-ப்பேன் *I will learn*
The 3rd pers. sing. masc. The 3rd pers. sing. fem.	படி-க்கிறான் *he learns* படி-க்கிறாள் *she learns*	படி-த்தான் *he learned* படி-த்தாள் *she learned*	படி-ப்பான் *he will learn* படி-ப்பாள் *she will learn*
The 3rd pers. sing. neut.	படி-க்கிறது *it learns*	படி-த்தது *it learned*	(படி-ப்பது) Here there is a variation. Less. 24.

(*g*) Sometimes the same root is used both with a causal or transitive and an intransitive signification; thus:

	Present.	*Past.*	*Future.*
From the root அழி are formed	அழி-கிறேன் *I perish*	அழி-ந்தேன்	அழி-வேன்
	அழி-க்கிறேன் *I destroy*	அழி-த்தேன்	அழி-ப்பேன்

In this case the *weaker* form is naturally *intransitive*, and the *stronger*, *transitive*. In களை and a few other verbs this is reversed.

The transitive or causal verb is பிறவினை (*other action*): the action ends in some other. The intransitive verb is தன்வினை (*self-action*): the action ends in the subject. [G. 99-104.]

§ 16. **Vocabulary.**

படி, *read.*
அழி, *perish, destroy.*
மேய், *feed, graze* (trans. and intrans.).
மேய்ப்பன், *a herdsman, shepherd.*
கொடு (pres. கொடுக்கிறான், past கொடுத்தான், fut. கொடுப்பான்), *give.*
மாடு, *an ox,* any animal of the genus Bos.
தந்தை, *father.*
பசு, *a cow.*
பிள்ளை, *a child.*

☞ He gave it, அவன் அதை[க்] கொடுத்தான், (*he it gave.*)

Exercise 3.

§ 17. [1] படிக்கிறேன். [2] மேய்க்கிறேன். [3] மேய்கிறேன். [4] அழிகிறேன். [5] அழிக்கிறேன். [6] பெரிய பசு. [7] வைத்தியன் படிக்கிறார். [8] கணக்கன் என்னை அழிப்பான். [9] நல்ல பையன் படிப்பான். [10] மேய்ப்பன் நாயைக் கொடுத்தான். [11] மாடு மேய்கிறது. [12] பிள்ளை படித்தது. [13] புதிய மாடு மேய்ந்தது. [14] சின்ன மகளும் தாயும். [15] மேய்ப்பன் மேய்க்கிறான். [16] நல்லவன் படிக்கிறான். [17] பசுமாடு வந்தது. [18] பெரிய பிள்ளை படிக்கிறது.

[1] He perishes. [2] I destroy. [3] I feed. [4] The cow grazes. [5] The shepherd grazes (trans.). [6] The accountant destroyed it. [7] The little child reads. [8] The cow perishes. [9] The little dog destroys it. [10] The bad boy will destroy them (neut.). [11] He gave it. [12] I will give. [13] The physician will give it. [14] The old cow gave. [15] The mother will give. [16] The father gave.

LESSON 4.

THE OBJECTIVE CASE. [G. 58–70.]

§ 18. The 2nd case (§ 3) of பசு (*a cow*) is பசுவை; of மரம் (*a tree*), மரத்தை; of மாடு (*an ox*), மாட்டை; of பிள்ளை (*a child*), பிள்ளையை; of ஆறு (*a river*), ஆற்றை; of கல் (*a stone*), கல்லை; and of காது (*an ear*), காதை.

(*a*) பசுவை is nom. பசு + வ் + ஐ (comp. § 3). Why is the வ் inserted? When the vowels அ, ஆ, உ, ஊ, ஏ, ஒ, ஓ, ஔ are followed by a vowel, வ் is inserted for the sake of euphony (ஏ may take either ய் or வ்), p. 20.

(*b*) பிள்ளையை is nom. பிள்ளை + ய் + ஐ. Why is ய் inserted? When the vowels இ, ஈ or ஐ are followed by a vowel, ய் is inserted for the sake of euphony (p. 20).

(*c*) மாட்டை is nom. மாடு + ஐ, the final உ of the noun being elided, and the ட் doubled; thus, மாட், மாட்ட், மாட்டை. The rule is, when any noun ends in டு, not preceded by one short syllable, (1) the ட் is doubled, (2) the உ is elided, and (3) the termination of the case is added.

(*d*) From ஆறு is formed ஆற்றை, in the same way, substituting ற் for ட்.

(*e*) மரத்தை is மரம் + ஐ, the ம் being changed into த்த்; or, which is the same thing, cast away அம், insert அத்து, and add the termination of the case.

(*f*) கல்லை is nom. கல் + ல் + ஐ. The final consonant of a short monosyllable is doubled before a vowel (p. 19).

(*g*) காதை is nom. காது – உ + ஐ. The final உ of all words not consisting of two short syllables, and not included in the above rules, is elided before a vowel.

§ 19. **Vocabulary.**

வீடு, *a house.*
நாடு, *a country.*
காடு, *a jungle.*
ஆடு, *sheep.*
ஆறு, *a river.*
சேறு, *mud.*
புஸ்தகம், புத்தகம், *a book.*
தகப்பன், பிதா, *a father* [தகப்பன் is Tamil, and பிதா Sanskrit; the former is more familiar, and answers to மகன், as பிதா to குமாரன்].
வானம், *the heaven.*
பூமி, *the earth.*
கை, *a hand.*

Exercise 4.

§ 20. [1] மாட்டை[க்] கண்டேன். [2] நல்ல மேய்ப்பன் ஆட்டை மேய்த்தான். [3] பசுவையும் பையனையும் கண்டேன். [4] பிதாவை[க்] கூப்பிட்டான். [5] வர்த்தகன் ஒரு மரத்தை[க்] கொடுப்பான். [6] வானமும் பூமியும். [7] அது சேறு. [8] பிள்ளையை[த்] தொட்டான். [9] கையை[த்] தொட்டான். [10] கணக்கன் புதிய வீட்டை அழித்தான். [11] கையை[க்] கொடு.

[1] I saw a house. [2] He destroyed the country. [3] I fed the cow. [4] I will give a book. [5] I saw the mud. [6] He called the good father. [7] The little boy learns the new book. [8] He touched the dog. [9] I did it. [10] I saw the heaven. [11] It destroyed the jungle. [12] The big boy saw the father and mother. [13] The physician gave a book. [14] I read a good book.

LESSON 5.

DECLENSION OF THE NOUN. [G. 55–64.]

§ 21. The Tamil noun is said to have eight cases. These are,

(*a*) The first (or nominative), which (in the singular) is the noun or the stem itself. [Less. 74. G. 56.]

(*b*) The second (accusative or objective), which adds ஐ to the stem. [§ 18 and Less. 75.]

[The added particles, signs of case, &c., are called உருபு = *form*. *Nannūl*, 240.]

(*c*) The third (or instrumental), which adds ஒடு, or ஆல், of which the former means *together with*, and the latter *by*. This is in reality two cases. [Less. 76.]

(*d*) The fourth (or dative), which adds கு = *to* (or க்கு or உக்கு) to the stem. [உ is inserted euphonically and க் is doubled according to rule.] If ஆக be also added it gives the meaning of *for*. [Less. 77.]

(*e*) The fifth (or ablative of motion), which adds இல் (sometimes இன்), இலிருந்து or இனின்று to the stem. [Less. 78.]

(*f*) The sixth (genitive or possessive case), which adds உடைய (§§ 22, 185) or இன் to the stem. [Less. 79.]

(*g*) The seventh (or locative), which adds இல் or இடத்தில் to the stem. [Less. 80.]

(*h*) The eighth (or vocative), which (1) adds ஏ to the stem; or (2) lengthens its last syllable; or (3) omits the final consonant, and lengthens the remaining vowel.

Paradigm.

SINGULAR.

CASE (1) மனிதன், *a man.*

(2) மனிதனை, *a man* (+ ஐ).

(3) மனிதனால், *by a man* (+ ஆல்).

மனிதனோடு, *together with a man* (+ ஒடு).

(4) மனிதனுக்கு, *to a man* (+ உக்கு).

மனிதனுக்காக, *for a man* (+ உக்கு + ஆக).

(5) மனிதனில், மனிதனிலிருந்து, மனிதனினின்று, *from a man* (+ இல் or இல் + இருந்து [lit. [1]*being from*], or இல் + நின்று [ல் + ந = ன; lit. [1]*standing from*]).

(6) மனிதனுடைய or மனிதனின், *of a man, belonging to a man* (+ உடைய or இன்).

(7) மனிதனிடத்தில், மனிதனில், } *with a man* (+ இடத்தில் or இல்), *at a man, in a man.*

(8) மனிதனே, *O man!* (+ ஏ).

[NOTES.—1. The Tamil noun has really but *one declension*.

2. The signs of the cases are the same for all nouns; and are the same in the plural as in the singular.

3. The only difficulty in declining nouns which differ from the above paradigm is

[1] These are adverbial participles, § 77.

in ascertaining the modifications, chiefly euphonic, which the nominative (*casus rectus*) undergoes in order to prepare it for the reception of the inflexional particles.

The stem, or inflexional base (*casus obliquus*), being ascertained, there is no difficulty.

4. For this inflexional base, where it differs from the nom., see § 18.
5. This is often used for the genitive or 6th case. (§ 248.)
6. It is generally the inflexional base that is used when a noun is made the first member of a compound. (§ 131.)
7. It is not the etymological root in all cases.
8. It is not quite identical with the crude form in Sanskrit.
9. In nouns in ம், the ம் is *not radical.* ம் and (வ் or) வு (which are often interchangeable in Tamil and its kindred dialects) are used euphonically as terminations of nouns.
10. This final ம் gives way to the stronger த்து before the vowel of a suffix (and in poetry sometimes before the consonant). Before a consonant the nasal is generally retained, but, of course, assumes the forms ங், ஞ், ந், before க், ச், and த்.]

§ **22.** இன் is very often inserted between the inflexional base of the noun and the termination of the case. This is evidently for the sake of euphony. [அன் is sometimes used for இன், in poetry. G. 65 and 108.]

§ **23.** ஏ may be added to most of the case-terminations. Sometimes this is emphatic; but, *for the most part*, merely euphonic.

Exercise 5.

§ **24.** 1 மரத்துக்கு. (§ 18. *e.*) 2 தாய்க்காக. 3 கணக்கனுடைய மரம். 4 வர்த்தகனிடத்தில். 5 வர்த்தகனோடே. 6 காட்டிலிருந்து. (§ 18. *c.*) 7 பிள்ளையே! (§ 18. *b.*) 8 நல்லபையன் வீட்டில் படித்தான். 9 காட்டிலே (§ 23) சேறு. 10 பசு காட்டிலே மேய்கிறது. 11 மேய்ப்பன் மாட்டை மேய்க்கிறான். 12 பையனே படி! 13 பெரிய வைத்தியன் வீட்டுக்கு வந்தான். 14 சின்ன மாடு காட்டில் மரத்தை அழித்தது.

1 He came with the child (Tam. 'with the child he came.' ALWAYS INVERT THE ORDER.) 2 He called the dog from the jungle. 3 The herdsman will feed the cow in the country. 4 By the physician's son. 5 From the accountant's little child. 6 He called me with the mother. 7 I saw him in the house. 8 The physician perished in the country. 9 Do this for the little daughter. 10 From the river. 11 In heaven and earth. 12 By the child.

A complete view of the noun-inflexions is given in the table of synopsis of nouns.

LESSON 6.

§ **25.** Very useful words formed with அ, இ, எ. [G. 5, 6.]

☛ By the aid of the following words, attending to § 6, a vast number of useful sentences of two words may be formed; thus, அவன் எங்கே, *where* [*is*] *he?*

SYNOPSIS OF NOUNS. (§ 21. G. 70.)

	COMMON FORM.	FORMS WHICH INSERT A LETTER.			ELISION OF A LETTER.	FORMS WHICH STRENGTHEN THE ROOT IN INFLEXION. (i)		
I. **The Nominative.** (§ 233.) SUBJECT. ஆனவன், ஆனவள், ஆனது, ஆனவை, &c. added. (§ 151. G. 56, 57.)	I. (a) *கணக்கன், an accountant.* Quite regular; terminations simply added.	II. (b) *கல், a stone.* A short monosyllable. ல் is doubled before the terminations. (See p. 20.)	III. *நரி, a fox.* ய் is inserted. (See p. 29.)	IV. *பசு, a cow.* வ் is inserted.	V. *காது, an ear.* Final உ is elided before the vowel of a termination.	VI. (c) *மாடு, a bullock.* Final உ is elided and ட் doubled. (G. 68.)	VII. *ஆறு, a river.* Final உ is elided and ற் doubled. (G. 68.)	VIII. (d) *மரம், a tree.* ம் changed into த்த். (G. 66.)
II. **Accusative.** (§ 236.) + ஐ: OBJECT. (§§ 3, 21. G. 58.)	கணக்கனை. (h)	கல்லை. கல்லினை.	நரியை.	பசுவை.	காதை.	மாட்டை. (l)	ஆற்றை.	மரத்தை.
III. **Abl. of Connexion.** (§ 239.) (I) BY MEANS OF: + ஆல். (II) TOGETHER WITH: + ஓடு. (m) (G. 59.)	கணக்கனால். (n) கணக்கனோடு.	கல்லால். கல்லோடு.	நரியால். நரியோடு.	பசுவால். பசுவோடு.	காதால். காதோடு.	மாட்டால். மாட்டோடு.	ஆற்றால். ஆற்றோடு.	மரத்தால். மரத்தோடு.
IV. **Dative.** (§ 242.) TO or FOR: + கு or உக்கு. + ஆக = *for.* Comp. Hind. *-ko.* (G. 60.)	கணக்கனுக்கு. கணக்கனுக்காக.	கல்லுக்கு. கல்லுக்காக.	நரிக்கு. நரிக்காக.	பசுவுக்கு. பசுவுக்காக.	காதுக்கு. காதுக்காக.	மாட்டுக்கு. மாட்டுக்காக.	ஆற்றுக்கு. ஆற்றுக்காக.	மரத்துக்கு. மரத்துக்காக.
V. **Abl. of Place from whence.** (§ 245.) FROM: + இல் (e) + இருந்து or நின்று. (G. 61.)	கணக்கனில் or கணக்கனிலிருந்து. கணக்கனினின்று (இன் inserted). (o)	கல்லில். கல்லிலிருந்து. கல்லினின்று.	நரியில். நரியிலிருந்து. நரியினின்று.	பசுவில். பசுவிலிருந்து. பசுவினின்று.	காதில். காதிலிருந்து. காதினின்று.	மாட்டில். மாட்டிலிருந்து. மாட்டினின்று.	ஆற்றில். ஆற்றிலிருந்து. ஆற்றினின்று.	மரத்தில். மரத்திலிருந்து. மரத்தினின்று.
VI. **Gen. or Possessive.** (§ 248.) OF: + உடைய, இன். (f) *Poet.* அது, ஆது, அ. (l) (G. 62.)	கணக்கனுடைய. கணக்கனின். கணக்கனது.	கல்லினுடைய. (f) கல்லின். கல்லினது.	நரியினுடைய. நரியின். நரியினது.	பசுவினுடைய. பசுவின். பசுவினது.	காதினுடைய. காதின். காதினது.	மாட்டினுடைய. மாட்டின். (k) மாட்டினது.	ஆற்றினுடைய. ஆற்றின். ஆற்றினது.	மரத்தினுடைய. மரத்தின். மரத்தினது.
VII. **Loc. or Abl. of Place wherein or whither.** (§ 251.) AT, IN, WITH: + இல் or இடத்தில். (g) (G. 63.)	கணக்கனில். கணக்கனிடத்தில். (p)	கல்லில். கல்லினிடத்தில்.	நரியில். நரியினிடத்தில்.	பசுவில். பசுவினிடத்தில்.	காதில். காதினிடத்தில்.	மாட்டில். மாட்டினிடத்தில்.	ஆற்றில். ஆற்றினிடத்தில்.	மரத்தில். மரத்தினிடத்தில்.
VIII. **Vocative.** + ஏ or final syllable lengthened. (G. 64.)	கணக்கனே! (குதிரைக்காரா!) (§ 21. *h.*)	கல்லே!	நரியே! (தம்பீ! பிள்ளாய்!)	பசுவே!	காதே! (j)	மாடே!	ஆறே!	மரமே!

(a) கணக்கன் makes nom. plur. கணக்கர் or கணக்கர்கள், to which the terminations are added. (§ 29.) (b) கல் makes the nom. plur. கற்கள் (ல் + க் = ற்க்) or கல்லுகள் (உ inserted). (c) மாடு, ஆறு make nom. plur. மாடுகள், ஆறுகள், to which the terminations are added. (d) மரம் makes nom. plur. மரங்கள் (ம் + க் = ங்க்). (§ 29.) (e) This case must not be confounded with the 1st form of the 7th. (f) இன். This is sometimes called the oblique case. It may be inserted between the stem and the casal termination. (§ 22.) This is more common in poetry than in prose, but in many cases euphony absolutely requires it. The ear will soon become accustomed to this. (g) கண் (with இன்) is used as a termination of the 7th case in *poetry*, கணக்கனின்கண். (h) In poetry தன் is sometimes inserted between the noun and its casal term. Thus: கணக்கன் தன்னை. (i) There is reason to suppose that in many nouns, the real root is to be sought in the oblique cases (மாட்ட், ஆற்ற், மரத்த்), as in the classical languages. (j) The vocative, as in all other languages, takes the weaker stem of the noun. (k) The examples given are தனுதுதலை, *his head*, and தனகைகள், *his hands.* (l) For the cases in which such nouns as மாடு, ஆறு and மரம் are governed by following nouns, see § 131. (m) ஓடு is sometimes shortened to ஒடு: கணக்கனொடு. (n) ஏ may be added to any termination in ல். This is for euphony; sometimes it imparts a little emphasis. (§ 23.) (o) இடத்தில் from the 7th case may be inserted: கணக்கனிடத்திலிருந்து. (p) இடத்து is sometimes used for இடத்தில்: கணக்கனிடத்து. (§ 151. *f.*)

[*To face p.* 32.

PRACTISE THESE WELL WITH A TEACHER.

(*a*) அவன், *he, that man.*
இவன், *he, this man.*
எவன், *who, what man?*

(*b*) அவள், *she, that woman.*
இவள், *she, this woman.*
எவள், *who, which woman?*

(*c*) அது, *that thing.*
இது, *this thing.*
எது, *which thing?*

(*d*) அங்கே, *there* (illic).
இங்கே, *here* [vulg. இஞ்சே].
எங்கே, *where?*

(*e*) [1] அப்படி, *so, in that way.*
இப்படி, *thus, in this way.*
எப்படி, *how, in what way?*

(*f*) அந்த, *that, those* [demonstrative adjective].
இந்த, *this, these.*
எந்த, *which?*

(*g*) [2] அப்பொழுது (commonly அப்போது or அப்போ), *then.*
இப்பொழுது (com. இப்போது or இப்போ), *now.*
எப்பொழுது (com. எப்போது or எப்போ), *when?*

(*h*) அவ்வீடு, *that house.*
இவ்வீடு, *this house.*
எவ்வீடு, *which house?*

(*i*) அத்தனை, *so many* (§ 212).
இத்தனை, *this many.*
எத்தனை, *how many?*
தனை means *number* or *quantity*, and is not used alone.

(*j*) அவ்வளவு, *so much* (§ 115).
இவ்வளவு, *thus much.*
எவ்வளவு, *how much?*
Here வ் is inserted euphonically and doubled (p. 21).

(*a, b, c*) ன் is the masculine termination, ள் the feminine, and து the neuter. Those ending in ன் and ள் are declined like மனிதன். Those in து elide the final உ.

(*a–j*) Initial அ, இ, எ are used respectively to point out things *distant*, things *near*, and to ask a *question*. Compare the English *thAt, thIs, WHat.* [உ is used, in poetry only, to point out things in the *middle* or *behind*. G. 5.]

(*h*) These three letters may be prefixed to any noun, in which case the initial letter of the noun is generally doubled (p. 20).

NOTE.—Adverbs of place and manner are also formed in old Tamil by prefixing அ, இ, எ, உ to -ன், -ங்கு, -ங்கணம், &c.

Thus அவன், அங்கு, அங்கணம்,
இவன், இங்கு, இங்கணம்,
எவன், எங்கு, எங்கணம்,
உவன், உங்கு, உங்கணம்.

So கண், 'place'; ஆறு, 'manner'; and a multitude of similar words are used. அங்கண் (nasal inserted), 'there'; எவ்வாறு, 'in what way?' 'how?'

Exercise 6.

§ **26.** [1] எவன் கண்டான்? [2] எப்பொழுது கண்டான்? [3] எங்கே கண்டான்? [4] எப்படி[க்] கண்டான்? [5] இப்பொழுது பசுவை மேய்த்

[1] Often pronounced by the common people அம்படி or ஆம்படி.

[2] பொழுது = காலம் = *time.*

தான். 6 எங்கே கணக்கனுடைய தாய்? 7 அந்த மனிதன் எங்கே? 8 எப்படி நாட்டை அழித்தான்? 9 பெரிய பசு இங்கே மேய்கிறது. 10 எவன் தொட்டான்? 11 வைத்தியனுடைய புது வீடு எது? 12 சின்ன[ப்] பையன் அந்த[ப்] புஸ்தகத்தை[ப்] படித்தான். 13 இப்போ செய். 14 அதெங்கே? 15 எத்தனை வீடு? 16 அங்கே எவ்வளவு பணம்?

எங்கே வந்தாய்? [☞ An idiom, and = *What have you come for? What do you want?*]

1 How did he make it? 2 Where [is] the merchant's son? 3 Come now. 4 He saw her then. 5 That [is] his house. 6 He did so. 7 Thus he perished with his son. 8 When will he learn? 9 He will learn now. 10 The good shepherd will feed the sheep now. 11 Which is his new house? 12 Where is it? 13 Who is he? 14 Who is she? 15 Which is that?

LESSON 7.

IMPERATIVE MOOD. [G. 84.]

§ 27. **Vocabulary.**

வா, *come.* போ, *go.*
கொண்டுவா (pronounced always கொண்டா), *bring* (= *having taken come*).
கொண்டுபோ, *take away* (= *having taken go*).
எடு, *lift up.*
நில்லு, *stand, stop, remain* (neut.).
நிறுத்து, *stop, bring to a stand* (active).
கேள், *hear, ask, obey.*
சொல்லு, *say, tell.*
கொடு, *give.*
தா, *give, bestow.*

(*a*) The root, or crude theme of the verb, is the second person singular imperative: கொடு, *give!* போ, *go!*

(*b*) By adding உம் (or ம்), this becomes the *honorific*, or polite imperative, thus: எடும், போம், நில்லும், கேளும், சொல்லும், கொடும், நிறுத்தும், வாரும், *come* (irregular, from root வா), தாரும் (irregular, from root தா), *give.*

(*c*) By adding கள் to the above, or உங்கள் (or ங்கள்) to the root, we obtain the plural, which is often used as a still higher *honorific*, thus: போங்கள், *go ye.* எடுங்கள், *lift ye.* வாருங்கள், *come ye.* கேளுங்கள், *hear ye.* சொல்லுங்கள், *say ye.* கொடுங்கள், *give ye.* தாருங்கள், *bestow ye.*

Exercise 7.

§ 28. 1 அங்கே போ. 2 இங்கே வா. 3 எங்கே மேய்க்கிறான்? 4 சின்ன[ப்] பையன் எந்தப் புஸ்தகத்தைப் படிக்கிறான்? 5 கணக்கு சொல்லு. 6 பிள்ளையை எடு. 7 அங்கே நில்லு. 8 வீட்டிலே படி.

⁹ மாட்டை நிறுத்து. ¹⁰ வர்த்தகனுடைய குமாரனுக்கு [மகனுக்கு]க் கொடுங்கள். [The Tamil மகன் is more homely than the Sanskrit குமாரன்.] ¹¹ தேவன் எங்கே?

¹ Come to the house (=come home). ² When did he do [it]? ³ Where [is] the great ox? ⁴ Go to the river. ⁵ Lift it from the mud. ⁶ Bring the little child here. ⁷ Take the physician's cow there. ⁸ Whom did that man call? (Tam. 'that man whom he called.') ⁹ This (இவன்) is the shepherd's son. ¹⁰ That (அவன்) is the great physician's son.

LESSON 8.

THE PLURAL NUMBER. [G. 69.]

§ 29. (*a*) The plural of nouns is generally formed by adding கள் to the singular; thus, வீடு, *house*, வீடுகள், *houses*.

☞ [கள் is strictly the pluralizing particle of the neuter, or rather of the *Low-caste*.]

(*b*) Masculine nouns ending in ன் mostly change ன் into ர். They also very generally, but improperly, add கள் also; thus, மனிதன், *a man*, plural மனிதர்கள், or sometimes simply and more correctly மனிதர்.

(*c*) The cases of the plural are formed by adding the same terminations as in the singular, thus (p. 32):—

1	வீடுகள்	*houses.*
2	வீடுகளை	*houses* (after a transitive verb).
3	வீடுகளால்	*by* (*means of*) *houses.*
	வீடுகளோடு	(*together*) *with houses.*
4	வீடுகளுக்கு	*to houses.* வீடுகளுக்காக, *for houses.*
5	வீடுகளில்	*from houses.*
	வீடுகளிலிருந்து	
	வீடுகளினின்று	
6	வீடுகளின்	*of houses.*
	வீடுகளினுடைய	
7	வீடுகளில்	*with, at, unto, or in houses.*
	வீடுகளிடத்தில்	
8	வீடுகளே	*O houses!*

☞ Observe here the difference between the Tamil on one side, and the Sanskrit and Classical languages on the other.

[The plural endings are கள், ர், வை, அ, மார் (§ 151), ம். அவன், *he*, makes அவர் or அவர்கள். அது, *it*, அவை or அவைகள் (து into வை). நான், *I*, makes நாம்: here ம் is the sign of the plural.]

(*d*) Sometimes the க் is doubled; thus, பசுக்கள்.

(*e*) Final ம் is always changed into ங் before க்; thus, மரம் + கள் = மரங்கள். See p. 22.

Exercise 8.

§ 30. 1 கல்லுகளை எடு. 2 மனிதரே! கேளுங்கள். 3 மனிதனே! கேள். 4 பையன்களுக்குக் கொடு. [Here ன் remains.] 5 அந்த வைத்தியர்களின் வீடுகள். 6 காய்களைநிறுத்து. 7 அந்த வர்த்தகருக்குச் சொல்லு. 8 தகப்பனிடத்தில் வந்தான். 9 தாயே! இந்த[ப்] பிள்ளைகளை எடு. 10 அவனுடைய மாடுகளுக்கு. 11 இவர்களுடைய வீடுகளில். 12 தகப்பனே! வாருங்கள்.

1 Go with the merchants to the house. 2 The accountant's good houses. 3 The new physician's old trees. 4 He is feeding the big bullocks in the jungles. 5 He saw those cows with the shepherd. 6 He learnt thus in the book. 7 They are merchants. 8 Where [are] the merchants? 9 Where are those (persons)?

☞ Tamil grammarians do not use the terms *singular* and *plural* at all. ஒருமை (= *one-ness*) and பன்மை (= *many-ness*, பல் + மை) are used to express the ideas. This arrangement will appear at first sight rather complex. [G. 52, 53.]

Nouns are divided into two CASTES (திணை = *genus*):

I. உயர்திணை (உயர், *high* + திணை, *class*) = PERSONAL nouns.

II. அஃறிணை (அல், *no* + திணை, *class:* for the transm. see Introd., p. 22) = IMPERSONAL nouns.

Personal nouns are the names of rational beings.

Impersonal nouns are all others.

There is a further division into five பால் (= *species*).

These are

I. These belong to உயர்திணை:
- (I.) ஆண்பால் [= *male-species*]. This includes the singular masculine of rationals.
- (II.) பெண்பால் [= *female-species*]. Singular feminine of rationals.
- (III.) பலர்பால் [= *many-persons-species*]. Plural epicene rationals.

II. These belong to அஃறிணை:
- (IV.) ஒன்றன் பால் [= *of-one-thing-species*]. ஒன்றன் = ஒன்றின், a poetic form. Singular masculine, feminine or neuter of irrationals.
- (V.) பலவின் பால் [= *of-many-things-species*]. Plural masculine, feminine or neuter of irrationals.

LESSON 9.

THE PRESENT TENSE OF THE VERB. [G. 83.]

§ 31. (*a*) We have seen (Lesson 3) that there are three parts in any tense-form; viz. the *root*, the *middle particle denoting time*, and the *personal termination*. The following is a full list of the *ordinary personal* terminations:—

Person.	*Singular.*	*Plural.*
1	*Masc. and fem.* என் .	ஓம்.
2	*Masc. and fem.* ஆய் .	ஈர், ஈர்கள்.
3	*Masc.* ஆன் . .	ஆர், ஆர்கள்.
	Fem. ஆள் . . .	
	Neuter அது . .	[அ (அன), seldom used.]

☞ [These are fragmentary and modified forms of the personal and demonstrative pronouns.]

(*b*) The third person neuter plural is seldom used, the singular being substituted for it, as in Greek.

(*c*) The third masculine plural in ஆர் is used as a *polite form* when speaking of an equal or superior. ஆர்கள் is the higher honorific.

(*d*) The second plural in ஈர் is used when we should say 'you' in English, to a single person. ஈர்கள் is the higher honorific.

(*e*) Almost every plural form, both of verbs and pronouns, may be used honorifically for the singular. Thus அவர், அவர்கள், plurals of அவன் (§§ 25, 29) are used for *He* when speaking of an equal or superior.

(*f*) For ஆய் of the second singular ஐ is used in vulgar talk, and in some poetic forms.

§ 32. Vocabulary.

(*a*) Verb-roots which insert the middle particle கிறு simply: [WEAK]

செய், *do.*
வரு, *come.*
போ, *go.*
சொல்லு, *say.*
போடு, *put.*
எழுது, *write.*

(*b*) Verb-roots which insert the middle particle கிறு with க் prefixed (or க்கிறு): [STRONG]

நட, *walk.*
தை, *sew.*
தேய், *rub.*
துடை, *wipe.*
குடி, *drink.*
வாசி, *read aloud.*
படை, *create, form.*
இரு, *be, sit.*

§ 33. [ன் may be euphonically inserted between the கி and the று; thus, கின்று and க்கின்று, but this is rather pedantic.

In high Tamil ஆநின்று is also (but very rarely) used as the temporal particle of the present. G. 80.]

§ **34.** A full paradigm of the ordinary form of the present tense of செய் and படி :—

Person.	*Singular.*	*Plural.*
1st	செய்கிறேன், *I do* . . படிக்கிறேன், *I learn* .	செய்கிறோம், *we do.* படிக்கிறோம், *we learn.*
2nd	செய்கிறாய், *thou doest* . படிக்கிறாய், *thou learnest* .	செய்கிறீர், *ye or you do.* செய்கிறீர்கள், ,, படிக்கிறீர், *ye or you learn.* படிக்கிறீர்கள், ,,
3rd *m.*	செய்கிறான், *he does* . . செய்கிறார், ,, . . படிக்கிறான், *he learns* . படிக்கிறார், ,, . .	செய்கிறார், *they do.* செய்கிறார்கள், ,, படிக்கிறார், *they learn.* படிக்கிறார்கள், ,,
3rd *f.*	செய்கிறாள், *she does* . படிக்கிறாள், *she learns* .	
3rd *n.*	செய்கிறது, *it does* . . படிக்கிறது, *it learns* . படிக்கின்றது, ,, .	செய்கின்றன, *they do.* படிக்கின்றன, *they learn* (seldom used). படிக்கிறதுகள் (vulgar).

[Also படிக்கின்றேன் &c., படியாநின்றேன் &c. For the remaining poetical forms see G. 83.]

§ **35.** In very common Tamil படிக்குது and even படியுது are used for படிக்கிறது. It is necessary *to understand* these forms, even if we do not *use them.*

☞ Observe that *I read, I am reading, I do read* are all forms of the *present* tense, and = படிக்கிறேன்.

Exercise 9.

§ **36.** 1 நல்ல பையன்கள் புஸ்தகத்தைப் படிக்கிறார்கள். 2 இப்போ வாசி. 3 புஸ்தகத்தைத் துடை. 4 எங்கே போகிறீர்கள்? (common போறீர்கள்?) 5 கணக்கனும் வர்த்தகனும் எழுதுகிறார்கள். 6 குமாரனுக்குக் கொடு. 7 அவருடைய வீடு எங்கே? 8 இவள் பிள்ளையை[க்] கொண்டுபோகிறாள். 9 தாய் வீட்டுக்கு வருகிறாள். 10 மாடுகளை நிறுத்துகிறார்கள். 11 சின்ன மகள் தைக்கிறாள். 12 வர்த்தகனும் கணக்கனும் குடிக்கிறார்கள். 13 மாடுகளை[த்] தேய்க்கிறான். 14 புஸ்தகத்தை[த்] தைக்கிறான்.

SYNOPSIS OF PRONOUNS. (LESSON X. § 25.)

	SINGULAR.					PLURAL.				
	1ST PERSON.	2ND PERSON.	3RD PERSON.	3RD PERSON NEUTER.	REFLEXIVE.	1ST PERSON.	2ND PERSON.	3RD PERSON.	3RD PERSON NEUTER.	REFLEXIVE.
I. **The Nominative.** (§ 10.)	நான் (POET. யான்), *I*.	நீ, *thou*.	Masc. அவன், *he*. Fem. அவள், *she*.	அது. (POET. அஃது.)	தான், *self*. (COM. GEN.) (§ 108.)	நாம், நாங்கள். (§ 11. *c*.) (யாம் POET.)	நீர், நீங்கள். (*a*) (நீவிர் POET.)	Com. { அவர்கள். அவர். (*b*)	Neut. அவை, அவைகள். (அதுகள்.) (*d*)	தாம். தாங்கள். (*c*)
II. **Accusative.** (§ 10) NOMINATIVE shortened and changed. + ஐ.	என்னை.	உன்னை. (POET. நின்னை.)	அவனை. அவளை.	அதை, அதனை. (அன் inserted.)	தன்னை.	நம்மை, எங்களை. (எம்மை POET.)	உம்மை, உங்களை. (நும்மை POET.)	அவர்களை. அவரை.	அவைகளை. அவற்றை. (அற்று inserted.)	தம்மை. தங்களை.
III. **Abl. of Connexion.** (I) BY MEANS OF: ஆல்.	என்னால்.	உன்னால். (நின்னால்.)	அவனால். அவளால்.	அதால், அத்தால். (அதினால், அதனால்.)	தன்னால்.	நம்மால், எங்களால். (எம்மால்.)	உம்மால், உங்களால். (நும்மால்.)	அவர்களால். அவரால்.	அவைகளால். அவற்றால். அவற்றினால்.	தம்மால். தங்களால்.
(II) TOGETHER WITH: ஒடு.	என்னோடு.	உன்னோடு. (நின்னோடு.)	அவனோடு. அவளோடு.	அதோடு. (அதினோடு, அதனோடு.)	தன்னோடு.	நம்மோடு, எங்களோடு. (எம்மோடு.)	உம்மோடு. உங்களோடு. (நும்மோடு.)	அவரோடு. அவர்களோடு.	அவைகளோடு. அவற்றினோடு.	தம்மோடு. தங்களோடு.
IV. **Dative.** TO or FOR: + கு. [The shortened ROOT takes அக்கு, not உக்கு.]	எனக்கு. எனக்காக.	உனக்கு. உனக்காக. (நினக்கு, நினக்காக.)	அவனுக்கு. அவனுக்காக. அவற்கு POET. அவளுக்கு. அவளுக்காக.	அதிற்கு, அதற்கு. அதுக்கு VULG. அதனுக்கு POET.	தனக்கு.	நமக்கு, எங்களுக்கு. (எமக்கு.) எங்கட்கு.	உமக்கு, உங்களுக்கு. (நுமக்கு.)	அவர்களுக்கு. (அவர்கட்கு.) அவருக்கு. (அவர்க்கு.)	அவைகளுக்கு. அவற்றிற்கு.	தமக்கு. தங்களுக்கு. (தங்கட்கு.)
V. **Abl. of Place from whence.** FROM: இல், &c. Final ன் doubled in monosyllables, p. 19.	என்னில். என்னிலிருந்து. என்னினின்று.	உன்னில், &c. (நின்னில்.)	அவனில். அவளில்.	அதில், அதனில்.	தன்னில்.	நம்மில். நம்மிலிருந்து. எங்களில். எங்களிலிருந்து. (எம்மில்.)	உம்மில், உங்களில். உம்மிலிருந்து. உங்களிலிருந்து. (நும்மில்.)	அவர்களில். அவரில், &c.	அவைகளில், &c. அவற்றில், &c.	தம்மில், &c. தங்களில், &c.
VI. **Gen. or Possessive.** OF: உடைய. Simple shortened ROOT often used.	என். எனது. என்னுடைய. என்னின்.	உன் (நின், &c.). உனது. உன்னுடைய. உன்னின்.	அவன், அவள். அவனது. அவனுடைய. அவனின்.	அதின், அதன். (அதினது, அதனது.) அதினுடைய. அதனுடைய.	தன். தனது. தன்னுடைய. தன்னின்.	நம், எங்கள் (எம்). நமது, எங்களது (எமது). நம்முடைய. எங்களுடைய. நம்மின், எங்களின்.	உம், உங்கள். உமது, உங்களது. உம்முடைய. உங்களுடைய. (நும், நுமது.)	அவர். அவர்கள். அவருடைய. அவர்களுடைய.	அவைகளுடைய. அவற்றினுடைய.	தம், தங்கள். தமது, தங்களது. தம்முடைய. தங்களுடைய.
VII. **Abl. of Place wherein or whither.** AT, IN, WITH: இல், இடத்தில்.	என்னில். என்னிடத்தில்.	உன்னில். (நின்னில்.) உன்னிடத்தில்.	அவனில். அவளில். அவனிடத்தில். அவளிடத்தில்.	அதில், அதனில். அதினிடத்தில். அதனிடத்தில்.	தன்னில். தன்னிடத்தில்.	நம்மிடத்தில், நம்மில். எங்களிடத்தில். எங்களில். (எம்மில்.)	உம்மில். உம்மிடத்தில். உங்களில். உங்களிடத்தில். (நும்மில்.)	அவரில். அவர்களில். அவரிடத்தில். அவர்களிடத்தில்.	அவைகளில். அவைகளிடத்தில். அவற்றில்.	தம்மில். தம்மிடத்தில். தங்களில். தங்களிடத்தில்.

N. B.—Compare the notes to synopsis of nouns.

(*a*) நீர் is used politely, as 'you' in English. (§ 11. *b*.) (*b*) அவர் is used politely or as an honorific. (*c*) தாங்கள் is used as an honorific. (§ 108. *b*.) (*d*) அதுகள், the regular plural, is sometimes used, but is rather antiquated.

[1] She does it. [2] They learn the book in the house (Tam. 'they—in the house—the book—read'). [3] We feed sheep in the jungle. [4] We go to the house now. [5] The mother brings the child to the good merchant's house. [6] The child learns (*is learning* or *does learn*). [7] She sews. [8] The father walks. [9] We learn them. [10] When does he learn this? [11] They are perishing. [12] Where are they perishing? [13] He is going home. [14] The child walks. [15] How does the child walk? [16] The boy reads the book [aloud]. [17] They say so. [18] You [hon.] are coming here. [19] Write that in this book. [20] The cows drink in the river.

LESSON 10.

PERSONAL PRONOUNS. [§ 10. G. 72, 73.]

§ 37. Pronouns when declined take the same case-terminations as nouns; but in the oblique cases they change the root, and are thus irregular in Tamil, as in other languages. See table of synopsis of pronouns.

For the 6th case the simple stem is often used, when it makes a kind of compound with the nouns to which it is attached. அது is sometimes used as a termination of the same case.

[அது being the neuter pronoun *that* (§ 10), and being in apposition with the noun following, the form எனது can only, strictly speaking, be used when the following noun also is neuter. Thus, எனது கை = என் + அது + கை = *my hand*. But எனது பிதா would be incorrect. In poetry ஆது is used for அது occasionally, and அ when the following noun is plural. Thus, எனாது கை, *my hand*; என கைகள், *my hands*. Comp. G. 62.]

Exercise 10.

§ 38. [1] எங்கள் பிதாவே! (§ 18. *a.*) [2] என் வீடு. [3] எனக்குக் கொடு. [4] என்னோடு வா. [5] நம்மிடத்தில். [6] என்னுடைய மரம் அங்கே. (§ 6.) [7] என்னிடத்தில் வா. [8] நம்மால் அழிந்தான். [9] அவன் அதை இப்படி [ச்] செய்தான். [10] பிள்ளைகள் என்னோடு நடக்கிறது. (§ 31. *b.*) [11] உன்னுடைய புஸ்தகத்தை [ச்] சின்ன [ப்] பையனுக்கு [க்] கொடு. [12] உன் தகப்பன் வீட்டில் இருக்கிறார். [13] நம்முடைய பசு காட்டிலே மேய்கிறது. [மேயுது. § 35.]

[14] [அகத்தின் அழகு முகத்தில் தெரியும், *the mind's beauty will be reflected in the face.*]

[1] Come to me (7th case). [2] Where is their good bullock? [3] My bullock [is] here. [4] He does this for us. [5] Who will do this for us? [6] How did he do this for us? [7] A good cow is in our house. [8] They are destroying my new house. [9] How does he write it? [10] I [am] a physician. [11] This [is] my book. [12] Read

it to me. [13] Learn it with him. [14] He is wiping my new book. [15] They are rubbing down your big bullocks. [16] These are my little books. [17] When does our cow feed in the jungle? [18] Where is my father? [19] Which of us (5th case) is reading (aloud)? [20] Which of you (5th case) is learning? [21] The little child is in the house with them.

LESSON 11.

'MUST.' ADVERBS. INFINITIVE MOOD.

§ 39. Vocabulary.

முன்ஷி, *a munshi* or *native teacher* (Pers.).

பாடம், *a lesson.*

தெரியும், *it is understood.*
  எனக்குத் தெரியும், *I understand it* (it is intelligible to me).

தெரியாது, *it is not intelligible.*
  எனக்குத் தெரியாது, *I don't understand it* [to me, &c.].

உச்சரி, *pronounce* (pres. உச்சரிக்கிறேன், past உச்சரித்தேன், fut. உச்சரிப்பேன். [§ 15.] Write out the whole of the present tense as in § 34).

சரியாய் [சரி + ஆய்], *rightly.*

செம்மையாய் [செம்மை + ஆய்], *correctly.*

தெளிவாய் [தெளிவு + ஆய்], *clearly.*

Defective verbal forms:

வேண்டும், *it is necessary, one must* (vulg. வேணும்), *please.*

வேண்டாம், *it is unnecessary*, one *must not, need not, please don't* (vulg. வேணாம் or வாணாம்).

These are also used in entreating.

§ 40. A noun may generally be converted into what may be called an ADVERB by adding ஆய் [or ஆக] to it. In English *ly* is added in the same way, but to an adjective. So *wise* gives *wisely*, but the Tamil says *wisdomly* (ஞானமாய்). (§ 136.)

This is carried to a great extent; thus, பங்கு = *a share*, but பங்காக = *in partnership.*

§ 41. To make a form answering in many respects to our INFINITIVE MOOD: when any verb has க்கிற in the present tense, change க்கிற into க்க; and when it has கிற, add அ, ய or வ to the root. Examples will be found in Ex. 11.

☞ Form for yourself the (so-called) infinitive mood of all the verbs in the preceding lessons.

We	*must*	*read,*
நாம்	வாசிக்க	வேண்டும்.
We	to read	it is necessary.

[The infinitive is here a verbal noun. The pronoun may be regarded as forming with it a compound. Thus, நாம் வாசிக்க = *our reading*. A word may intervene; thus, நாம் செம்மையாய் வாசிக்க = *our rightly reading*. Beware of using a dative: நமக்கு வாசிக்க வேண்டும் would mean, *you must read to us*.]

Exercise 11.

§ **42.** [1] பையன் படிக்க வேண்டும். [2] எனக்கு இப்போ வேண்டும். [3] இப்படி [ச்] செய்ய வேண்டாம். [4] செம்மையாய் உச்சரிக்க வேண்டும். [5] இந்தப்பாடம் எனக்குத் தெரியும். [6] அவனுக்கு[த்] தெரியாது. [7] இப்பொழுது வா. [8] முனிஷி வருகிறார். [9] வானத்தையும் பூமியையும் படைத்தார். (§ 15. *f*.) [10] மாட்டை கிறத்த வேண்டும். [11] நான் எப்படி உச்சரிக்க வேண்டும்? [12] வேண்டாம், போ! [13] தகப்பனே, இதை[ச்] செய்ய வேண்டும். [14] தாயே, அப்படி[ச்] சொல்ல வேண்டாம். [15] உனக்கு எப்படி[த்] தெரியும்?

[The terms *Father* and *Mother* are constantly used by Tamilians as signs of respect and affection.]

[1] You must read rightly. [2] Read rightly. [3] You must pronounce clearly. [4] Speak clearly. [5] Do it rightly. [6] You must do it rightly. [7] The little boy learns the lesson. [8] He does not understand the lesson. (To him, &c.) [9] This must be done. (இதைச் செய்ய [inf. mood] வேண்டும்.) [10] This must not be done. [11] How must I do this? [12] When must they do this? [13] He must rub down our bullocks now. [14] The new munshi is coming now into the house. [15] The physician understands it well. [16] You must go home. [17] Don't read. [18] Don't walk in the mud. [19] The accountant does not understand that account.

LESSON 12.

AFFIRMATION AND NEGATION.

§ **43.** உண்டு, *there is* (or *are*).

இல்லை, *there is* (or *are*) *not* [§ 133. Less. 38].

அல்ல, *not*, *no*.

☞ இங்கே மரங்கள் உண்டு, *there are trees here.*

இங்கே மரங்கள் இல்லை, *there are no trees here.*

அவைகள் மரங்கள் அல்ல, *those are not trees.*

எனக்கு உண்டு = *I have.* எனக்கு இல்லை = *I have not.*

As in Latin, *I have* is often expressed by a dative with the verb *to be*. [Less. 77.]

[The roots இல் and அல் are not really negatives, but are mostly found in the negative aorist (§ 110). Less. 57. The following are chiefly used in poetry:—

1. இல்லேன்.	அல்லேன்.
2. இல்லாய்.	அல்லாய்.
3. இல்லான் (*m.*).	அல்லான்.
இல்லாள் (*f.*).	அல்லாள்.
இல்லது, இன்று (*n.*).	அல்லது, அன்று.
1. இல்லோம் (இல்லேம், இல்லம்).	அல்லோம் (அல்லேம்).
2. இல்லீர்.	அல்லீர்.
3. இல்லார் (*m. f.*).	அல்லார்.
இல்ல, இல்லன (*n.*).	அல்ல.]
(இல்லவே = இல்லை).	

§ **44.** The difference between the two negatives, இல்லை and அல்ல, is that the former denies the EXISTENCE of anything, while அல்ல denies *something that is said concerning it.* இல்லை denies the SUBJECT: *trees are not here.* அல்ல denies the PREDICATE: *those* (which are there) *are not trees* (but something else).

[The same distinction obtains between ILLA and ALLA in Kanarese (McKerrell, p. 182), between KĀDU and LĒDU in Telugu (Brown's Gram. p. 193), and between AYIN and LO or AL in Hebrew (Nordheimer's Gram. §§ 1062–1065).]

Exercise 12.

§ **45.** 1 காட்டிலே மரங்கள் உண்டு. 2 ஆற்றிலே சேறு உண்டு. 3 தாய் வீட்டிலே இல்லை. 4 இவள் என்னுடைய தாய் அல்ல. 5 ஆடுகளுக்கு மேய்ப்பன் இல்லை. 6 இந்தவைத்தியன் மேய்ப்பன் அல்ல. 7 முனிஷியோடு படிக்க வேண்டும். 8 இவைகள் நல்ல மரங்கள். 9 நீங்கள் சரியாய்ச் சொல்ல வேண்டும். 10 பிள்ளைகள் உண்டு. 11 இங்கே நல்ல மரங்கள் இல்லை. 12 இவர் முனிஷி அல்ல. 13 எனக்கு மகனுமில்லை, மகளுமில்லை.

1 There is a good physician here. 2 There is a cow in that jungle. 3 He is not a little child. 4 Put that here. 5 You must put that there. 6 We must take this up. 7 I must read with the munshi. 8 We must pronounce clearly. 9 The little boy must come to my house. 10 The mother must not walk in the mud. 11 She has children. 12 There are cows there. 13 Where [are] the cows?

LESSON 13.

INTERROGATIVES.

§ **46.** When we wish to ask a question, we can generally do so by putting ஆ or ஓ at the end of an affirmative sentence, after the manner of the Latin enclitic *ne*.

Thus, வருகிறான் = *he comes*; { வருகிறானா? *does he come?* / வருகிறானோ? *(but) does he come?*

These particles may be appended to any word in a sentence on which stress is to be laid; thus, அவனா வந்தான்? *did* HE *come?* அப்படியா? *is it so?*

ஆ simply asks the question, ஓ often suggests that there is an alternative or doubt.

ய் and வ் are inserted when necessary, to prevent hiatus, as in § 18. *a*, *b*.

In replies, or emphatic affirmations, use ஏ; வருகிறானே.

[Ā and Ō are used in precisely the same way in Telugu. In Kanarese Ā and E are both used as the Tamil ஆ, and Ō as the Tamil ஓ. Ō alone is found in Malayāḷam.]

§ 47. In Lesson 6 we see that எ also is an interrogative letter, but only at the beginning of a word.

ஏ and யா prefixed to words are sometimes used in the same way. ஆர் (or யார்) is commonly used for *who?*

என்ன is used for *what?* and differs from எது which means rather, *whether of the two?* or *which among many?* ஏன் is *why*, § 214.

என்னம் is used for என்ன occasionally, and is then declined like a noun.

§ 48. **Vocabulary.**

பராபரன், *God.* (The Christian word for GOD *absolutely*; தேவன் is A GOD. சர்வேஸ்பரன் also is used. It is Sanskrit, சர்வ + ஈஸ்பரன் = *universal Lord.*)

விசுவாசி, *believe* (pres. விசுவாசிக்கிறேன், *I believe*; past விசுவாசித்தேன், *I believed*; fut. விசுவாசிப்பேன், *I shall believe.* The Christian usage of this word is not quite idiomatic).

சுறுசுறுப்பு, *industry.*

சுறுசுறுப்பாய் (§ 40), *industriously.*

காவற்காரன், *a watchman* (p. 22).

Exercise 13.

§ 49. [1] பராபரனை விசுவாசிக்கிறேன். [2] இதை விசுவாசிக்க வேண்டும். [3] எதைச்செய்ய வேண்டும்? [4] என்ன செய்கிறாய்? [5] என்னத்தைச் சொல்லுகிறான்? [6] ஆருக்குத் தெரியும்? [7] சின்னப் பையன் சுறுசுறுப்பாய்ப் படிக்கிறானா? [8] சுறுசுறுப்பாய்ப் படிக்கிறானோ? [9] சுறுசுறுப்பாய்ப் படிக்கிறான். [10] இவன் கணக்கனா? [11] இது உன்னுடைய வீடோ? [12] அங்கே மரங்கள் உண்டோ? [13] இங்கே மரங்கள் இல்லையா? [14] இது மரம், அல்லவா? [15] எனக்கு என்ன தெரியும்? [16] காவற்காரனுக்குச் சொல்லு. [17] காவற்காரா! (§ 21. *h*. 3.) வா. [18] நீ என்னத்தை விசுவாசிக்கிறாய்?

[1] When will you read? (§§ 15. *f*, 31. *a*.) [2] Is that my lesson? [3] Where is the munshi? [4] What does the physician say? [5] Is the watchman there? [6] The watchman is not there. [7] He is not the watchman. [8] Who is the watchman? [9] Is there a watchman? [10] Is there mud in the river? [11] Are there trees in the jungle? [12] Are there children in my house? [13] Are there not little children in the father's house? [14] Dost thou believe in God?

☞ Tamil uses no auxiliary like *do*. Thus the emphatic *he does learn* is படிக்கிறானே, and the interrogative *does he learn?* is படிக்கிறானா?

LESSON 14.

ELLIPSIS.

§ 50. In conversation the signs of cases are often interchanged; and those of the 2nd and 6th cases are sometimes omitted altogether.

[In the higher style of Tamil this is very frequent.]

உப்புக் கொடு, *give* [me] *the salt* (not உப்பை = உப்பு + ஐ).

தண்ணீர் கொண்டுவா, *bring me* [some] *water* (not தண்ணீரை).

தண்ணீர் is commonly pronounced தண்ணி, and கொண்டுவா becomes கொண்டா.

பாவஞ் செய்தான், *he committed sin* (not பாவத்தைச் செய்தான்). Such forms may be considered as compounds.

The learner should consider carefully whether the omission of the casal sign would occasion ambiguity. If not, he may omit it in most cases.

From this must be excepted nouns signifying rational beings (உயர்திணை), both masc. and fem., which have the case-termination in full, in common Tamil. In poetry ellipsis is the rule.

It may be stated, as a law, that *the sign of the 2nd case sing.* of impersonal nouns (அஃறிணை) should not be expressed.

Compare this with the usage of Indo-European languages in which neuter nouns have the nominative and accusative alike.

After nouns of number the plural sign கள் also is often omitted; thus,

நாலு வீடு கட்டினான்,
He built four houses. (§ 173.)
நாலு பெயர் வந்தார்கள்,
Four persons came. (Camp. Tel. Gram. 158.)

No ambiguity can arise here.

§ 51. ம் before ச் may become ஞ் }
" க் " ங் } The nasal is changed into that of the class to which the following consonant belongs.
" த் " ந் }
" ம் may disappear altogether (p. 22).

☞ The whole system of the transmutations of letters, their insertion and their elision, is very complicated. It must, however, be thoroughly understood by every student of the poetical dialect. These changes are gradually going out of use. A few only which affect the pronunciation are retained. They will be explained as occasion requires. Compare also p. 20.

§ 52. **Vocabulary.**

தண்ணீர், *cold water* (தண், *cool*, நீர், *water*).
பத்து, *ten*.
உப்பு, *salt*.
பாவம், *sin*.
பணம், *money*.
வேளை, *time*, *opportunity*.
வேலை, *work*.
வேலைக்காரன், *a servant* (காரன் = *a doer, an agent*. [So காவல், *a guard or watch*, காவல்காரன், *a watchman*]).
இரும்பு, *iron*.
கூப்பிடு, *call* (கூப்பு + இடு, § 68).
மேசை, *a table*.
அடி, *beat* (pres. -க்கிறேன், past -த்தேன், fut. -ப்பேன், § 15. *f*).
பாரம், *a burden* (சுமை).
பண்டி, *a bandy*, *conveyance*.
செபம், *prayer* [Skt. *japa*].

§ 53. ல் before க் may become ற்; thus, காவல் + காரன் = காவற்காரன்.

Exercise 14.

§ 54. [1] பாடம் படித்தான். (§ 15. *f*.) [2] தண்ணீர் எங்கே? [3] செபம் படிக்கிறான். [4] அவனிடத்தில் பணம் உண்டு. [5] காவற்காரனைக் கூப்பிடு. [6] பாவஞ் செய்ய வேண்டாம். [7] மேசை இங்கே போடு. [8] நாய் அடித்தான். [9] மாட்டை அடிக்க [or மாடடிக்க] வேண்டாம். [10] என்னுடைய வேலைக்காரர் எங்கே? [11] பத்துப்பாரம் இரும்பு எடுக்கிறார்கள். [12] பண்டி கொண்டுவரச் சொல்லு. [13] வேலைக்காரன் பண்டி கொண்டுவரவில்லையா?

[1] He is learning a lesson in the house. [2] He is reading a book in the jungle. [3] Does he learn a lesson? [4] Is there water in the house? [5] I want [some[1]] salt (to me salt is necessary). [6] He sins. [7] Bring the money to me. [8] Read this to me. [9] Call my servant. [10] Bring ten loads of salt. [11] Did he give money to the servants? (§ 15. *f*.)

LESSON 15.

PAST AND FUTURE TENSES. EXHAUSTIVE CLASSIFICATION OF VERBS.

§ 55. The personal terminations of the present tense are used also for the past and future tenses, with slight exceptions. *The middle particle determines the tense.*

[1] The word *some* is seldom expressed in Tamil, unless it means emphatically *a little*.

[Carefully go over again Lessons 3 and 9, and write out in full the past and future tenses of all the verbs you meet with, except the 3rd person future, singular and plural, which will be given in § 72. Note that every verb comes under one of the six forms in the next section.]

§ 56. The middle particle of the present is கிறு or (க்) கிறு. For this a few general rules will be given, but the dictionary must be consulted.

GENERAL RULES FOR THE PAST AND FUTURE.

I. கிறு of the present has ந்த் in the past and வ் in the future. These are generally *intransitive* and WEAK forms, with some exceptions.

Ex.:—

Root.	*Pres.*	*Past.*	*Fut.*	*Inf.*
அடை, *Obtain, attain to.*	அடைகிறேன், *I obtain.*	அடைந்தேன், *I obtained.*	அடைவேன், *I shall obtain.*	அடைய, *To obtain.*

Thus are conjugated அறி, *know*; ஈ, *give*; கடை, *churn*; அறை, *smite*; விழு, *fall*; கழி, *pass off* or *away*; and a large number of others.

☞ Many roots take two forms, according to their use as active or neuter.

II. Roots in உ [not included in special rules (II) or in § 68] have கிறு in the present, இன் in the past, and வ் in the future. These are common to *both transitive and intransitive* verbs.

They may be called MIDDLE forms.

Ex.:—

Root.	*Pres.*	*Past.*	*Fut.*	*Inf.*
அடங்கு, *Submit, go under.*	அடங்குகிறேன், *I submit.*	அடங்கினேன் (அடங்கு + இன் + ஏன்), *I submitted.*	அடங்குவேன், *I will submit.*	அடங்க, *To submit.*

☞ [Final உ before the vowel of a following word, or of a termination, is often elided, for the sake of euphony; thus, அடங்கு + இன் = அடங்கின் (p. 23). This is never done when உ is preceded by one short syllable; thus, பசு + இன் = பசுவின், not பசின். (G. 24.) The உ is evidently not radical. It is added euphonically to aid the enunciation. அ is added in the same way in Malayāḷam.]

III. க்கிறு of the present requires த்த் in the past, and ப்ப் in the future. These harsher forms are mostly TRANSITIVE [§ 160].

These are STRONG forms.

Ex.:—

Root.	*Pres.*	*Past.*	*Fut.*	*Inf.*
கடி, *Bite.*	கடிக்கிறேன், *I bite.*	கடித்தேன், *I bit.*	கடிப்பேன், *I will bite.*	கடிக்க, *To bite.*

SPECIAL RULES.

(I.) Roots ending in அ (and the greater number of the few in ஆ) take க்கிறு in the present, and follow GENERAL RULE I in the past and III in the future. [§ 66.]

STRONG in present, future, and infinitive; WEAK in past only.

Ex.:—

Root.	*Pres.*	*Past.*	*Fut.*	*Inf.*
நட, *Walk.*	நடக்கிறேன், *I walk.*	நடந்தேன், *I walked.*	நடப்பேன், *I shall walk.*	நடக்க, *To walk.*
வமா, *Exult.*	வமாக்கிறேன், *I exult.*	வமாந்தேன், *I exulted.*	வமாப்பேன், *I shall exult.*	வமாக்க, *To exult.*

(II.) Roots ending in கு, டு, று, preceded by one short syllable, and which take கிறு in the present, are exceptions to rule II, as far as concerns the past tense, *to form which they simply double the consonant and drop the* உ. Some of these admit of the regular form also.

IRREGULAR WEAK forms [§ 68].

Ex.:—

Root.	*Pres.*	*Past.*	*Fut.*	*Inf.*
புகு, *Enter.*	புகுகிறேன், *I enter.*	புக்கேன், *I entered* (but also, and more commonly, புகுந்தேன்).	புகுவேன், *I will enter.*	புக, *To enter.*

Root.	*Pres.*	*Past.*	*Fut.*	*Inf.*
பகு[1], *divide* (INTR.)	பகுகிறேன், *I divide.*	பக்கேன், *I divided.*	பகுவேன், *I shall divide.*	பக, *To divide.*
படு[2], *Suffer.*	படுகிறேன், *I suffer.*	பட்டேன், *I suffered.*	படுவேன், *I shall suffer.*	பட, *To suffer.*
பெறு, *Obtain, bring forth, or beget.*	பெறுகிறேன், *I obtain.*	பெற்றேன், *I obtained.*	பெறுவேன், *I shall obtain.*	பெற, *To obtain.*

(III.) Roots in ன் (னு), ல் (லு), ண் (ணு), ள் (ளு) have mostly கிறு in the present, த் in the past, and in the future வ் after a vowel, and ப் after a consonant. There are certain changes which take place for the sake of euphony, § 70.

EUPHONICALLY MODIFIED WEAK forms (p. 22).

☞ [*a.* த் coming after ன் becomes ற்.

b. When ல் and த் come together they become ன்ற் or ற்ற்.

c. த் coming after ண் becomes ட்.

d. When ள் and த் come together they become ண்ட்.]

	Root.	*Pres.*	*Past.*	*Fut.*	*Inf.*
1	தின் [தின்|னு], *Eat.*	தின்கிறேன் தின்னுகிறேன்	தின்றேன் (*a*)	தின்பேன்	தின்க
2	ஈனு, *Bring forth (of cattle).*	ஈனுகிறேன்	ஈன்றேன் (*a*) (உ of the root dropped).	ஈனுவேன்	ஈன
3	செல் [செல்|லு], *Go, pass.*	(செல்கிறேன்) செல்லுகிறேன்	சென்றேன் (*b*)	செல்லுவேன்	செல்ல
4	உண் [உண்|ணு], *Eat.*	உண்கிறேன்	உண்டேன் (*c*)	உண்பேன்	உண்ண or உண்க

[1] This is also used as TRANS. and strong, § 64.

[2] But see § 60.

	Root.	*Pres.*	*Past.*	*Fut.*	*Inf.*
5	ஆள் [ஆளு], *Rule.*	ஆளுகிறேன்	ஆண்டேன் (*d*) (உ of the root dropped).	ஆளுவேன்	ஆள
6	கொள் [கொள்|ளு], *Have, contain, hold, buy, take.*	கொள்ளுகிறேன்	கொண்டேன்	கொள்ளுவேன்	கொள்ள
7	மீள்	மீட்கிறேன், மீளுகிறேன்	மீண்டேன்	மீளுவேன்	மீள, மீட்க

☞ Exceptions and irregularities are illustrated in the following exercises, which should be frequently gone over.

LESSON 16.

§ 57. REGULAR WEAK FORMS. [§ 56. I.]

Pres.	*Past.*	*Fut.*	*Inf.*
—கிறு	—ந்த்	—வ்	—ய

[Mostly INTRANSITIVE : many exceptions.]

Exercise 15.

1 மேய்ப்பனிடத்தில் ஆடு மேய்கிறது. 2 எப்படி அழிந்தான்? 3 நாள்[1] கழிந்தது. 4 அழிவார்கள். 5 நல்ல வைத்தியன் நமக்கு அதை ஈவார் [not very common]. 6 கணக்கன் இதைச் சரியாய் அறிவான். 7 காவற்காரர் அந்தப்பணத்தை அடைவார்கள். 8 தாயும் மகளும் கடைகிறார்கள். 9 வீடுகளையும் பணத்தையும் அவனாலே அடைவோம். 10 ஆர் இதை அறிய வேண்டும்? 11 அவர்கள் இவரை அறைந்தார்கள். 12 நீங்கள் இதை அறிய வேண்டும். 13 நீ அந்த ஆட்டைக்கொல்லவேண்டாம்.

1 The day has passed away. 2 We must churn in the house. 3 They perished in the jungle. 4 God knows our sins. 5 The accountant and the watchman will obtain those cows from him. 6 The watchman perished with his son. 7 The good boy knows the lesson correctly. 8 I know it by the lesson. 9 You must not smite the child. 10 The bullock fell down. 11 He fell in the mud.

[1] நாள் = *the 24 hours.* பகல் = *the day time, 12 hours.*

LESSON 17.

WEAK FORMS WITH IRREGULAR PAST TENSE.

§ 58. Exceptions to the FIRST GENERAL RULE. [§ 56. I.]

		Root.	*Pres.*	*Past.*	*Fut.*	*Inf.*
THESE OMIT க் IN THE PAST.	I.	பெய், *Rain.*	பெய்கிறேன்	பெய்தேன்	பெய்வேன்	பெய்ய
		செய், *Do.*	செய்கிறேன்	செய்தேன்	செய்வேன்	செய்ய
		நெய், *Weave.*	நெய்கிறேன்	நெய்தேன்	நெய்வேன்	நெய்ய
		வை, *Abuse.*	வைகிறேன்	வைதேன்	வைவேன்	வைய
CONTRACTED.	II.	ஆ, *Become* [ஆகு, ஆயு], *be finished, completed.*	ஆகிறேன் (ஆகுகிறேன்). [Cp. § 268.]	ஆனேன் [occasionally also ஆயினேன் for ஆகினேன் as if from root ஆயு].	ஆவேன் [or ஆகுவேன்][1].	ஆக
		போ, *Go* (போயு, போகு).	போகிறேன் [Cp. § 258.]	போனேன் [poet. போயினேன்].	போவேன் [or போகுவேன்][1].	போக
	III.	சா, *Die* (சாகு).	சாகிறேன்	செத்தேன்	சாவேன் [or சாகுவேன்][1].	சாக (சாவ)
	IV.	வே, *Burn* (வேகு).	வேகிறேன்	வெந்தேன்	வேவேன் [or வேகுவேன்][1].	வேக (வேவ)
		நோ, *Ache, suffer pain* (நோகு).	நோகிறேன்	நொந்தேன்	நோவேன் [நோகுவேன்].	நோக (நோவ)

[1] In these rather pedantic forms கு is inserted for euphony.

மழை, *rain.*
வெண்ணெய், *butter* (வெள், *white,* நெய், *ghee*).
ஏன், *why?*
புடவை, *a woman's cloth, garment.*
தலை, *a head.*
கால், *leg and foot.*

Exercise 16.

§ 59. [1] மழை பெய்கிறது [பெய்யுது, பெய்குது, § 35]. [2] இதைச் சரியாய்ச் செய்வேன். [3] புடவையை [or புடவை, § 14] நெய்தான். [4] அவள் வேலைக்காரனை வைகிறாள். [5] என்னை வைதார்கள். [6] அந்தப் பையன் கணக்கன் ஆவான். [7] வீட்டுக்குப் போவோம். [8] அந்த மாடு காட்டிலே செத்தது. [9] தாயினுடைய வீடு அப்பொழுது வெந்தது. [10] எனக்குத் தலை நோகிறது [நோகுது in common talk]. (I suffer pain in my head.) [11] அங்கே போனானோ? [12] புது மாடு செத்ததா? [13] அந்த வேலை ஏன் ஆக இல்லை? [ஆகவில்லை.]

[1] It rains. [2] His leg pains. [3] She is churning for butter. [4] He will die in the jungle. [5] Did the house burn? [6] Who died? [7] When did he die? [8] When will they go home (to the house)? [9] [Is] this your leg? [10] Why do they revile the watchman? [11] They weave cloths in the house. [12] Who [are] you? (You—who?) [13] Who [is] there? [14] Go to the watchman's house.

LESSON 18.

§ 60. SECOND GENERAL RULE. Exceptions to § 56. II. Roots in உ.

	Root.	*Pres.*	*Past.*	*Fut.*	*Inf.*
I. 1	படு, *Lie down.*	படுக்கிறேன், *I lie down.*	படுத்தேன், *I lay down.*	படுப்பேன், *I will lie down.*	படுக்க, *To lie down.*
2	உடு, *Clothe, put on.*	உடுக்கிறேன்	உடுத்தேன்	உடுப்பேன்	உடுக்க
II. 3	இரு, *Be.*	இருக்கிறேன்	இருந்தேன் irregular in this tense only.	இருப்பேன்	இருக்க

☞ And so all in உ with க்கிறு in the present.

	Root.	Pres.	Past.	Fut.	Inf.
III. 4	தீர் [or தீரு], *Be cleared off.*	தீருகிறேன்	தீர்ந்தேன் regular from root தீர், §56. I.	தீருவேன்	தீர
5	வளர் [or வளரு], *Grow.*	வளருகிறேன்	வளர்ந்தேன்	வளருவேன்	வளர
6	தவிர் [or தவிரு]. *Put away.*	தவிருகிறேன்	தவிர்ந்தேன்	தவிருவேன்	தவிர
7	சேர் [or சேரு], *Draw near to.*	சேருகிறேன்	சேர்ந்தேன்	சேருவேன்	சேர
8	வாழ் [or வாழு], *Prosper.*	வாழுகிறேன்	வாழ்ந்தேன்	வாழுவேன்	வாழ
9	தாழ் [or தாழு], *Be humble.*	தாழுகிறேன்	தாழ்ந்தேன்	தாழுவேன்	தாழ
10	தவழ் [or தவழு], *Crawl.*	தவழுகிறேன்	தவழ்ந்தேன்	தவழுவேன்	தவழ

☞ And so all roots (not short monosyllables) in ர் or ழ், which may optionally add உ.

These omit the nasal ந் in the past tense.		Root.	Pres.	Past.	Fut.	Inf.
	IV. 11	பொரு, *Fight.*	பொருகிறேன்	பொருதேன் [Cp. § 58. I.]	பொருவேன்	பொர
	12	அழு, *Weep.*	அழுகிறேன்	அழுதேன்	அழுவேன்	அழ
	13	உழு, *Plough.*	உழுகிறேன்	உழுதேன்	உழுவேன்	உழ
	14	தொழு, *Worship.*	தொழுகிறேன்	தொழுதேன்	தொழுவேன்	தொழ

Short monosyllables in ழு, ரு or ய் are weak forms.

☞ Roots in ழு or ரு [except தரு, வரு], or ய், and the root வை, preceded by one short syllable, and having the present in கிறு, take single த் in the past and வ் in the future.

வஸ்திரம், *a garment.*	முழங்கால், *the knee, from the knee to the ankle.*
ஊர், *a village.*	முழம், *a cubit.*
ஊரான், *a man of the village.*	கால், *leg.*
ஊரார் [§ 29. *b*], *people of the village.*	

Exercise 17.

§ 61. 1 வஸ்திரங்களை உடுக்கிறார்கள். 2 வீட்டிலே என்ன உடுத்தேன்? 3 எங்கே படுத்தான்? 4 காட்டில் வளர்ந்தது. 5 காட்டிலே என்ன மரம் வளர்ந்தது? 6 இங்கே இருக்கிறாளா? 7 பாவம் தீர்ந்தது. 8 பாவம் தீர்ந்ததா இல்லையா? 9 ஊரார் வாழ்ந்தார்கள். 10 பிள்ளை முழங்காலாலே தவழ்ந்தது. 11 தாய் என்னத்திற்காக[1] [or ஏன்] அழுதாள்? 12 தாயே! அழவேண்டாம். 13 அவன் படுக்கப் போகிறான். 14 தேவனைத் தொழுதான். 15 ஊரார் உழவேண்டும். 16 [தொழுதனன் றொழுதெழுந் தனன்.]

1 The child grew. 2 The trees grow in the jungle. 3 Why do you crawl? 4 The villagers will plough the jungle. 5 The villagers must worship God. 6 You must not crawl; you must walk. 7 I was in the house with the accountant. 8 Shall I flourish? 9 Must I become humble? 10 They must be industrious. 11 Have you a pain in your head, or in your foot? 12 Is the cow dead, or the bandy-bullock? 13 The villagers lay down [to sleep] in the jungle.

LESSON 19.

§ 62. Examples of the SECOND GENERAL RULE, § 56. II. Roots in உ. These may be called MIDDLE FORMS. They are mostly derived from nouns: so பூணு from பூண், *an ornament;* and பூட்டு from பூட்டு, *a lock.*

☞ Both transitive and intransitive verbs are found in this class.

1 From என்னம், 4th case sing. [Comp. § 47.] இன் inserted. [§§ 18. *e*; 22.] ன் + க் = ற்க் = *for what, wherefore.*

	Root.	*Pres.*	*Past.*	*Fut.*	*Inf.*
1	ஆக்கு [from ஆகு *become*], *Make, cause to become, convert into.*	ஆக்குகிறேன் [ஆக்கிறேன்]	ஆக்கினேன்	ஆக்குவேன்	ஆக்க
2	தூங்கு, *Sleep.*	தூங்குகிறேன் [தூங்கிறேன்]	தூங்கினேன்	தூங்குவேன்	தூங்க
3	பேசு, *Speak, converse with.*	பேசுகிறேன்	பேசினேன்	பேசுவேன்	பேச
4	எழுது, *Write.*	எழுதுகிறேன்	எழுதினேன்	எழுதுவேன்	எழுத
5	பண்ணு, *Make* (out of).	பண்ணுகிறேன்	பண்ணினேன்	பண்ணுவேன்	பண்ண
6	தேடு, *Seek.*	தேடுகிறேன்	தேடினேன்	தேடுவேன்	தேட
7	தேற்று [from தேறு, §160.*d*], *Comfort.*	தேற்றுகிறேன்	தேற்றினேன்	தேற்றுவேன்	தேற்ற
8	கட்டு, *Tie, build, tie on.*	கட்டுகிறேன்	கட்டினேன்	கட்டுவேன்	கட்ட
9	காட்டு [from காணு, § 160. *f*. *g*], *Show.*	காட்டுகிறேன்	காட்டினேன்	காட்டுவேன்	காட்ட
10	செலுத்து, *Cause to go, expend, pay* [§§ 160.*d*, 161.]	செலுத்துகிறேன்	செலுத்தினேன்	செலுத்துவேன்	செலுத்த
11	மூடு, *Cover.*	மூடுகிறேன்	மூடினேன்	மூடுவேன்	மூட

[In the past tense இ is probably the real middle particle of time, ன் being an euphonic increment. (Comp. Telugu verb *koṭṭu*.)]

நெல், *rice unhusked.*
அரிசி, *raw husked rice.*
சோறு, *boiled rice.*

Exercise 18.

§ 63. [1] ஒரு வஸ்திரத்தைக் கட்டினான். [2] தாயிடத்தில் பிள்ளை தூங்குகிறது. [3] காட்டிலே உனக்கு என்னத்தைக் காட்டினான்? [4] தாய் பிள்ளைகளைத் தேற்றுகிறாள். [5] என் பாடத்தைச் செம்மையாய் எழுதினேன். [6] அவன் என்னிடத்தில் பேசினான். [7] தண்ணீரைத் தேடுகிறார்கள். [8] இப்பொழுது தூங்கவேண்டுமோ? [9] அவள் சோறு ஆக்கினாள் (she made rice: she *converted* அரிசி into சோறு). [10] ஒரு வீடு (or வீட்டை) கட்டினான்[1].

[1] We must build a new house. [2] Tie the cow there. [3] Who tied the bullock? [4] Where did he write the book? [5] The munshi wrote it. [6] He seeks a physician. [7] Who made this? [8] Who did this? [9] Show the house to the watchman. [10] You must comfort your good mother. [11] Did she seek the little boy? [12] What do they seek here? [13] We will write clearly to the munshi. [14] Has the mother boiled the rice? [15] Did he seek the cow, or did he go to sleep in the house? [16] The accountant has paid the money, so the debt is cleared off.

LESSON 20.

§ 64. Regular STRONG forms: THIRD GENERAL RULE.

Pres.	*Past.*	*Fut.*	*Inf.*
—க்கிறு	—த்த்	—ப்ப்	—க்க்

[Mostly *transitive:* strengthened forms of those in § 57: with some exceptions.]

	Root.	*Pres.*	*Past.*	*Fut.*	*Inf.*
1	பார், *Behold, see, look at.*	பார்க்கிறேன்	பார்த்தேன்	பார்ப்பேன்	பார்க்க
2	கா[2], *Preserve.*	காக்கிறேன்	காத்தேன்	காப்பேன்	காக்க

[1] Tamil houses originally consisted simply of leaves &c. *tied* together.

[2] In common talk கார் is often used for this root; thus, imp. hon. காரும், *preserve ye.*

	Root.	*Pres.*	*Past.*	*Fut.*	*Inf.*
3	மன்னி [1], *Forgive.*	மன்னிக்கி றேன்	மன்னித் தேன்	மன்னிப் பேன்	மன்னிக்க
4	இரட்சி, *Save, deliver.*	இரட்சிக்கி றேன்	இரட்சித் தேன்	இரட்சிப் பேன்	இரட்சிக்க
5	குளி, *Bathe.*	குளிக்கிறேன்	குளித்தேன்	குளிப் பேன்	குளிக்க
6	கழி, *Purge out, remove, pass.*	கழிக்கிறேன்	கழித்தேன்	கழிப்பேன்	கழிக்க

காலம், *time.*
குளம், *tank.*
தீமை, *evil.*
காப்பு, *defence.*

Exercise 19.

§ 65. [1] தாய் பிள்ளையைக் காக்கிறாள். [2] நாய் வீட்டைக் காக்கிறதா? [3] அந்தப் பையன் புதுப் பாடத்தைப் பார்த்தான். [4] கணக்கன் மன்னிப்பானோ? [5] பிள்ளைகள் வீட்டிலே குளிக்கிறார்களா? [6] பிதாவே! எனக்கு மன்னிக்க வேண்டும். [7] காலத்தைக் கழித்தான். [8] காலம் கழிகிறது. [9] எனக்கு அந்த அரிசியைக்காட்டு. [10] அது தீமையா அல்லவா சொல்லு. [11] ஊரார் என்னிடத்தில் பேசுவார்களா எழுதுவார்களா? [12] தீமைக்குத் தீமை செய்ய வேண்டுமோ?

[1] I saw (looked at) him in the house. [2] I shall see him then. [3] Did you see it? [4] We must preserve the children. [5] God forgives our sins. [6] Forgive us our sins. [7] Deliver us from evil. [8] This [is] evil. [9] We must not do evil. [10] He will bathe in the house. [11] He took care of the house. [12] Pay the money now to the accountant. [13] He has done evil for money. [14] Will he bathe in the river or in the tank? [15] Time passes very swiftly.

[1] The root மன்னி requires a dative of the person, as in Latin.

LESSON 21.

§ 66. FIRST SPECIAL RULE. [§ 56. (I.)] Roots in அ, and a few in இ.

Pres.	*Past.*	*Fut.*	*Inf.*
—க்கிறு	—ந்த்	—ப்ப	—க்க

☞ [Verbs of this class are *transitive*: many exceptions; but *an action is mostly implied.*]

	Root.	*Pres.*	*Past.*	*Fut.*	*Inf.*
1	மற, *Forget.*	மறக்கிறேன்	மறந்தேன்	மறப்பேன்	மறக்க
2	பற, *Fly.*	பறக்கிறேன்	பறந்தேன்	பறப்பேன்	பறக்க
3	கல [both *trans.* and *intrans.*], *Mingle, coalesce.*	கலக்கிறேன் [comp. கலங்கு and கலக்கு].	கலந்தேன்	கலப்பேன்	கலக்க
4	திற, *Open* [*trans.*], *be open.*	திறக்கிறேன்	திறந்தேன்	திறப்பேன்	திறக்க
5	கட, *Pass over, transgress.*	கடக்கிறேன்	கடந்தேன்	கடப்பேன்	கடக்க
6	பிற, *Be born, go forth.*	பிறக்கிறேன் [§ 257]	பிறந்தேன்	பிறப்பேன்	பிறக்க
7	இற, *Pass away, die.*	இறக்கிறேன்	இறந்தேன்	இறப்பேன்	இறக்க
8	கற, *Milk, yield milk.*	கறக்கிறேன்	கறந்தேன்	கறப்பேன்	கறக்க
9	கிட, *Lie down.*	கிடக்கிறேன்	கிடந்தேன்	கிடப்பேன்	கிடக்க

குருவி, *a little bird.*
கதவு, *a door.*
பால், *milk.*
மற|தி, *forgetfulness.*

Exercise 20.

§ 67. [1] கதவைத் திறக்கவேண்டாம். [2] வேலைக்காரன் என்னத்திற்காகக் கதவைத் திறக்கிறான்? [3] ஆர் ஆற்றைக் கடப்பார்கள்? [4] நீ எப்படி அந்த வீட்டைத் திறந்தாய்? [5] பையனே! நீ இதை மறக்கவேண்டாம். [6] பிள்ளை பிறந்ததா? [7] அந்த வீட்டிலே ஆர் இறந்தது? [8] அபபடி நடந்தது. [9] நல்ல மனிதன் அப்படி நடப்பானா?

[1] Open the door. [2] They crossed over the river. [3] She mingled water with the milk. [4] The little boy forgot the old lesson. [5] I forgot the book. [6] You must not walk so. [7] In that pot water and milk are mingled. [8] The accountant walked with the watchman. [9] The bird flies there. [10] She looked at the little bird. [11] A child is born. [12] The servant died then. [13] The bird is there. [14] Where is the milk?

LESSON 22.

§ 68. SECOND SPECIAL RULE. [§ 56. (II.)] WEAK with irregular past.

Roots in டு, கு, று. Pres. in கிறு, past ட், க், ற் doubled, fut. வ், inf. அ.

	Root.	*Pres.*	*Past.*	*Fut.*	*Inf.*
1	விடு, *Leave.*	விடுகிறேன் [§ 254]	விட்டேன்	விடுவேன்	விட
2	இடு, *Give, apply to.*	இடுகிறேன் [§ 263]	இட்டேன்	இடுவேன்	இட
3	நடு, *Plant.*	நடுகிறேன்	நட்டேன்	நடுவேன்	நட
4	அறு, *Cease.*	அறுகிறேன்	அற்றேன் அறுந்தேன்[1]	அறுவேன்	அற
5	உறு, *Be, suffer.*	உறுகிறேன்	உற்றேன்	உறுவேன்	உற
6	மிகு, *Exceed.*	மிகுகிறேன்	மிக்கேன் (மிகுந்தேன்)	மிகுவேன்	மிக

[1] This is often used; thus, கயிறு அறுந்து போச்சுது [§ 123. *a*], *the rope has broken.*

	Root.	Pres.	Past.	Fut.	Inf.
7	நகு, *Laugh.*	நகுகிறேன்	நக்கேன்	நகுவேன்	நக
8	தொடு, *Touch.*	தொடுகிறேன்	தொட்டேன்	தொடுவேன்	தொட
9	போடு, *Put* [irreg.]	போடுகிறேன் [§ 256]	போட்டேன்	போடுவேன்	போட

☞ To this rule there are some exceptions: பொறு, *bear a burden, bear with, endure,* makes -க்கிறேன், -த்தேன், -ப்பேன்: so ஒறு, *mortify, afflict, punish.* These follow § 64.

நாற்று, young plants fit for transplanting ; மூன்று, three ; கட்டளை, a command. கட்டளை இடு, vouchsafe, grant graciously ; உள், within ; பெறு, obtain, beget, bear offspring ; சுமை, burden, from சும (§ 66), *bear, carry.*

Exercise 21.

§ 69. [1] என்னை அப்பொழுது காட்டிலே விட்டான். [2] என்னை நீர் விடவேண்டாம். [3] வேலைக்காரருக்குச் சோறு போட்டார்களா? [4] இப்படிக் கட்டளை இட்டார். (*He thus commanded* = he vouchsafed it thus. Observe the idiom.) [5] எனக்கு இதைக் கட்டளை இடவேண்டும். [6] ஊரார்நாற்று நடுகிறார்கள். (§ 59.) [7] அவன் எனக்குச் சோறு இட்டான். [8] காவற்காரன் என்வீட்டுக்குள் புகுந்தான். [9] பிள்ளைப் பெற்றாள் (*she bare a child.* Idiom). [10] மூன்று பிள்ளைகளைப் பெற்றான். [11] ஆற்றிலே போட்டான். [12] மாட்டுக்குப் போட்டானோ நாய்க்குப் போட்டானோ? [13] இதிலே தலை இட்டானா? [14] அந்த வேலைக்குப் போகவேண்டாம்.

[1] What shall I give you? [2] Why do they plant that tree there? [3] Why did the villagers leave the village? [4] Who suffered? [5] What did you obtain by this sin? [6] He went into the jungle. [7] Where did he plant? [8] Serve out the rice. [9] Did he put it on his head or on his foot? [10] Don't meddle in that business. [11] You must bear your burden! [12] The mother that bare him did not know her son.

LESSON 23.

§ 70. (I.) THIRD SPECIAL RULE [§ 56. (III)], and *irregular forms* in general: OF CONSTANT USE.

Pres. -கிறு. In the past the final consonant of the root often changed and ற் or ட் inserted. The fut. takes ப் or வ். Inf. in அ.

	Root.	*Pres.*	*Past.*	*Fut.*	*Inf.*
1	என், *Say.*	என்கிறேன்	என்றேன்	என்பேன்	என, என்க
2	வெல் (லு), *Conquer.*	வெல்லுகிறேன்	வென்றேன்	வெல்லுவேன்	வெல்ல
3	கொல் (லு), *Kill.*	கொல்லுகிறேன்	கொன்றேன்	கொல்லுவேன்	கொல்ல
4	நில் (லு), *Stand, stop.*	நிற்கிறேன்[1] (நில்லுகிறேன்)	நின்றேன்	நிற்பேன்[4] (நில்லுவேன்)	நிற்க
5	கல், *Learn.*	கற்கிறேன்	கற்றேன்	கற்பேன்	கற்க
6	சொல் (லு), *Speak, say.*	சொல்லுகிறேன்	சொன்னேன் (for சொல்லினேன்)	சொல்லுவேன்	சொல்ல
7	காண் (கண்), *See.*	காண்கிறேன் [§ 260]	கண்டேன்	காண்பேன்	காண
8	கேள், *Hear, obey, ask.*	கேட்கிறேன்[2]	கேட்டேன்[3]	கேட்பேன்	கேட்க
9	தரு, *Give.*	தருகிறேன்	தந்தேன்	தருவேன்	தர
10	வரு, *Come.*	வருகிறேன்	வந்தேன்	வருவேன்	வர

[1] ல் + க் = ற்க். [2] ள் + க் = ட்க். [3] ள் + த் = ட்ட். [4] ல் + ப் = ற்ப்.

☞ [In regard to the last two verbs it may be doubted whether the roots are தரு and வரு or தா and வா. They are both conjugated regularly as from roots தரு and வரு, except in the past tense and the imperative (§ 27). வரு has a poet. imp. also, வம்மின் (for வாமின்); and so தம்மின். It is difficult to avoid the conviction that தா = Sanskrit DĀ and DHĀ; (it has all the meanings of both in some or other of the S. Indian languages) in which case analogy would point out வா as the root of its companion. In Telugu the root is RĀ and 'semi-vowels are easily interchangeable' (Bopp, 20).

The irregularity in the past is analogous to that in the verbs வே and சோ (§ 58). Compare also சா-செத்தேன்.

The regular past tenses of all these verbs [§ 56. (I)] would be, according to analogy, வாந்தேன், தாந்தேன், வேந்தேன், சோந்தேன். In each case the root vowel is shortened.

In the plural imperative we have தாரும், வாரும் (for தாவும், வாவும்). I apprehend ர் is used to prevent hiatus, instead of வ், in order to distinguish these forms from the derivatives of the roots தாவு and வாவு. [Compare காரும் from கா.] This use of ர் instead of வ் is not unknown in the cognate dialects.

It may be remarked also, in confirmation of the above, that colloquially தாறேன் and வாறேன் (for தா-கிறேன், வா-கிறேன்) are used for தருகிறேன் and வருகிறேன்.]

§ 70*. PARADIGM OF THE PAST TENSE. Read again Lesson 3.

	படி, *learn, read.*		வாங்கு, *buy, obtain.*	
	Sing.	*Plural.*	*Sing.*	*Plural.*
1st Pers.	படித்தேன், *I learned.*	படித்தோம், *We learned.*	வாங்கினேன், *I bought.*	வாங்கினோம், *We bought.*
2nd	படித்தாய் (for ஆய், ஐ is found in common Tamil).	படித்தீர், *You* [hon.] *learnt.* படித்தீர்கள், *Ye learnt.*	வாங்கினாய், *Thou boughtest.*	வாங்கினீர், *You bought* [hon.] வாங்கினீர்கள், *Ye bought.*
3rd *m.*	படித்தான், *He learnt.*	படித்தார், *They* or *he* [hon.] *learnt.*	வாங்கினான், *He bought.*	வாங்கினார், *They* or *he* [hon.] *bought.*
f.	படித்தாள், *She learnt.*	படித்தார்கள், *They* (m. and f.) *learnt.*	வாங்கினாள், *She bought.*	வாங்கினார்கள், *They* (m. and f.) *bought.*
n.	படித்தது, *It learnt.*	படித்தன[1], *They* (n.) *learnt.*	வாங்கினது, வாங்கியது[2], *It bought.* [Contracted வாங்கிற்று.]	வாங்கின[1], *They* (n.) *bought.*

[1] This form is seldom used, the singular taking its place.

[2] ய் is substituted elegantly for ன் *in this form only.*

Exercise 22.

§ 71. [1] நான் இந்த ஊர்க் கணக்கன் என்றான். [2] நீர் அவனை வெல்ல வேண்டும். [3] ஊரார் எங்கே நிற்கிறார்கள்? [4] உனக்கு ஆர் அப்படிச் சொன்னார்கள்? [5] தாயே! அப்படிச் சொல்லவேண்டாம். [6] இப்பொழுது தருவேன் என்றான்[1]. [7] என் பசுவைக் காட்டிலே கண்டீரோ? [8] பராபரனுடைய கட்டளைகளைக் கேட்டார்கள். [9] தாயும் பிள்ளையும் ஊராரும் இப்போ வருவார்கள். [10] நீங்கள் என்னத்தை அவனிடத்திலே கேட்கிறீர்கள்? [11] வர்த்தகனிடத்தில் என்ன வாங்கினாய்? [12] உப்பு வாங்கவில்லையா? (§ 113.)

[1] Who comes there? [2] Who gave you this? [3] Don't say that lesson (வேண்டாம்). [4] The servants must stop here. [5] We will go into the house with the watchman. [6] The son conquered the villagers. [7] He said he must stop here (trans. 'I must stop here'). [8] Who made this? [9] Who did this? [10] Who created this? [11] Where did he buy the rice? [12] What did you hear in the village? [13] Did you see the good doctor in the house? [14] What lesson has the little boy learnt with the munshi?

LESSON 24.

PARADIGM OF THE FUTURE TENSE.

§ 72. In the 3rd person neuter of the future (the singular and plural of which are alike) there is an anomaly. It is formed by adding உம் to the root of verbs whose present has கிறு (ய் and வ் being inserted when necessary [§ 18]) and க்கும் to those whose present has க்கிறு.

☞ But (1) நில் makes நிற்கும்; கல், கற்கும்; கேள், கேட்கும் (compare their present tenses); (2) சாகும், நோகும், ஆகும், போகும் (*it will die, pain, become, go*) are contracted into சாம், நோம், ஆம், போம்.

[1] When என் (§ 70) is used, the whole of that to which it refers may be considered to be within quotation marks. The quotation is direct: '*He said, "I will come."*' This will be more fully illustrated hereafter (§ 82).

	Root செய். (*Pr.* செய்கிறேன்.) WEAK.		*Root* படி. (*Pr.* படிக்கிறேன்.) STRONG.	
	Sing.	*Plural.*	*Sing.*	*Plural.*
1st Pers.	செய்வேன், *I shall do.*	செய்வோம், *We shall do.*	படிப்பேன், *I shall learn.*	படிப்போம், *We shall learn.*
2nd	செய்வாய், *Thou wilt do.*	செய்வீர், *You will do* [hon.] செய்வீர்கள், *Ye will do.*	படிப்பாய், *Thou wilt learn.*	படிப்பீர், *You will learn* [hon.] படிப்பீர்கள், *Ye will learn.*
3rd *m.*	செய்வான், *He will do.*	செய்வார், *They* or *he* [hon.] *will do.*	படிப்பான், *He will learn.*	படிப்பார், *They* or *he* [hon.] *will learn.*
f.	செய்வாள், *She will do.*	செய்வார்கள், *They* (m. and f.) *will do.*	படிப்பாள், *She will learn.*	படிப்பார்கள், *They* (m. and f.) *will learn.*
n.	செய்யும், *It will do.*	செய்யும், *They* (n.) *will do.*	படிக்கும், *It will learn.*	படிக்கும், *They* (n.) *will learn.*

§ 72*. **Vocabulary.**

நீர், *water* : தண்ணீர்.
யாக்கை, *the body* (only used in poetry).
ஆகும் = *it will become, serve for,* &c., contracted into ஆம்.
எழுத்து, *a letter, a writing.*
முகம், *face.* சூது, *gaming.*
வாது, *disputation.*
வேதனை, *torment.*
வியாதி, *sickness.*

Exercise 23.

§ 73. [1] அந்த மாடு என்ன செய்யும்? [2] அது எப்படி ஆகும்? [3] மரம் ஊரிலே இருக்குமா? இல்லை, காட்டிலே இருக்கும். [4] பாவம் தீருமா? [5] மாடுகளும் ஆடுகளும் இப்போ அந்தக் காட்டிலே மேயும். [6] பிள்ளை தவழுமா? நடக்குமா? [7] குருவி பேசுமா? இல்லை, பறக்கும். [8] 'நீரில்

E 2

எழுத்தாகும் யாக்கை.' [Poetical.] [9] இது முகத்துக்கு ஆம். [10] அந்த வியாதி போமா? [11] 'சூதும் வாதும் வேதனை செய்யும்.' [12] இப்படிச் செய்யப் போமா? [13] பசுமாடு கேட்குமா? [மாடு is any animal of the genus *Bos*. Here பசு indicates the species.] [14] அந்தச் செட்டிக்கு என்னத்தைக் கொடுப்பாய்?

[1] What shall I do? [2] What will the child learn? [3] The cow will come now. [4] Do you know that letter? [5] It will happen so (Tam. 'it will walk so,' நட). [6] The command will come to the villagers. [7] Who must go to the munshi? [8] When will the tree grow? [9] Where can the book be (Tam. 'where will it be')? [10] Will the house fall? No, it will stand. [11] Will the village perish? [12] Will that house suit you? [13] Will the child weep for its mother? [14] We will write a letter to the boy's father.

LESSON 25.

RELATIVE PARTICIPLES.

§ **74.** We have gone through the present, past, and future tenses of the Tamil verb. We have also seen how a form answering in many respects to the English infinitive mood is obtained. The imperative mood too has been given. We come now to a form, probably differing from any with which the learner is acquainted in any language, but which is found in all the South-Indian dialects: *a relative participial form.*

The Tamil has no relative pronoun. How then can it express 'the shepherd *who* feeds the sheep' and 'the sheep *which* graze in the jungle'? Thus, ஆடுகளை மேய்க்கிற மேய்ப்பன் and காட்டிலே மேய்கிற ஆடுகள். Here மேய்க்கிற and மேய்கிற mean 'who feeds' and 'which graze.' This form, which includes the English verb and relative pronoun, is obtained by throwing away the personal terminations of the present and past tenses and adding அ. Thus, மேய்க்கிறேன்: take away ஏன் and add அ, you have மேய்க்கிற, the *relative participle of the present tense.* So மேய்த்தேன்: take away ஏன், add அ, and மேய்த்த, the *relative participle of the past tense*, is the result. The 3rd person neuter of the future tense is also used as the *relative participle of the future* or *aorist:* மேய்க்கும்.

There is a corresponding negative form, § 121. (4.)

[The அ which is added seems to be the remnant of a relative pronoun, like the Greek ὅς, ἥ, ὅ, only placed after the verb instead of before it: ὃν εἶδον ἄνδρα = நான் கண்ட மனிதன்.]

Example :—

Pres.	மேய்க்கிறேன், *I feed*.	மேய்க்கிற, *who*, *which* or *that feeds*.
	மேய்கிறேன், *I graze*.	மேய்கிற, *who*, *which* or *that grazes*.
Past.	மேய்த்தேன், *I fed*.	மேய்த்த, *who*, *which* or *that fed*.
	மேய்ந்தேன், *I grazed*. . . .	மேய்ந்த, *who*, *which* or *that grazed*.
	அனுப்பினேன், *I sent*. . . .	அனுப்பின, அனுப்பிய, *who*, *which* or *that sent*. [§ 70. (2.)]
Fut.	மேய்க்கும், *It will feed*. . .	மேய்க்கும், *who*, *which* or *that will feed*.
	மேயும், *It will graze*. . . .	மேயும், *who*, *which* or *that graze*.
	(Quite indef. as to time.)	

The constructions resulting from this will appear strange till the learner has accustomed himself to them.

1. This participial form is used as an *adjective*; 2. yet it has the same governing power as any other part of the verb, as will be seen in the following sentences. 3. It qualifies nouns of any gender, case, or number; 4. but (like the English adjective) itself suffers no change.

☞ After the final அ of these forms, the initial consonant of a following word is never doubled.

Exercise 24.

§ **75.** [1] நான் படித்த பாடம். [2] வீட்டில் இருக்கிற பிள்ளை அழுகிறது. [3] பிள்ளை வீட்டில் அழுகிறது. [4] வீட்டில் அழுகிற பிள்ளை. [5] ஊரில் இருக்கும் வைத்தியன். [6] இப்பொழுது வந்த வேலைக்காரன். [7] ஊரார் நட்டமரங்கள். [8] தேவன் இட்ட கட்டளை. [9] அவர்கள் எனக்காகத் திறந்த கதவு. [10] என் பிதா கடந்த ஆறு. [11] எங்களைக் காத்த பராபரன். [12] மனிதரை இரட்சிக்கும் தேவன். [13] பிள்ளைகள் குளிக்கிற தண்ணீரைக் கொண்டுவா. [14] நான்செய்த பாவங்களை நீர் மன்னிக்க வேண்டும். [15] நான் போகிற வீட்டுக்கு நீவரவேண்டாம். [16] நான் எழுதின (§ 62) பாடத்தை முனிஷி பார்க்க வேண்டும். [17] நான் சொல்லும் பொழுது உனக்குத் தெரிய வரும். [18] [வெல்லும் வெம்படை வேந்தன்.] [19] அவனுக்குச் சாங் [சாகும்] காலஞ் சமீபித்தது.

[1] The books which the boy sought. [2] The daughter whom the mother comforted. [3] The daughter who comforted the mother. [4] The trees which grew in that jungle. [5] The garments which the son put on. [6] The son who put on garments. [7] The

rain which will fall here. [8] It will rain here. [9] The leg which pained me. [10] The boy who went to the village died there. [11] The cloth which he wove. [12] The table which they made. [13] Beat the dog which bites the little children. [14] Where is the rice I saw in the house?

§ 76. The relative participle is called பெயர் எச்சம் or *noun-defect* (பெயர், *noun*, எச்சம், *defect*), because it requires a noun to fill up the meaning. We call it relative, because it relates to the noun that follows. In analysis it is, with its dependent words, an attributive enlargement of the noun, equivalent in English to *an adjective clause.* [Pope's III. G. 87.]

LESSON 26.

ADVERBIAL PARTICIPLE, OR GERUND.

§ 77. There is another form which is called வினை எச்சம் or *verb-defect*, because it requires a following verb to fill up the meaning. It is a kind of gerund, is indeclinable; and, though belonging to the past tense, *takes its time from the finite verb which closes the sentence.* In analysis it (with the words depending upon it) is an adverbial extension of the predicate.

It is formed from the 1st person singular of the past tense.

[This is the most convenient way of considering the subject. It is probable that the tense is formed from the participle, in which case analogy would suggest a pres. part. in கிறு, and a future in வு or ப்பு, to which the personal terminations were added, the உ being elided.]

(*a*) In all the verbs included in § 56. II, MIDDLE forms [not those in (I), (II), (III)], throw away ஏன்: அடங்கினேன் makes அடங்கி = *having submitted.*

From this EXCEPT

சொல்லு (§ 70), which makes சொல்லி, *having said*, as though from a regular past tense, சொல்லினேன்.

(*b*) In all other cases throw away ஏன் and add உ: படித்தேன் makes படித்து = *having learnt.*

[The Telugu and Kanarese have a *present* verb. part. also. (Comp. Camp. *Tel. Gram.* § 313; McKerrell's *Kan. Gram.* p. 86.)]

Its use will be best learnt from a few examples:

(1) அவன் கண்டு பேசினான் = *he saw and spoke.* Here கண்டு takes the place of the finite verb 'saw.' *The Tamil admits of only one finite verb in a sentence, simple or compound.*

(2) நான் அந்தப் பாடத்தைக் கேட்டு வாசித்து எழுதினேன்.
I heard, read, and wrote that lesson.

கண்டு, கேட்டு, வாசித்து may be translated '*having seen*,' '*having heard*,' and '*having read*.'

(3) சின்னப் பையன் நடந்து வந்தான்.
(The little boy having walked came.)
The little boy came walking, or *on foot*.

☞ The verbal participle *often has the force of an adverb*. Upon the proper appreciation of this will depend much of the learner's progress.

As a general rule, *whenever a subject has two or more finite verbs in English, render all but the last by the* வினை எச்சம், or *adverbial participle*.

Tamil delights in the accumulation of verbal forms, sometimes adding scarcely anything to the meaning. By means of these a sentence may be indefinitely lengthened out, while the meaning is preserved from all ambiguity. [Comp. Lessons 81–93.]

English co-ordinate sentences are thus thrown into one sentence, with extensions. [This is quite analogous to the use of the aorist participles in Greek.]

By their use the principal verb may be modified with a precision scarcely attainable in any other way[1].

(4) நான் அங்கே போய் வருவேன்.
I WILL *go there and come* (back).
அவன் பொசித்துக் [பொசி, *eat*, § 64] குடிக்கிறான்.
He IS *eating and drinking*.

The *tense* of the subordinate verbal forms போய், பொசித்து is determined by the finite verb. [G. 86.]

Exercise 25.

§ 78. [1] தீமையை நீக்கி எங்களை இரட்சியும். [2] இந்தப் பாடத்தைப் படித்து அறியவேண்டும். [3] காவற்காரன் நம்முடைய வேலைக்காரனை வைது அடித்தான். [4] எவன் உம்மைக் கண்டு பேசினான்? [5] எந்தப் பாடத்தைப் படித்து எழுதினீர்? [6] ஊரார் அடங்கிப் (= submissively) பேசினார்கள். [7] இதைத் தெளிவாய் உச்சரித்துச் சொல்லவேண்டும்.

[1] I cannot refrain from quoting the following passage from an essay by Professor Schoff 'On the Tartaric Languages,' quoted in Prof. Max Müller's *Survey of Languages*. It is perfectly applicable to the construction of Tamil, *mutatis mutandis*: 'How peculiar and truly Tartaric this wonderful concatenation of sentences and intervening of words! A sentence runs on in long periods . . . like a majestic stream. . . . The terminations and suffixes are like the small vassals, depending on the powerful and high-sounding gerunds; and these again govern and hold together the larger members of a period, like so many pashas.' In the profoundly learned, but unhappily unfinished, researches into the Tartar dialects of M. Abel Remusat a similar description is given.

[8] ஊருக்குப் போய்ப்[1] பார்க்கவேண்டும். [9] பையன் தேடின புஸ்தகங்களை எடுத்துக்கொண்டு வா. [க், ச், த், ப் always doubled after த்து or இ of this form.] [10] எந்த வீட்டிலே தேடிவந்தாய்? [11] என்னுடைய வேலைக்காரர் இறந்துபோனார்கள் [செத்துப்போனார்கள்]. [12] ஏன் அவனைக் காட்டிலே விட்டுவந்தாய்?

[1] They came and spoke with him. [2] The dog bit and killed the bird. [3] She entered the house and saw the mother. [4] He obtained money and gave to the villagers. [5] We must plough and plant trees. [6] The little boy lay down and slept in the jungle. [7] The mother sought the child weeping. [8] Which servants died in the jungle? [9] Which are the books that the boy was seeking in the house? [10] Why did the boy leave the sheep in the jungle?

LESSON 27.

PERFECT AND PLUPERFECT TENSES.

§ 79. These are not given in native Tamil grammars, but compound forms equivalent to them are in constant use.

In modern Tamil the use of auxiliary verbs is increasing, and ought to increase. As languages grow they require auxiliary verbs to give greater precision. Tamil might vie with English in this respect, if its auxiliaries were fully brought into use.

(1) A PERFECT is formed by adding இருக்கிறேன், *I am* (§ 60. II), to the verbal participle last treated of.

Ex. படித்து இருக்கிறேன் (more generally written படித்திருக்கிறேன்), *I have learnt* (lit. I am, having learnt).

அடங்கி இருக்கிறான், *he has submitted* (lit. he is, having submitted).

(2) A PLUPERFECT is formed by adding இருந்தேன், *I was* (§ 60. II), to the same.

Ex. படித்து இருந்தேன் (படித்திருந்தேன்), *I had learned* (lit. I was, having learned).

பேசி இருந்தேன், *I had spoken* (lit. I was, having spoken).

§ 80. Thus also may be formed a FUTURE PERFECT, படித்திருப்பேன், *I shall have learned;* a PERFECT INFINITIVE, படித்திருக்க, *to have learned;* and a PERFECT, PLUPERFECT, and FUTURE PERFECT of the relative and verbal participles, படித்திருக்கிற,

[1] போய், § 58. II (for போயி), the verb. part. of போ, *having gone*, very common. So ஆய், § 58. II (for ஆயி or ஆகி).

படித்திருந்த, படித்திருக்கும், படித்திருந்து, *who* (*which* or *that*) *has*, *had*, or *shall have learned* or *is having learned*.

☞ This perfect is sometimes used for the present to denote a *state of being*: the *static perfect*. Thus, தரித்திருக்கிறார், *he dwells* (தரி, *dwell*, *stop*, TARRY, § 64); அறிந்திருக்கிறேன், *I know*.

Exercise 26.

§ 81. [1] ஆர் வீட்டிலே வந்திருக்கிறார்கள்? [2] முனிஷி அப்படிச் சொல்லி இருந்தார். [3] அந்தப் பையன் படித்த பாடங்களை இப்பொழுது மறந்திருக்கிறான். (§ 66.) [4] கணக்கன் பணத்தை எனக்குக் கொடுத்திருந்தான். [5] நான் செய்திருக்கும்[1] பாவங்களை மன்னியும். [6] வேலைக்காரர் கட்டியிருந்த வீடு விழுந்தது. [7] நல்லவனாய் இருக்கிறான். (ஆய் for ஆயி from ஆயினேன் [§§ 58. II, 77. *a*], lit. he is, having become good = *he is a good man.*) [8] எங்கே போய் இருக்கிறான்? [9] இதைப் பார்த்திருக்கிறாயா? ஊரார் உனக்குச் சொல்லி இருக்கிறார்களா? [10] அதை அவன் பார்க்கவில்லை, ஊராரால் கேட்டிருந்தான் (கேட்டிருப்பான்).

[1] I have written the lesson. [2] You had sought the child in the jungle. [3] The door which he had opened for the little boy. [4] The villager who had planted the tree came. [5] The tree which the villager had planted grew. [6] I have forgotten and forgiven the evils he has done to me. [7] The milk was mingled with water. [8] The bird drank the milk mingled with water.

LESSON 28.

QUOTATIONS. THE USE OF என்று, '*that*.'

§ 82. In § 70 we had the root என், *speak*, of which the past is என்றேன், and consequently the verbal participle (§ 77) என்று = *having said*.

This is used, when in English a DIRECT quotation is made, instead of quotation marks; and when the quotation is INDIRECT, as equivalent to 'that.' It is the Greek ὅτι. Translate it, when necessary, by 'that.'

[The infin. என occurs in poetry and sometimes colloquially for என்று. So என்பது (§ 88) and என்கிறது. To these ஆய் (§§ 40, 81) and ஆக, § 136, are added when *the exact words used are not quoted*. Compare §§ 168, 136. *d*.]

[1] The future is used indefinitely for any time: 'which at any time I may have committed.'

☞ *He said he would come,* வருவேன் என்று சொன்னான்.
('*I will come,*' —— *he said.*)

I believe there is, உண்டென்று விசுவாசிக்கிறேன்.
('*There* is' —— *I believe.*)

Compare

[அவர் உண்டென்பதை விசுவாசிக்கிறேன்.
I believe that (*which will say*) 'GOD IS.'

அவர் உண்டென்கிறதை விசுவாசிக்கிறேன்.
I believe that (*which says*) '*God is.*'

விசுவாசிக்கிறேன் { என்பதாய்ச் / என்பதாகச் } சொன்னான்.
He said (*what amounted to*) '*I believe.*']

§ **83**. When என்று is used more than once in a sentence உம் is added to each (என்று + உம் = என்றும்).

☞ பராபரன் உண்டென்றும் அவர் என்னைப் படைத்தார் என்றும் விசுவாசிக்கிறேன்.
I believe that God is and that he created me.
('God is'—and 'he me created'—I believe.)

§ **84**. **Vocabulary.**

Before, முன், முன்னம், முன்னமே, முன்பு.
After, பின், பின்பு, பிறகு, பிற்பாடு.
[முன் and பின் must be regarded as nouns, signifying 'the before time' and 'the after time.' (§ 251.) They govern the 4th case generally, but sometimes the 6th, and may themselves be partially declined.]

நன்றாய், *well* (நன்று = *that which is good* + ஆய். § 40).
பழம் *fruit.*
கன்று, *a calf.*
முடி (§ 57), *be finished, come to an end;* (§ 64) *finish, complete.*
இதோ, *see, behold* this; அதோ, *see, behold* that. [இது, அது + ஓ.]
நினை, *think* (§ 64).
ஆஸ்தி, *wealth.*

☞ The desire to obtain more.
இன்னஞ் சம்பாதிக்க வேண்டும் என்கிற ஆசை.
[Still | to acquire | [one] must | which says | the desire.]

This idiom is frequently used. Beware of translating it இன்னஞ் சம்பாதிக்க ஆசை!

§ **85**. முன், &c. are used with the *future* relative participle; and பின், &c. with the *past* relative participle: they form adverbial phrases of time and place (§ 74).

அவன் அதைச் செய்யும் [செய்கிறதற்கு, செய்வதற்கு, §§ 87, 88] முன் [முன்னமே] வந்தேன், *I came before he did it* (lit. the before time that he will do it).

அவன் அதைச் செய்தபின் வந்தேன், *I came after he had done it* (lit. the after time that he did it). [Less. 71.]

Exercise 27.

§ 86. [1] அவர்கள் வீட்டைக் கட்டும் (§ 62, [கட்டி முடிக்கும்] முன்னமே மழை பெய்தது. [2] நாம் பிள்ளையைத் தேடின பிற்பாடு கணக்கனுடைய வீட்டில் இருக்கிறது என்று காவற்காரன் வந்து சொன்னான். [3] [கன்றை] ஈன்ற பசு (§ 56. III) இதோ இருக்கிறது என்று சொன்னான். [4] இவள் பிள்ளையைப் பெற்ற (§ 56. II) தாயோ, என்று கேட்டார். [5] அந்தநாயை அடிக்கவேண்டாம் என்று கட்டளை கொடுத்தேன் [சொன்னேன்]. [6] காவற்காரனுக்குப்பின் ஊரார் வந்தார்கள். [7] அதற்குப்பின் பத்துப்பாரம் வந்தது. [8] பின்னென்ன! [9] முன்னே போகச்சொன்னேன் அல்லவா? ஏன் பின்னே வந்தாய்? [10] இவன் என்றும் அவன் என்றும் எனக்குத் தெரியவில்லை [தெரியாது].

[1] Before you sleep. [2] He said that before the villagers ploughed, it rained (§§ 58, 59). [3] Think well before you do this said I. [4] His head ached (§ 58) after he ate [§ 56. (III)] that fruit. [5] You read your lesson well after he went home. [6] Where is the boy who read his lesson well? (§ 107.) [7] After this what will you do? they asked. [8] Before I came should you not have wiped the table? [9] Tell him to rub down the bandy-bullock after it has come from the jungle. [10] He has a desire to acquire wealth.

LESSON 29.

PARTICIPIAL NOUNS.

§ 87. A multitude of *participial nouns* in very common use, and at the same time elegant, are formed from the present and past relative participles, or பெயர் எச்சம், by adding personal terminations.

(*a*) Thus, from படைக்கிற, pres. rel. part. of படை (§ 74), *create*, are formed:—

Singular.

படைக்கிறவன், *one* (masc.) *who creates.* [அன் added and வ் inserted.]

படைக்கிறவள், *one* (fem.) *who creates.* [அள் added and வ் inserted.]

படைக்கிறது, *that which creates*, or *the creating.* [து (for அது) added.] This is also the 3rd sing. neut. ind. pres.

Plural.

படைக்கிறவர், *one* (honorific) *who creates.* [அர் added and வ் inserted.]

படைக்கிறவர்கள், *those who create* (masc. and fem.). [அர்கள் added and வ் inserted.]

படைக்கிறவை or படைக்கிறவைகள், *those* (neut.) *which create.* [வை (or அவை) and வைகள் added.]

(*b*) From படைத்த, the past rel. part. are formed:—	From அனுப்பின, past rel. part. of அனுப்பு, *send* (§ 56. II):—
Singular.	
படைத்தவன், *one who created*, &c. (படைத்தோன்).	அனுப்பினவன் or அனுப்பியவன்[1].
படைத்தவள், *one* (f.) *who created.*	அனுப்பினவள் or அனுப்பியவள்.
படைத்தது, *that which created*, or *the having created.* [This is also the 3rd sing. neut. ind. past.]	அனுப்பினது or அனுப்பியது.
Plural.	
படைத்தவர் (படைத்தோர்).	அனுப்பினவர் or அனுப்பியவர்.
படைத்தவர்கள்.	அனுப்பினவர்கள் or அனுப்பியவர்கள்.
படைத்தவை-கள், படைத்தன.	அனுப்பினவை or அனுப்பியவை, or அனுப்பின.

These forms are of perpetual occurrence; accustom yourself to form them with verbal roots you meet.

☞ Even in the common dialect படைத்தோன், படைத்தோர், [ஓன், ஓர் for அவன், அவர்] are used occasionally for படைத்தவன், படைத்தவர்.

The neuter singular, besides its primary use, corresponds often in meaning to the participial noun in 'ing' used as a noun: *the creating*, &c.

The following are examples:—

1. அப்படிச் செய்வது (செய்கிறது) சரி அல்ல.
   It is not right to do so.
   [Lit. that which will do so is not right.]

The future gives a more general idea = *at any time.*

[1] [ய substituted for ன. This is not so common as the other form.]

2. அவன் கண்டது உண்டோ?
Has he seen it? = அவன் கண்டானோ?
[But is his having seen it a fact?]

3. பொன் இங்கே இருப்பது இல்லை [or omit இருப்பது].
Gold is not here. (§ 114.)

§ 88. Participial nouns with a future signification are formed by adding ப்ப to the root of strong verbs, and வ to weak ones. In this latter case வ may be used for வ in the neut. singular.

Thus, அழை, *call*, makes அழைக்கிறேன், *I call*, and
செய், *do*, „ செய்கிறேன், *I do*.

Fut. அழைப்பேன்.		Fut. செய்வேன்.
அழைப்பவன்	*one* (masc.) *who will call*,	செய்பவன்.
அழைப்பவள்	&c. [ப்ப is added to the	செய்பவள்.
அழைப்பது	root, to which are joined	செய்வது (என்பது).
அழைப்பவர்	the terminations, அன்,	செய்பவர்.
அழைப்பவர்கள்	அள், அது, அர், அர்கள், வை,	செய்பவர்கள்.
அழைப்பவை-கள்	வைகள், as before.]	செய்பவை-கள்.

The neut. sing. செய்வது, &c. is constantly used, but the remaining forms of the future are not so common.

☞ § 89. These nouns govern the same cases as the verbs from which they are derived.

Thus: என்னை அழைத்தவர் அவர். [என்னை is 2nd case governed
It is he that called me. by அழைத்தவர்.]

அவனை அடிப்பது நியாயம் அல்ல.
It is not right to beat him.

§ 90. **Vocabulary.**

வானம், *heaven, the sky.*
பரமண்டலம், *heaven* (பர, *other*, மண்டலம், *sphere*).
பூமி, *the earth.*
பூமண்டலம், *the earthly sphere —the world.* (பூ, *earth*, in compounds.)
அற்ற, அற்றவன், அற்றவள், அற்றது, &c., from அறு, *cease* (§ 56. I), *without, less; he, she* or *it that is without.*
காப்பாற்று, *guard* (§ 56. II).
திக்கு, *a quarter of the heavens.*
திக்கற்றவன் (திக்கு + அற்றவன்), *one who has nowhere to turn to, a helpless person.*
தெய்வம், *divinity, providence.*
துணை, *help.*
தோன்று (§ 56. II), *appear.*
மறை (§ 56. I), *disappear* (§ 64), *hide.*
மூடு (§ 56. II), *cover, shut up.*
வேளை, *time, opportunity.*
வை, *put, place, keep* (§ 64). [In § 58 a totally different word.]

Exercise 28.

§ 91. [1] *பிறந்தன* (§ 66) இறக்கும்; இறந்தன பிறக்கும்; தோன்றின மறையும்; மறைந்தன தோன்றும். [2] வானத்தையும் பூமியையும் படைத்தவர். [3] பரமண்டலங்களில் இருக்கிற எங்கள் பிதாவே! [4] ஆடுகளை மேய்க்கிறவன் மேய்ப்பன்; ஊரைக் காக்கிறவன் காவற்காரன். [5] வானத்தில் பறக்கிறது குருவி. [6] இதைச் செய்பவன் எவன்? [7] திக்கற்றவனுக்குத் தெய்வமே துணை. [8] நான் வீட்டுக்கு வருவதறிந்து [து + அ = த] (§ 50) கதவைத் திறக்கவும் மற்றவேளை (§ 50) மூடிவைக்கவுஞ் சொன்னேன். [வரு + வ + து. § 88.] [9] அப்படிச் செய்வது தீமை நினைப்பதும் தீமை. [10] சம்பாதித்ததைக் காப்பாற்ற வேண்டும். [11] காப்பாற்றினதை விர்த்திபண்ண வேண்டும். [12] கொழுத்தவன் கைக்கு இளைத்தவன் துரும்பு [*the weaker goes to the wall*].

[1] Who is it that gives the money to the little boy? [2] Who struck the watchman? [3] This (man) protects me. [4] This is what I said. [5] Who did this? [6] How did he do it? [7] Are you he that did it? [8] Art thou he that should come (வருபவர்)? [9] He who has called us [is] God. [10] I sent 10 loads of salt; have you seen them? [11] It appeared in the heaven and disappeared. [12] This is a jungle without water. [13] This is not heavy. [14] You must take care of what you have acquired. [15] You must increase your wealth and knowledge.

LESSON 30.

THE (SO-CALLED) PASSIVE VOICE. [§ 262.]

§ 92. The Tàmil has no *passive voice*, but a compound verb may be formed, which in many respects supplies its place. This form, which is foreign to the idiom of the language, must be very sparingly used.

It is made by adding படு, *suffer* [§ 56. (II)], in all its inflexions to the (so-called) infinitive mood of the verb. படுத்து (§ 56. II) added in the same way makes a causal, concerning which more will be said hereafter. (§§ 160, 161.)

Thus: செய்ய, *to do*, செய்யப்பட, *to be done.*
அழைக்க, *to call*, அழைக்கப்படுகிறேன், *I am called.*
அடிக்க, *to beat*, அடிக்கப்பட்டான், *he was beaten.*
தேட, *to seek*, தேடப்படுவார்கள், *they will be sought.*

In some few cases the simple root is prefixed to படு.

☞ *Who did this?*
இதுயார் செய்தது?
இதுயாரால் செய்யப்பட்டது?

§ 93. **Vocabulary.**

கெட்ட, *bad* (past rel. part. of கெடு, *be spoiled*, §§ 68, 74].
தச்சன், *a carpenter.*
வெட்டியான், *the man who burns the dead and performs menial offices in a village.*
கூப்பிடு, *call* [கூப்பு, *a call* + இடு, *give*, § 68].
{காகிதம், *a paper, letter.*
{கடுதாசி, *a letter.*
{விண்ணப்பம், *a petition.*
{மனு, *a petition.*
{அர்ஜி, *a report* or *petition.*
துரை, *a gentleman*, 'Mr.,' *a governor.*
சுவாப்கவீஸ், *a clerk, interpreter, one who reads petitions and drafts answers.*
புன்செய், *land only fit for dry cultivation* [புன், *inferior* + செய், *field*].
நன்செய், *paddy-land, wet-cultivation* [நன், *good*].
தெரிய|ப்|படுத்து (§§ 56. II, 161), *cause to understand, make known.*

Exercise 29.

§ 94. [1] கெட்டபையன் அடிக்கப்படுவான் (or அடிபடுவான். Here அடி = a beating). [2] இந்தமேசை தச்சனாலே செய்யப்பட்டது. [3] இதுதச்சன் செய்த மேசை. [4] அந்தமேசை தச்சன் செய்தது. [5] வெட்டியானையுங் காவற்காரனையுங் கூப்பிட்டுவா. [6] நான் துரைக்கு ஒரு அர்ஜி எழுதினேன். [7] அந்த மனு சுவாப்கவீஸினாலே வாசிக்கப்பட்டது. [8] என் கடுதாசியைத் தகப்பன் (§ 50) கையில் கொடுத்தேன். [9] இது நன்செயோ புன்செயோ? [10] நன்செய் என்றும் புன்செய் என்றும் மனுவில் எழுதி இருக்கிறான். [11] உம்மிடத்தில் விண்ணப்பஞ் செய்தேன். [12] எழுதுகிறதற்கு[1] காகிதம் என்னிடத்தில் இல்லை. [13] உமக்கு அந்த விண்ணப்பத்தில் என்காரியத்தைத் தெரியப்படுத்தினேன். [14] ஊராருக்கு விண்ணப்பம் எழுதத் தெரியுமா?

[1] Tell the gentleman that Mr. Smith has come. [2] This (இவர்) is the gentleman's interpreter. [3] The petition which he wrote is in my hand. [4] Have you dry land or irrigated? [5] I have both dry land and irrigated land. [6] Tell the gentleman that the person who gave the petition is here. [7] Tell him this is not wet land, but dry land. [8] Ask him who wrote the petition for him. [9] Where was this written? [10] By whom was that evil done?

[1] The 4th case of the participial noun (neuter, singular), எழுதுகிறது (§ 87), *that which writes* + அன் (= இன், § 22) + கு = *to the writing, for the writing.* This form corresponds often to our infinitive used as a noun.

[11] By whom is this village governed? [12] What is the cow eating? [13] You must submit. [14] Don't bite. [15] Was this cloth she wore woven? [16] Has he paid for the garment?

LESSON 31.

'IF.'

FORMS CORRESPONDING TO THE ENGLISH SUBJUNCTIVE (OR CONDITIONAL) MOOD.

§ 95. (*a*) One of these conditional forms is obtained from the past tense (§ 70*), 1st person singular, by changing ஏன் into ஆல் :

Thus, அனுப்பினேன், *I sent.* . அனுப்பினால், *if* (I, you, &c.) *send.*
செய்தேன், *I did.* . . . . செய்தால், *if* (I, you, &c.) *do.*
என்றேன், *I said.* . . . . என்றால், *if* (I, you, &c.) *say.*

Ex.: 1. இவனுக்கு உடனே சூடு போட்டால் ஒருவேளை பிழைப்பான் [போடு, § 68].
Perhaps he may live if you brand *him at once.*

2. அளவுக்கு (§ 242) மிஞ்சினால் அமிர்தமும் நஞ்சு.
[*Even ambrosia, taken in excess, is poison.*]

This is the ordinary form for *adverbial clauses of condition.*

(*b*) Another form, not much used in prose, is obtained by adding இல் or இன் to the root of verbs whose present takes கிறு ; and க்கில் or க்கின் to those which have க்கிறு.

Thus, செய்யில் or செய்யின் (§ 58. I); (Poet. எனில், எனின்);
படிக்கில் or படிக்கின் ;
ஆகில், ஆயின் [§ 58. II. Root, ஆ or ஆகு].

So நிற்பின் (*if . . . stand*); இருப்பின் (*if . . . be*).

These are 3rd and 7th cases of verbal nouns. Thus ஆனால் = '*by the having become,*' and ஆகில் = '*in the having become.*'

§ 96. **Vocabulary.**

சூடு, *a brand, burning.*
தண்டனை, *punishment.*
தண்டி, *punish* (§ 56. III).
அதிகம், *much, more.* அதிகமாய், *too much* (adv. § 40).
விளை, *spring up, grow, be produced* (§ 56. I).
துன்பம், *affliction* (opposed to இன்பம்).
நிலம் [நில், *stand*], *land.*
பயிர், *corn, produce in general.*
பயிர்செய், *cultivate* (§ 58. I).
வழக்கு, *dispute, suit.*
தீர்ப்பு, *decision* (§ 190).
ஒருவேளை, *perhaps* [ஒரு = *one*].
உடனே, *at once* [lit. *together with*, allied to ஒடு, ஓடு, signs of the 3rd case].
நல்லது, *very well* [நல், *good*, அது, *that* (is)] = நன்று.
குற்றம், *a fault.*

Exercise 30.

§ 97. [1] நீ இப்படிச் செய்தால் தண்டனைவரும். [2] காவற்காரன் அப்படிச் சொன்னால் அவன் தண்டிக்கப்பட வேண்டும். [3] அவன் அதிகமாய் நடந்தால் கால்நோகும். [4] நாய் கடித்தால் அதை அடிக்க வேண்டும். [5] கணக்கனை அனுப்பினால் கேட்பார்கள். [6] தீமைசெய்தால் துன்பம் விளையும். [7] நல்லது, என்மகன் இந்த வழக்கைக்குறித்துச் (= *concerning*, § 115) சரியாகத் தீர்ப்புச் செய்தால். [8] உன்னைக் கண்டால் அவனுக்குச் சந்தோஷமாயிருக்கிறது. (Translate : whenever he sees.) [9] ஊரார் பயிர்செய்தால். [10] இந்த வழக்குத் தீர்ந்தால் எனக்கு நிலம் உண்டு. [11] அந்த வியாதி போகச் சொன்னால் போமா? [12] கரும்பைக் கழுதைமுன் போட்டால் கழுதைக்குத் தெரியுமா கரும்பின் உருசி?

[1] If you call he will come. [2] If they plough the land corn will be produced. [3] If afflictions come you must bear [them]. [4] If it rain the villagers will plough. [5] If the child cries we must go. [6] If he pronounces clearly I shall understand. [7] What lesson is he reading to the munshi? [8] If the gentlemen decide this dispute rightly. [9] If you leave me thus, what shall I do? [10] If the villagers stand there, what will the gentleman say? [11] If we boil rice they will pay the money. [12] If the boy forget his lesson he must be beaten.

☞ [The நன்னூல் (Sūt. 343) enumerates twelve forms to which it assigns the common name of வினை எச்சம் (§ 77) = *infinite forms of the verb*.

Taking the root செய், these are said to be—

I. For the past:	II. For the present:	III. For the future:
1. செய்-து (§ 77).	6. செய (or செய்ப, § 41).	7. செயின் (§ 95).
2. செய்-பு.		8. செய்-யிய.
3. செய்-யா.		9. செய்-யியர்.
4. செய்-யூ.		10. செய்-வான்.
5. செய்-தென. (+ து + என, § 82.)		11. செய்-பான்.
		12. செய்-பாக்கு.

To these the commentator adds for the future—

13. செய்-தால் (செய்து + ஆல் (§ 95. *a*) = BY *having done*, § 21).
14. செய்-தக்கால் (செய் + து + அ + கால் = *the time of having done*).
15. செய்-தலும் (செய்து + அல் + உம், § 148 = *together with the doing*).

Of these the majority are poetical and obsolete.

The வினை எச்சம் is thus defined in Sūt. 342 :—

'That is a வினை எச்சம் in which the action and the time appear, but a finite verb, with its terminations indicating gender and number, is wanting to complete the sense.'

In Sūt. 344, it is laid down as a rule that 'the first four of these forms, and the last three must have the same nominative as the finite verb, the others may have a different nominative.'

The more advanced student will find it of advantage to study these Sūtrams. (Compare III. G. 86.)]

LESSON 32.

QUASI-CONJUNCTIONS FORMED FROM VERBS.

§ 98. Some of these *subjunctive forms* are in use as *quasi-conjunctions* :—

a. ஆனல், ஆகில் are subjunctives of ஆ, 'become' (§ 58. II) = *if* [it] *become.*

ஆனல், ஆகில் (poet. ஆயின்) are used for 'if.'

☞ அப்படி ஆனல், அவன் ஏன் இப்படிச் சொல்லுகிறன்?
If (*it be*) *so*, *why does he* *speak thus?*

இவன் கணக்கன் ஆனல், நாம் பணத்தைக் கொடுக்கவேண்டும்.
If he is the accountant, *we* *must give the money.*

b. என்றல், எனில் are subjunctives of என், 'say' (§ 70) = *if* [you] *say.*

என்றல், எனில் (poet. எனின்) are used to express a reason = *for*, *because.* They then follow an interrogative.

Thus எப்படி எனில் = *if you say*, '*how?*'
ஏன் என்றல் = *if you say*, '*why?*'

These and similar forms are to be used sparingly. The sentences in which they occur may often be more elegantly expressed otherwise.

Thus, நான் நன்றய்ப் படிக்கவேண்டும்; ஏன் என்றல், இந்தப் பாடம் கடினமாய் இருக்கிறது.
I *must learn*; *for*, *this lesson* *is hard.*
Better thus: இந்தப்பாடங் கடினம் ஆனதால் நன்றய்ப் படிக்க வேண்டும்.—அது எனக்கு நன்றய்த் தெரியும்;
I know that well;
எப்படி எனில், அதைக் கண்டேன். *for*, *I saw it.*
Better: அதை நான் கண்ணிஞலே கண்டபடியால் எனக்கு நன்றய்த் தெரியும்.

☞ In common talk, the future or past, with ஆனல் or ஆகில், is used for the subjunctive. Thus

கொடுப்பாய் ஆனல் = கொடுத்தால், *if thou wilt give.*

ஏ is sometimes added.

கொடுப்பாயே ஆனல்.

அவன் செய்வானே ஆகில், *if he will do so.*
So also கொடுத்தானே ஆனால், *if he gave.*
எல் is a contraction of ஆகில். (See my குறள் Lex.)

Exercise 31.

☞ In Tamil the HYPOTHESIS (protasis) MUST ALWAYS PRECEDE THE CONCLUSION (apodosis).

§ 99. [1] இங்கே வருவாயே ஆனால் (வந்தால்) அந்தப் பணத்தை உனக்குத் தருவேன். [2] நீ அந்த ஊருக்கு இப்பொழுது போகவேண்டும்; ஏன் என்றால், உன் தகப்பன் உன்னை வரச் சொன்னார். [3] இந்தப்பாடத்தைப், படித்தாயே ஆனால், இது உனக்குத் தெரியும். [4] பசு கன்றை ஈன்றதானால் (ஈன்றது ஆனால்) நாம் போய் அதைப் பார்க்கவேண்டும். [5] ஆனால், பரீட்சை செய்வோம். [6] குற்றம் பார்க்கில் (§ 95. *b*) சுற்றம் இல்லை. [Poet.] (சுற்றம் = attached relatives.) [7] ஆனால் என்ன? என் மீசையிலே மண்படவில்லை.

[1] What did you eat? [2] If you slept in the house you must have heard it. [3] If he has said this I shall go. [4] If he will pay (§ 62) me (*dat.*) the money I will write the petition. [5] They came before I wrote the letter, because they had heard it from (by) the villagers. [6] This is evil, for many will be destroyed by it. [7] Shall we try it? [8] Whose fault is this? [9] Did your father tell you to go? if so, go at once. [10] If you cultivate will it grow up at once? [11] Is what he said right, or is it not? [12] If they build houses in the jungle who will know it?

LESSON 33.

ADVERBIAL CLAUSES OF CONCESSION. 'ALTHOUGH,' 'BUT,' ETC.

§ 100. (*a*) Although I said = நான் சொல்லியும் (lit. *and I having said*): Hypothesis affirmed: I *did* say, but yet . . . The fact is conceded, but the result, or expected consequence, is denied: though the bird sang (*conceded fact*), she did not hear: குருவி பாடியும் அவள் கேட்க வில்லை (§ 113).

(*b*) Although I say (shall say, may say) = நான் சொன்னாலும் (lit. *and if I say*): Hypothesis simply conceived as possible.

(*a*) Here உம் = *and* (§ 7) is added to the adverbial participle (§ 77).

(*b*) In this உம் is added to the subjunctive form (§ 95).

These two forms are of perpetual use, and present no special difficulties.

The following are all the varieties of formation. [III. G. 141, 142.]

(1) Verb. part. (§ 77) with உம் = *although*, with the past.
அனுப்பியும், *although* [I] *sent* (and having sent), § 77. *a.*
படித்தும், *although* [he] *has learnt* (and having learnt), § 77. *b.*

(2) Subjunctive with உம் = *although he may, shall*, &c.
அனுப்பினாலும், *although* [I] *may send* (§ 95. *a*).
படித்தாலும், *although* [he] *should read.*
ஆகிலும், ஆனாலும், *although it be* (§ 95. *b*). (Poet. எனினும், ஆயினும்.)

☞ Let the reader impress it upon his mind, that it is very rarely the case that any Tamil form of this kind corresponds precisely to an English particle or phrase. Do not translate 'but' by ஆனால் or ஆனாலும், *as a matter of course*, wherever you meet with it; but, weigh well the meaning and force of the particle, and translate accordingly.

§ 101. **Vocabulary.**

ஆகிலும், *nevertheless, yet.*
ஆனாலும், *but.*
தீர்வை, *tax.*
கிஸ்தி, *kist* = கிஸ்திப்பணம், *instalment of land tax.*
வாய்தாபணம், *the same.*
பகுதி, *tax* (government share).
வரி, *tax, tribute.*
மாசூல், *the produce of a field.*
அற, *cut, reap* (§ 56. III).
சாத்து, *shut* (§ 62).
கதவு சாத்து, *shut the door* (§ 50).
பொருந்து (§ 56. II), *agree.*

கடல், *the sea.*
வாரம், *a share.*
குடிவாரம், *the people's share* (குடி, *people, inhabitant*).
மேல்வாரம், *the proprietor's share* (மேல், *above*).
சர்க்கார், *the government, the Circar.*
திரை, *a wave* [not very common; அலை is the ordinary word].
திரவியம், *wealth.*
பிராணம், *life.*
சேதம், *destruction.*

Exercise 32.

§ 102. [1] சர்க்காருக்கு என்ன செல்ல வேண்டும்? [§ 56. (III.)] [2] இவன் படித்திருந்தும் முனிஷி அல்ல. [3] அந்த ஊரார் மாசூல் அறுத்திருந்தும் கிஸ்திப்பணம் இல்லையென்றார்கள். [4] என்னே ஆண்டீரோ! [5] கணக்கன் ஊராரிடத்தில் வரியைக் கேட்கவேண்டும்; ஏனெனில், மாசூல் முன்னமே அறுத்திருக்கிறார்கள். [6] அந்த காயை அடித்தாலும்

கடிக்கும். [7] அந்தக் காட்டிலே மரங்களை வெட்டிருந்தாலும் (§§ 68, 79, 100) ஊரார் உழுது (§ 60. III) பயிர் செய்ய வேண்டும். [8] பொய் சொன்னாலும் பொருந்தச் சொல்ல வேண்டும். [9] பிராணச்சேதம் வந்தாலும் வரும். [10] 'திரைக் கடல் ஓடியுந் திரவியந்தேடு.' [Poet. ம் + த் = ந்த்.] [11] இவனை ஆகிலும் காண்போம். [12] அவர்கள் கற்றிருந்தாலும் அறிந்தவர்கள் அல்ல (§ 87).

[1] When will you pay your tax? [2] Have you reaped the produce? [3] Before I reaped the produce I paid my instalment of tax. [4] I have paid my dues (*பகுதி*) to Government. [5] Is this the cultivator's share or the proprietor's share? [6] Although he reaped then, he must now pay the tax. [7] Although he read with the munshi, he does not understand the lesson. [8] My foot pained me, yet I came with him. [9] The villagers came walking. [10] Although you shut the door. [11] How can you tell what the people's share is and what the proprietor's?

LESSON 34.

POTENTIAL MOOD. 'PERMISSION,' 'POSSIBILITY.'

§ **103**. 'May,' 'can'; 'might,' 'could.' [For the negatives see § 117.]

a. நான் படிக்கலாம், *I* MAY *learn.* } DIRECT.
b. நான் படிக்கக் கூடும், *I* CAN *learn.* }

c. அந்தப் பையன் படிக்கலாம் என்றான், *he said that the boy* MIGHT *learn.* } OBLIQUE.
d. அந்தப் பையன் படிக்கக் கூடும் என்றான், *he said that the boy* COULD *learn.* }

(1) A potential mood is formed in Tamil by adding ஆம், to signify *permission*, or கூடும், *ability*, *possibility*.

(2) ஆம் is probably a corruption of ஆகும், the 3rd pers. neut. fut. of ஆ (§ 72*), *become*;—if so, it is = *will become*.

(3) கூடும் is the 3rd pers. neut. fut. (§ 72) of கூடு, *come together*, *fit*, and is used impersonally = *it can be*.

(4) ஆம் is added to a verbal noun (hereafter to be considered, § 148) formed by joining அல் to the roots which have கிறு in the present, and க்கல் to those which have க்கிறு. (The analogy of these strong and weak forms is maintained throughout. Comp. §§ 41, 72.)

Thus: செய் + அல் + ஆம் = செய்யலாம் (ய் doubled for euphony), (I, &c.) *may do.*

படி + க்கல் + ஆம் = படிக்கலாம், (I, &c.) *may learn.*

(5) கூடும் is added to the infinitive mood.

செய்ய + கூடும் = (க், ச், த், ப் are always doubled after the inf. mood) செய்யக் கூடும், (I, &c.) *can do* (pp. 20, 40).

படிக்க + கூடும் = படிக்கக் கூடும், &c., (I, &c.) *can learn*.

☞ (1) For such sentences as *May you be happy!* see § 140.

(2) *Can* is sometimes idiomatically rendered in other ways:

Can you write? உனக்கு எழுதத் தெரியுமா? [Is (the manner of) writing intelligible to you?]

Can you read? நீ வாசிப்பாயா? [Will you read?]

'Can' may often be *rendered elegantly by the* simple future.

Exercise 33.

§ 104. [1] வேலைக்காரர் வந்து (§ 70) கதவைத்திறக்கலாமா? (§ 66.) [2] துரையுடைய சுவாப்கவீஸ் அந்தக் கட்டளையை எழுதி அனுப்பலாமா? [3] தாய் பிள்ளைகளை அப்படிக் காட்டிலே விட்டுவிடலாமா? (§ 68. விடு doubled gives emphasis = *to forsake utterly*, § 254.) [4] நீங்கள் பாவத்தை விட்டு விடவேண்டாமா? [5] பசுமாடு வீட்டிலே வரலாமா? [6] ஆடுகள் பேசக் கூடுமா? [7] இப்படி உச்சரிக்கக் கூடுமா? [8] அதிகமாகவே இருக்கலாம் என்று நினைக்கிறேன். [9] அந்த வேலைக்காரனை அப்படித் தண்டிக்கலாமா? [10] அந்தக் கடினமான (§ 133) பாடத்தைப்படிக்கக் கூடுமா? [11] இது யாராலே ஆகும் [ஆம்]? [12] குடிகளுக்குத் தெரியப் படுத்தலாமா? (§ 92.) [13] வானத்தையும் பூமியையும் படைத்தவர் இதையுஞ் செய்யக்கூடும்.

N. B.—கூடும் signifies (1) *possibility*; (2) *fitness, right*.

[1] May the little boy shut the door of the house? [2] Shut the door. [3] He may shut the door. [4] He can [is able to] shut the door. [5] May they open the door? Yes (திறக்கலாம்). [6] May I call the servants? Yes. [7] Can the boy lift this weight? Yes. [8] Although the people were come, he slept in the house. [9] Is it right to beat the little boy so? (கூடுமா?) [10] Although the mother comforted the little child, it wept. [11] Can you speak with the gentleman at this time? [12] Ought the little boy to come on foot (walking)? [13] May the munshi see the lesson you have written? [14] Must the child weep for its mother? [15] There are ten loads of iron, I think.

[N.B.— *Yes* is often rendered by ஆம் (or vulgarly ஆமா for ஆம் ஆம்); but the verb should be repeated: போகலாமா? Ans. போகலாம், not simply ஆம்.]

It will be desirable for the student to go over this

SYNOPSIS OF THE TAMIL VERB.

I. INDICATIVE MOOD.

	Weak Form.	*Strong Form.*
ROOT	செய் (single க), (§ 15. *f*)	படி (double க்).
PRESENT	செய்கிறேன், *I do* (§ 31) { செய்கின்றேன் (§ 33) செய்யாநின்றேன் (§ 264) }	படிக்கிறேன், *I learn* (§ 34).
IMPERFECT	செய்தேன், *I did* (§§ 55–71)	படித்தேன், *I learned* (§ 70*).
PERFECT	செய்திருக்கிறேன், *I have done* (§ 79)	படித்திருக்கிறேன், *I have learned* (§ 79).
PLUPERFECT	செய்திருந்தேன், *I had done* (§ 79)	படித்திருந்தேன், *I had learned* (§ 79).
I. FUTURE	செய்வேன், *I shall do* (§ 56)	படிப்பேன், *I shall learn* (§ 56).
II. FUTURE	செய்திருப்பேன், *I shall have done* (§ 80)	படித்திருப்பேன், *I shall have learned* (§ 80).

II. SUBJUNCTIVE MOOD. (If, although.)		
	Weak Form.	*Strong Form.*
PRESENT (SUPPOSITION)	செய்தால், செய்யில், *if* (I, &c.) *do* (§ 95) .	படித்தால், படிக்கில், *if* (I, &c.) *learn* (§ 95).
PERFECT (SUPPOSITION)	செய்திருந்தால், *if* (I, &c.) *have done* (§ 79) .	படித்திருந்தால், *if* (I, &c.) *have learned* (§ 79).
PAST (AFFIRMATION)	செய்தும், *although* (I, &c.) *did* (§ 100) . .	படித்தும், *although* (I, &c.) *learned* (§ 100).
PERFECT (AFFIRMATION)	செய்திருந்தும், *although* (I, &c.) *have done* (§ 79)	படித்திருந்தும், *although* (I, &c.) *have learned* (§ 79).
FUTURE (SUPPOSITION)	செய்தாலும், *although* (I, &c.) *should do* (§ 100)	படித்தாலும், *although* (I, &c.) *should learn* (§ 100).
FUTURE PERFECT (SUPPOSITION)	செய்திருந்தாலும், *although* (I, &c.) *should have done* (§ 79)	படித்திருந்தாலும், *although* (I, &c.) *should have learned* (§ 79).
III. POTENTIAL MOOD. (May or can.) Page 81.		
ALL TIMES . .	செய்யக்கூடும், (I, &c.) *can do* (§ 103) . .	படிக்கக்கூடும், (I, &c.) *can learn* (§ 103).
	செய்யலாம், (I, &c.) *may do* (§ 103) . .	படிக்கலாம், (I, &c.) *may learn* (§ 103).

IV. Imperative Mood.		
	செய், *do* (§ 27)	படி, *learn* (§ 27).
V. Optative Mood.		
	செய்யக்கடவேன், &c. (§ 140), *may* (I) *do*, &c. (நான், &c.) செய்க	படிக்கக்கடவேன் (§104), *may* (I) *learn*, &c. (நான், &c.) படிக்க.
VI. Infinitive Mood. (§ 168.)		
PRESENT . .	செய்ய, *to do* (§ 41)	படிக்க, *to learn*.
PERFECT . .	செய்திருக்க, *to have done* (§ 80) . . .	படித்திருக்க, *to have learned*.
VII. Participles.		
ADVERBIAL (§ 77)	செய்து செய்திருந்து } *having done*	படித்து படித்திருந்து } *having learned*. ஆனுப்பி.
RELATIVE OR ADJECTIVE (§ 74)	PRES. செய்கிற, *that does* . . . . PAST செய்த, *that did* . . . . . FUT. செய்யும், *that will do*	படிக்கிற, *that learns*. படித்த, *that learned*. படிக்கும், *that will learn*.

VIII. Verbal Nouns.

	Weak Form.	*Strong Form.*
FROM THE ROOT	செய்கை, செயல், செய்தல், செய்குதல், *a doing, deed* (§§ 143–148)	படிப்பு, படித்தல், படிக்குதல், *a learning, learning.*
FROM THE REL. PARTICIPLE	செய்கிறவன், ள், து, *one who does, &c.* (§§ 87, 88)	படிக்கிறவன், &c. &c., *one who learns* (§§ 87, 88).

IX. Negative Verb. Lessons 37–40.

ABSOLUTE . .	செய்யேன், *I* (do, &c.) *not do* (§ 110) . .	படியேன், *I* (do, &c.) *not learn* (§ 110).
COMPOUND . .	செய்யவில்லை, (I, &c., do, &c.) *not do* (§ 113)	படிக்கவில்லை, (I, &c., do, &c.) *not learn* (§ 113).
VERBAL NOUN + இல்லை	செய்கிறதில்லை, (I, &c.) *do not do* . . . செய்ததில்லை, (I, &c.) *did not do* (§ 114) . செய்வதில்லை, (I, &c.) *shall not do* . .	படிக்கிறதில்லை, (I, &c.) *do not* படித்ததில்லை, (I, &c.) *did not* படிப்பதில்லை, (I, &c.) *shall not* } *learn* (§ 114).
ADVERBIAL PARTICIPLES	செய்யாது செய்யாமல் } *not doing* (§§ 121, 122) . .	படியாது படியாமல் } *not learning* (§§ 121, 122).
WITH இரு .	செய்யாதிரு செய்யாமலிரு } through all tenses and moods (§§ 121–123)	படியாதிரு படியாமலிரு } (§§ 121–123).

RELATIVE PARTICIPLES	செய்யாத / செய்யா } *that does not* (§§ 121–124)	படியாத / படியா } *that learns not* (§§ 121–124).
VERBAL NOUNS	செய்யாமை, *the not doing* (§ 154) செய்யாதவன், &c., *who does not, &c.* (§§ 121–124)	படியாமை, *the not learning* (§ 154). படியாதவன், &c., *who does not learn* (§§ 121–124).
IMPERATIVE	செய்யாதே, *do not* (§ 121)	படியாதே, *learn not* (§ 121).

X. Passive Voice. (§ 92.)

THE INFINITIVES செய்ய and படிக்க with படுகிறேன், பட்டேன், and படுவேன் (§ 56. III) throughout.

PRESENT	செய்யப்படுகிறேன், *I am done* (§ 92)	படிக்கப்படுகிறேன், *I am read* (§ 92).
IMPERFECT	செய்யப்பட்டேன், *I was done* (§ 92)	படிக்கப்பட்டேன், *I was read* (§ 92).
FUTURE	செய்யப்படுவேன், *I shall be done*	படிக்கப்படுவேன், *I shall be read* (§ 92).

XI. Causal Form. (§§ 160, 161.)

செய் + வி + க்கிறேன், *I cause to do.* படி + ப்பி + க்கிறேன், *I cause to learn.*
Both conjugated throughout like படி ——

XII. Some Poetical or Obsolete Forms. Lesson 97.

PRESENT	செய்கின்றனன் = செய்கிறான். The form செய்யாநின்றேன் is sometimes used (§ 264).
PAST	உண்டனை = உண்டி = உண்டாய்.

FUTURE	உண்கு, உண்பல் = உண்பேன். உண்கும் = உண்போம். வருது = வருவேன். வருதும் = வருவோம். சேறு = செல்லுவேன். சேறும் = செல்வோம். கெடுவல் = கெடுவேன். நடமார் = நடப்பார்கள். செய்ப = செய்வார்கள். படியன்மார் = படிப்பார்கள்.
OPTATIVE	வாழ்க, வாழிய, வாழியர், *may* (I, thou, &c.) *prosper*. கொள்ளல் = கொள்ளக்கடவேன். (§ 140.)
INFINITIVE	For செய்ய are used செய்யிய, செய்யியர். For நடக்க, நடப்ப.
IMPERATIVE	செய்மின், *do ye*. ஆதி, *become thou*.
ADVERBIAL PARTICIPLES	செய்து, உண்குபு, உண்ணு, உண்ணூ, செய்யென், செய்வான், செய்பான், செய்பாக்கு are all used as adverbial participles. Page 77.
CONTRACTED RELATIVE PARTICIPLES	(§ 72). For வாவும் is used வாம். The middle particle and termination are sometimes omitted and the root only used: செய்வினை = செய்கிறவினை or செய்தவினை or செய்யும் வினை. THIS IS ONE OF THE GREAT PECULIARITIES OF TAMIL POETRY. (§ 270.)
NEGATIVE	நடந்திலன் = நடவேன், நடக்கின்றிலன், நடக்கிலன், நடக்கலன், நடவாதான் are all forms equivalent to நடவேன். செய்யேல் = செய்யல் = செய்யாதே, *pl.* செய்யன்மின், செய்யாதிருங்கள். (§ 270.)
CONJUGATED APPELLATIVES (§§ 184, 270)	வில், *a bow*, makes வில்லேன், *I a bow-man;* வில்லை, *thou a bow-man;* வில்லான், &c. These are declined as nouns, the first makes வில்லேனை, &c. முதல் makes முதற்று, *that which is the first;* முதல, *those which are the first.* In general all the personal terminations of the verb may be used with nouns in this way. For ஆன், ஒன் is also used; and for ஆர், ஓர்;—முன்னோன், முன்னோர்.

(*a*) The term. ஆன், ஆள், ஆர், என், ஒம், ஈர் are often shortened into அன், அள், அர், என், அம், and இர் respectively;—அன் being also inserted. For ஒம் are used எம், ஆம்: உண்டேம் = உண்டோம்.

(*b*) Particles such as இன், அன், கு, பு, அல், and many others, are inserted between the root and terminations of verbs in poetry.

LESSON 35.

Exercise 34.

A STORY.

§ 105. [Every word in this tale is in use, and every form deserves attention. Let the learner go over it often, and carefully consult all the references.]

மது-பிந்து-கலகம்[1].
The honey-drop-tumult.

ஒரு துலுக்கன் ஒரு பெரிய ஊரிலே கடைக்கு[ப்] போய்[த்]
A Muhammadan a great in town to the bazaar having gone,
1 13 21 21 78

தேன் வாங்கும்[2] போது ஒரு துளி[த்][3] தேன் கீழே சிந்தியது.
honey which will buy the time, a drop-honey below was spilt.
50 74 50 131 70 (2)

அதின் மேலே ஒரு ஈ வந்து மொய்த்தது. அந்த ஈயை
Of it upon a fly having come it alighted. That fly,
25, 21 77, 70 70 25 18

அங்கிருந்த (அங்கு இருந்த) பல்லி பிடித்து[க்] கொண்டது[4].
there-which-was ——————*(a) lizard having seized, took.*
74 77 70*

அந்த[ப்] பல்லியை[க்] கடைக்காரனுடைய பூனை பிடித்து[க்]
That lizard the bazaar-man's cat having seized,
25 18 52, 21 77

கொண்டது. அந்த[ப்] பூனையை[த்] துலுக்கனுடைய நாய் கடித்
took. That cat the Muhammadan's dog having
70 (2) 25 18 21 77, 56

து[ப்] போட்டது[5]. அந்த நாயை[க்] கடைக்காரன் அடித்து[க்]
bit it put. That dog the bazaar-man having beaten,
68. III 70 25 131 77

கொன்று போட்டான். அந்த[க்] கடைக்காரனை[த்] துலுக்கன்
having killed, he put. That bazaar-man the Muhammadan
78, 56 (III) 25 18

வெட்டி[ப்] போட்டான். அந்த[த்] துலுக்கனை மற்றை[க்]
having cut down, he put. That Muhammadan the other
77 70 (2) 25 18

கடைக்காரர்கள் வெட்டி[ப்] போட்டார்கள். அந்த[க்] கடைக்
bazaar-men having cut down, they put. Those bazaar-
29 77 25 29

காரரை[த்] துலுக்கர் வந்து, சுற்றி[க்]
men (*the*) *Muhammadans having come, having surrounded,*
29 77

கொண்டார்கள். துலுக்கர் சூழ்ந்து கொண்டதை[ப்]
took. The Muhammadans the having surrounded
29 77 87

பார்த்து[க்] கடைக்காரருக்காக வெகு பெயர் கூடினார்கள்.
having seen, for the bazaar-men many persons came together.
77, 64 29 70

அவர்களும் இவர்களும் கை கலந்து, சண்டை செய்து,
And those, and these, hand having mingled, a row having made,
10, 8 8, 10, 25 50, 77, 66 50, 77, 58. I

அந்த[ப்] பக்கத்திலே நூறு பெயர் இந்த[ப்] பக்கத்திலே நூறு
in that side a hundred persons, in this side a hun-
25 21 172 25 21

பெயர் சாகவே[b], பட்டணம் எல்லாம்
dred persons, to die indeed (when they had died), *the town all*
172 58 (III), 169 127

பயந்து அல்லகல்லோலப் பட்டு வலசை
having feared, utter confusion having suffered, a hurried removal
77, 66 77 161 50

வாங்கியது.
it took.
70 (2).

§ 106. Notes on the story.

(1) மது-பிந்து-கலசம். Compounds are often formed in Tamil, as in other languages, by merely putting the crude forms together.

This is simple Sanskrit. Compare § 131.

(2) தேன் வாங்கும் போது. Here போது (or பொழுது), meaning *time*, is used for 'when': வாங்கும் is the future relative participle (§ 74), but is used indefinitely for any time. Translate, 'When (he) was buying honey.'

Thus: அவன் போனான் போகும்போது, &c.
He went, and while he was going.

(3) துளித்தேன், *drop* [of] *honey:* மதுபிந்து. The words are put in apposition. Such constructions are frequent. So ஒரு குடம். தண்ணீர், *a pot* [of] *water.* சிந்தியது is here used intransitively.

(4) கொண்டது, from the root கொள் (ளு), (§ 56. III). It is used several times here, சுற்றிக் கொண்டார்கள், &c. This verb is frequently added as an auxiliary to the adverbial participle of another,—

(*a*) To give a MIDDLE or REFLEXIVE signification: வாங்கிக் கொண்டான், *he bought* (for himself). It may be thus added to very many verbs.

(*b*) To give the idea of HABITUAL REPEATED action: எழுதிக் கொண்டான், *he continued writing*. It is not used when the action is done once for all.

(*c*) Merely as an expletive, adding perhaps an idea of COMPLETENESS; as here, பிடித்துக்கொண்டது. (§ 259.)

(5) கடித்து[ப்] போட்டது. Here போடு is added to the adverbial part. கடித்து. This verb added to another makes its transitive character more apparent. It adds force in some cases. (§ 256.) போ is added to *intransitive* verbs in the same way. (§ 258.)

(6) சாகவே: ஏ emphatic added to the infinitive mood makes it equivalent to the *case absolute*=*they having died*. (§ 168.)

§ 107. Vocabulary to the Story.

துலுக்கன், *Muhammadan*.
கடை, *a bazaar*.
கடைக்காரன், *a bazaar-man*.
தேன், *honey*.
துளி, *a drop*.
வாங்கு, *buy, obtain, receive* (§ 56. II). பொழுது, போது, *time*, with rel. part.=*when, while*.
மற்றை, *other*.
கீழ்[1], *under* (ஏ is often added).
சிந்து, *spill* (§ 62).
மேல்[1], *over, above* (ஏ often added).
ஈ, *a fly*.
மொய், *swarm, alight upon as a winged insect* (§ 56. III).
அங்கு, *there*=அங்கே.
பல்லி, *a lizard* (from பல் = *a tooth*).
கூடு, *join* (§ 62).
சுற்று, *surround* (§ 62).
பிடி, *seize* (§ 56. III).
பூனை, *a cat*.
வெட்டு, *cut, cut down* (§ 56. II).
வெகு, *many, much*.
பெயர், *a name, a person, people*: பேர்.
சண்டை, *a row*—'*shindy*.'
பக்கம், *a side*.
நூறு, *a hundred* (§ 172).
பட்டணம், *a town*.
எல்லாம், *all, the whole*.
பய[2], *fear* [only the past பயந்து, &c. in use], (§ 66.)
அல்லகல்லோலம், *utter confusion* (an imitative word, like hubbub, &c.).
வலசை, *a hurried removal through fear*, &c., used with the verb வாங்கு, *emigrate*. [Ar. *wulsa*.]
சூழ், *surround* (§ 60).

[1] Both மேல் and கீழ் are nouns governing the 6th case with the termination இன்: வீட்டின் மேல், மேசையின் கீழ். அதன்மேல் ஏறினான், *he climbed upon it*. They may govern also the 4th case (§§ 248, 251).

[2] Nouns in ம் form verbs with root படு, *suffer*. They then lose ம் and ப் is doubled (§ 161).

LESSON 36.

THE REFLEXIVE PRONOUN தான்: 'SELF,' 'OWN,' 'INDEED.'

§ **108.** (*a*) தான் is thus declined :—

Case.	*Singular.*	*Plural.*
1	தான், *himself, herself, itself.*	தாம் or தாங்கள், *themselves.*
2	தன்னை (the stem shortened).	தம்மை „ தங்களை
3	தன்னால் தன்னோடு	தம்மால் „ தங்களால் தம்மோடு „ தங்களோடு
4	தனக்கு தனக்காக	தமக்கு „ தங்களுக்கு தமக்காக „ தங்களுக்காக

and so on like the 1st person (§ 37). Compare the forms of these pronouns carefully.

(*b*) The plurals தாம் and தாங்கள் are used perpetually as polite forms of address: *your honour, your excellency.*

☞ இது தங்களுக்கு வேண்டுமோ? *Do you want this?* (Is this wanting to themselves?)

தமக்கு is a little less respectful,
உமக்கு would be used to an equal, and
உனக்கு only to a junior or inferior.

(*c*) தான் is sometimes used as equivalent to *indeed*, and, at the end of a sentence, occasionally takes the place of the verb. It cannot be added to a finite verb. You must not say: போனான்தான், *he assuredly went;* but போனானே, or அவன்போனது நிசம்.

☞ இது தண்ணீர் தான், *this is indeed water* (water *itself* and nothing else).

ஆர் போனார்கள்? தாயும் பிள்ளையும் தான், *who went? The mother and the child* (went).

(This latter construction is hardly to be imitated. Repeat the verb, or give the whole sentence another turn):

நீ போக[த்] தான் வேண்டும், *you must, indeed, go.*

☞ The emphatic particle ஏ is more elegantly used in this case: நீ போகவே வேண்டும்.

(*d*) அந்தப் பையன் தன் (தன்னுடைய) பாடத்தைப் படித்துக்
That boy his lesson
கொண்டான். [§ 106. (4.)]
learnt.

Not அவனுடைய = *that person's.*

☞ Wherever the meaning is *his*, *her* or *its own*, referring to the subject (*suus*, *-a*, *-um*), use தன்னுடைய, தன் or தனது, and rarely அவனுடைய, அவளுடைய, அதினுடைய, &c.

§ 108 *. Vocabulary.

அவனவன், *each one* (he, he).
வல்லபம், *ability*.
காண்பி (§ 56. III), *cause to see, exhibit*.
சங்கீதம், *song*.
சித்தம், *will*.
பாடு, *sing* (§ 62).
அசை, *wag* (§ 64).
ஆலோசி (§ 64), *think, meditate*.
பாக்கியம், *happiness*.
நிசம், நிச்சயம், *certainty*.

Exercise 35.

§ 109. [1] வேலைக்காரர் கடைக்குப் போனார்கள். [2] நீ கணக்கனோ காவற்காரனோ? [3] நான் கணக்கன் அல்ல காவற்காரன்தான். [4] தாய் தன் பிள்ளையை இப்படிக் காட்டிலே விட்டுவிடலாமா? [5] தங்களுக்கு ஒரு வேலைக்காரன் வேண்டும் என்று வந்தேன். [6] தாங்கள் என்னைப் பார்க்க வேண்டும். [7] இந்தப் பக்கத்திலும் அந்தப் பக்கத்திலும் வீடுகள் உண்டு. [8] மரத்தின்மேலே என்ன உண்டு? [9] குருவிகள் தான் உண்டு. [10] சண்டை செய்யலாமா? [11] குடிகள் தீர்வையைச் செலுத்தினபொழுது மாசூல் அறுக்கலாம். [12] ஊரார் உன்னை வைதிருந்தாலும் (§ 58. I) நீ குடிகளை அடித்து[ப்] பிடித்து[ச்] சண்டை செய்யலாமா? [13] அவனவன் தன் தன் வல்லபத்தைக் காண்பித்தான். [14] தங்கள் சித்தம் என் பாக்கியம் என்றான். [15] தலை (§ 50) அசைத்துக் கொண்டு [§ 106. (4)] சங்கீதம் பாடினான். [16] தனக்குள்ளே ஆலோசித்தான். [17] அது நிசந்தான்.

[1] The bazaar-man beat his cat. [2] The Muhammadan killed his dog. [3] The people left their houses and emigrated. [4] There is honey in the jungle. [5] Is there honey in the jungle? [6] There is no honey in the jungle. [7] Give me a drop of water. [8] Is it right to catch flies? [9] Did the villagers kill the bazaar-man's dog? [10] No, the Muhammadan killed it. [11] Come when I write the letter. [12] Come when I have written the letter. [13] Go after you have seen the petition. [14] He came before the clerk had read the report to the gentleman.

LESSON 37.

THE NEGATIVE VERB.

§ 110. The Tamil has a peculiarity nearly confined [1] to the family of South Indian dialects; it has a negative inflexion of the verb. And this is formed by adding to the root the personal terminations *without any particle indicative of time.* Compare—

படி + க்கிறு + என் = படிக்கிறேன், *I read.*
படி + 0 + என் = படியேன், *I do not read.*

[The learner may imagine, if he please, that the absence of *any middle particle denoting time* signifies that the action of the verb takes place in no time whatever; and so *an absolute negative for all times* is formed.]

Paradigm.

Roots படி, நட, அனுப்பு.

Person.	*Singular.*	*Plural.*
1st	படியேன், நடவேன், அனுப்பேன்.	படியோம், நடவோம், அனுப்போம்.
2nd	படியாய், நடவாய், அனுப்பாய்.	படியீர், நடவீர், அனுப்பீர் (+ கள்).
3rd *m.*	படியான், நடவான், அனுப்பான்.	படியார்(கள்), நடவார்(கள்), அனுப்பார்(கள்).
f.	படியாள், நடவாள், அனுப்பாள்.	
n.	படியாது, நடவாது, அனுப்பாது, படியா.	படியா, நடவா, அனுப்பா (not common).

Obs. (1) ய் and வ் are inserted, and உ elided, in these three forms respectively.

(2) This whole form is concise and elegant, but rather pedantic. Some persons of it only are in *common use;* the compound forms in § 113, &c. being less liable to ambiguity.

[1] Compare Rask's Anglo-Saxon Grammar, preface, p. xxix. Old Scandinavian poetry affords traces of a negative not only in verbs, but also in pronouns. Some of the Caucasian dialects exhibit the same peculiarity.

§ **111.** **Vocabulary.**

கிடங்கு, *a 'godown,' store-room.*
தோட்டம், *a garden.*
குதிரை, *a horse.*
பண்டி, *a buggy, cart, vehicle.*
{காரியம், *thing, matter.*
{சங்கதி, *affair.*
{செய்தி, *news.*
விசாரி, *inquire* (§ 56. III).

நட, *walk* [§ 56. (I)], *go on, happen, take place.*
தெரி, *be plain, understood* (used impersonally), (§ 56. I).
ஐயா! *sir!* (voc. of ஐயன், *an honourable person*).
ஓடு, *run* (§ 56. II).

Exercise 36.

§ **112.** [1] அந்த ஊரார் 'இந்தக் காரியத்தை அறியோம்' (§ 56. I) என்றார்கள். [2] படித்துக் கொண்டால் [§ 106. (4)] அறிவோம். [3] அந்தச் சங்கதியை விசாரிக்கும் பொழுது 'அறியேன்' என்றான். [4] இந்தக் காரியம் நடவாது. [5] 'இந்தப் பணம் ஊரிலே செல்லாது' [§ 56. (III)] என்று சொன்னான் (§ 70). [6] 'இந்தப் பணம் செல்லுமோ செல்லாதோ' என்று தனக்குத் தெரியாது என்றான். [7] 'உனக்குத் தெரியுமா' என்று கேட்டேன் 'தெரியாது ஐயா!' என்றான். [8] இந்தச் சின்னக் குதிரை ஓடுமா? ஓடாது ஐயா! [9] அந்தப் பெரிய குதிரை பண்டியிலே போகுமா? [10] போகாது என்று நினைக்கிறேன்.

[11] மரங்கள் பருவத்தால் அன்றிப்பழா, *trees only fruit in their season.*

[12] நல்லறஞ் செய்வது செய்யாது கேள் (= இனம்).

[1] Is it in the store-room? I don't know. [2] That horse does not run. [3] Why does not the bullock run? [4] The gentleman must inquire into my affair. [5] Have you heard the news? [6] Do you not hear the command of the gentleman (கேளீரோ)? [7] He says, I don't know. [8] He said that he did not know. [9] When I inquired about those matters the villagers did not understand what I said. [10] Will that little horse go in my bandy? [11] I think that money will not pass in our village.

LESSON 38.

THE NEGATIVE VERB: COMPOUND FORMS.

§ **113.** The negative most frequently used (and, on the whole, the best) is obtained by adding இல்லை = *not* (§ 43), to the infinitive of the verb. This compound negative form is indefinite as to time, and is the same for all numbers and persons.

நான், நீ, அவன், &c.	நடக்கவில்லை	I, thou, he, &c. *do* / *did* / *shall* or *will*	*not walk.*

§ **114.** இல்லை is also added to other parts of the verb, especially to the neuter participial noun (§§ 87, 88).

நான், நீ, &c. &c.

செய்கிறது + இல்லை = செய்கிறதில்லை,	I, thou, &c., *do not do, am not doing.*
செய்தது + இல்லை = செய்ததில்லை,	I, thou, &c., *did not do, have not done.*
செய்வது + இல்லை = செய்வதில்லை,	I, thou, &c., *will not* (at any time) *do.*

This is more common, but perhaps somewhat less elegant, than the former.

☞ [இல்லை (really இல்லே) and அல்ல are negative forms (§ 110) of two old positive roots, இல் = இர் = *be*, and அல் = அர் = *befit* (§ 184). These often govern a case.]

§ **115.** **Vocabulary.**

சாட்சி, *testimony* (also *a witness*).
சாட்சிக்காரன், *a witness.*
சேவகன், *a peon.*
வாக்குமூலம், *a deposition.*
சரி, *right.* சரியாய், *rightly.*
காவல், (பாரா)[1], *guard, ward, prison.*
சீட்டு, *a note.*
கவனி, *attend to* (§ 56. III).
குறி, *indicate, regard* (§ 56. III).
உளுக்கார்[ரு], *sit down* (§ 60. III).
நியாயம், *reason, right.*
நீதி, *justice.*

நியாயஸ்தலம், *a court, a place of justice* (ஸ்தலம், *a place*).
கோர்ட்டு (COURT) is often used.
வாதி, *the complainant.*
பிரதிவாதி (பிரதி, *opposition*), *the defendant.*
வக்கீல், *a pleader.*
அளவு, *a measure.*
இவ்வளவு (this measure), *thus much* (§ 25).
அவ்வளவு (that measure), *so much.*
எவ்வளவு (what measure), *how much?*
கிழி (§ 56. III), *tear.*

Exercise 37.

§ **116.** [1] துரை சரியாய்க் கேட்கவில்லை. [2] நீ நன்றாய்க் கவனித்து வாக்குமூலம் வாங்க வேண்டும். [3] உளுக்காரும் ஐயா! [4] நீ என்னத்தைக்[2]

[1] A word written thus is to be considered as a synonym of the one after which it is put; but is either a foreign word, or a vulgar and objectionable one, though common one.

[2] Lit. 'having indicated what, do you speak so much?' குறித்து is equivalent to *regarding, concerning, about.* (§ 230.)

குறித்து இவ்வளவு பேசுகிறாய்? [5] வாதிக்கு எவ்வளவு செல்ல வேண்டும்? [6] உன்குற்றத்திற்காக (§ 22) நீ நியாயமாய்த் தண்டிக்கப்படுவாய். [7] நியாய ஸ்தலத்திலே சாட்சிக்காரன் சரியாய்ச் சொல்ல வேண்டும். [8] இங்கே நீதிநடக்கும். [9] காவலில் (பாராவிலே) போடப்பட்டான். [10] உனக்குச் சாட்சி இல்லையா? [11] நான் அங்கே போவதில்லை. [12] அவன் கவனிக்கிறதில்லை. [13] வக்கீல் என்னைக் கூப்பிட்டுக் கேட்கவில்லை. [14] நீ சொன்ன வாக்குமூலம் சரியா? [15] அந்தக் குற்றத்தை அவர் மன்னிப்பதில்லை.

[1]Why has he not written the deposition? [2]Why do the peons beat the witness? [3]The gentleman will do you justice. [4]What fault has the physician committed? [5]Why do these villagers not pay the instalment (due)? [6]The child does not sleep. [7]Although I have called the defendant's witnesses they come not. [8]Although the munshi read the lesson to him he does not pronounce it rightly. [9]Although his father beat him the little boy does not attend to his lessons.

LESSON 39.

SOME DEFECTIVE AND IRREGULAR NEGATIVES.

§ 117. From the roots மாட்டு, *hook on*, கூடு, *join*, போ, *go*, ஒண்ணு, *be possible*, எல், *agree*, தகு, *befit* (δίκη), போது, *suffice*, ஒ, *agree*, வேண்டு, *need*, according to § 110, are made the very common forms:

Sing. 1st pers. மாட்டேன், I *will not, cannot.*
2nd ,, மாட்டாய்-டீர், thou (you) *wilt not, canst not.*
3rd ,, மாட்டான்-ர், he *will not, cannot.*
மாட்டாள், she *will not, cannot.*
மாட்டாது, it *will not, cannot.*

Plur. 1st pers. மாட்டோம், we *will not, cannot.*
2nd ,, மாட்டீர்|கள், ye or you *will not, cannot.*
3rd ,, மாட்டார்|கள், they *will not, cannot.*

கூடாது, *it must not be, cannot be.*
போகாது, '*it is no go*' (vulg.).
ஒண்ணாது, '*it won't fit*' (vulg.).
எலாது, *it is not proper.*
தகாது, *it is not fit, right.*
போதாது, *it is not sufficient.*
ஒவ்வாது, *it does not agree.*

வேண்டாம், *it is not necessary.* (This is quite irregular. For வேண்டாவாம்: வேண்டா + ஆம்.)
முடியாது, *it ends not, comes not to pass* (§ 56. I).

§ 118. The affirmative of கூடாது is formed regularly (3rd part. neut. fut., § 72), கூடும்; of ஏலாது, ஏற்கும் (§ 70); of தகாது, தகும்; of ஒவ்வாது, ஒக்கும்; and of வேண்டாம், வேண்டும். These are all common.

§ 119. *a.* இந்தத் தேனைக் கிடங்கில் வைக்கலாமா? வைக்கக் கூடாது.
May this honey be put in the store-room? It must not. [Comp. § 103.]

b. இந்தக் குதிரை பண்டியில் போகுமா? போக மாட்டாது.
Will this horse go in the bandy? It will not.

c. வாதி கொடுத்த மனு ஏற்குமா? ஏலாது.
Is the petition which the plaintiff has presented a fitting one? It is not a fitting one.

d. அவனை வைகிறது தகுமா? வைகிறது தகாது.
Is it a fit thing to abuse him? To abuse is not becoming.

e. பிரதிவாதி கோர்ட்டிலே (ஒரு) மனுக் கொடுக்க வேண்டுமா?
Should the respondent present a petition in court?
கொடுக்க வேண்டாம்.
He need not (should not, &c.).

f. செய்கிறாயா? '*Will you do it?*' (pronounced செய்றியா).
செய்(கி)றேன் = *I will.*
செய்யமாட்டேன் = *I won't.*

Exercise 38.

§ 120. [1] இந்தப் பையன் பாடம் படிக்க மாட்டேன் என்கிறான். [2] ஊரார் மாகுலே அறுத்துக் கொண்டுபோய் இருந்தும் கிஸ்திப்பணத்தைச் செலுத்த மாட்டோம் என்று சொல்லுகிறார்கள். [3] அந்தக் கடைக்காரன் தீமைகளைச் செய்திருந்தாலும் அவனுக்கு நீர் மன்னிக்கவேண்டும். [4] அந்தச் சங்கதியைக்குறித்து (§ 116) உமக்கு என்ன தெரியும்? [5] உமக்குத் தெரிந்ததை (§ 87) எல்லாம் (§ 127) தெளிவாய்ச் சொல்லக் கூடாதா? [6] இப்படிப் பேசுவது (§ 88) தகுமா? இது சரியல்ல (§ 43). [7] இது எப்படி நடந்தது சொல்லு சரியாய் (idiom for சரியாய்ச் சொல்லு, which is more correct). [8] நான் ஒன்றும் (§§ 172, 126 = *anything at all*) அறியேன் என்றான். [9] வேண்டாம் அப்பா! [10] அந்தப்பணம் எனக்குப் போதாது ஐயா! [11] போதும் போதும்! [For போதாது we often hear பற்றாது or பற்ற மாட்டாது = *it won't touch* (suffice). Thus, அந்தச் சம்பளம் வயிற்றுக்குப் பற்றாது, *the wages won't* suffice *for my* வயிறு. This is often said by the common people.]

[1] The watchman said that the villagers beat him; but the witnesses did not give their depositions rightly. [2] Why will you make a disturbance in the village? [3] Although the defendant killed the dog you must forgive his fault. [4] They all sat down in the court. [5] They were seated in the place of justice when the gentleman came in. [6] This and that agree. [7] Tell him how the affair happened. [8] He says that he cannot learn the lesson. [9] The servant said he would not do that. [10] They denied all knowledge of the affair. [11] The munshi said that I need not write that lesson.

LESSON 40.

OTHER NEGATIVE FORMS OF THE VERB.

§ **121.** (1) To get an ordinary familiar negative imperative, or prohibitive, to the 3rd sing. neut. neg. add ஏ, for the sing.; ஏ + உம், for the polite form; and ஏ + உங்கள், for the plural.

Thus, from நட-வ-ாது, *it walks not* (*does not happen*), are formed—

நட-வ-ாதே, *don't walk.*
நட-வ-ாதேயும், *don't walk, sir!*
நட-வ-ாதேயுங்கள், *do not walk, I pray you.*

(2) The negative adverbial participle (§ 77) is formed by adding ஆது or ஆமல் to the root. One of the forms is therefore the same as the 3rd sing. neut. neg., § 110.

படி-ய-ாது, } *not learning.*
படி-ய-ாமல், }

This is also used adverbially: ஓயாமல், *unceasingly;* இடைவி டாமல், *without intermission;* அறியாமல், *unwittingly.*

In poetry, sometimes, படியாமே, படியாமை.

(3) By adding to the above the auxiliary verb இரு (sometimes போ and other roots), in all its parts, a complete negative verb may be constructed, though the forms are rather cumbrous. Thus:

படி-ய-ாமல் இருக்கிறான், } *he does not learn* (he is not learning).
படி-ய-ாதிருக்கிறான்,. }
நட-வ-ாதிரு, *do not walk.*
நீ நட-வ-ாமலிருந்தால், *if you do not walk.*

Further examples are not necessary, but compounds of this kind are constantly used.

(4) A negative relative participle for all tenses, and participial nouns, answering to the forms in §§ 74, 87, are formed by

changing உ of the verbal participle in ஆது into அ (or sometimes, chiefly in poetry, by simply omitting து).

நடவாது (−உ+அ=) நடவாத, *who or which walks not:* நடவா.

இவன் படியாத பையன், *he* [is] *a boy who learns not* (or has not learned).

நான் கட்டாத (§ 62) வீடு, *a house which I have not built.*

Ex. அறியாத நாள் எல்லாம் பிறவாத நாள், lit. '*every day that knows not is a day not born,*'=time passed in ignorance is wasted.

(5) And thence we obtain the following negative participial nouns:

Singular:
- நட-வ-ாதவன், *he who does not walk.*
- நட-வ-ாதவள், *she who does not walk.*
- நட-வ-ாதது, *that which does not walk.*

Plural:
- நட-வ-ாதவர், *he* (hon.) *who does not walk.*
- நட-வ-ாதவர்-கள், *they who do not walk.*
- நட-வ-ாதவை-கள், *things which do not walk.*

இல்-ல-ாதவன்=*one who is not:* இல்லான்.

அல்-ல-ாதவன்=*one who has not.*

§ 121*. Vocabulary.

பதறு, *hurry* (§ 56. II).
சிதறு, *be dispersed, come to nothing, fail* (§ 56. II).
ஞானம், *wisdom.*
அஞ்ஞானம், *folly, ignorance, heathenism.*
விடா=விடாத, *incessant.*
நூல், *thread; a scientific work.*
மாற்று, *the standard value of a metal, its fineness.*
உரை, *standard of gold.*
தேம்பு (§ 62), *sob.*
ஓய் (§ 57), *cease, rest.*
Neither—nor, உம்—உம் with a negative (§ 208).

Exercise 39.

§ 122. [1] நீ தீமை செய்யாமல் இருந்தால் வாழுவாய். [2] பையனே காட்டுக்குப் போகாதே! [3] என் பிதாவே! என்னைத் தண்டியாதிரும். [4] குடிகளே! சண்டை செய்யாதிருங்கள்! பேசாதேயுங்கள்! [5] நீ படியாமல் இருந்தால் (போனால்) பாடம் வராது. [6] அவன் படிக்க மாட்டானே ஆனால் பாடம் எப்படிவரும்? [7] பதறாத காரியம் சிதறாது. [8] தகாததைச் செய்பவன் (§ 88) படாததைப் படுவான். [9] பாவஞ் செய்யாதிரு மனமே! புத்தியற்ற [அறு, §§ 68, 133] அஞ்ஞான நூல் படியாதே! (§ 121.) [10] தான் தேடாப் பொன்னுக்கு மாற்றும் இல்லை உரையும் இல்லை (*what is got without effort is not valued*). [11] விடா (§ 254) மழையாகப் (§ 136) பெய்து கொண்டிருந்தது. [12] இவனை

அறியாமல் இவன்பின்னே போய்ச் சோதித்து வாருங்கள் (= *without his knowing it:* for இவன் அதை அறியாமல்). [These sentences can be rendered in various ways.] 13 தேம்பித் தேம்பி ஓயாமல் அழுதான். 14 இது என்னாலே முடியாது.

1 I had not seen him. 2 If he will not come. 3 Why do not the servants open the doors? 4 If they do not open the doors when I tell them what can I do? 5 If the attorney does not properly represent the affair in court what can the plaintiff do? 6 This is a thing which has not happened and cannot happen. 7 Silence! this is an impossible thing. 8 What is not possible to us is possible to Him.

LESSON 41.

HINTS FOR CONVERSATION. CORRUPT FORMS.

§ 128. (*a*) The form படித்தேன் (§ 70. 2), &c., is vulgarly pronounced (ச்ச் for த்த்) படிச்சேன், and படித்தது is படிச்சுது or படிச்சு. This is not to be imitated, but in very common conversation can hardly be quite avoided. Thus, போச்சுது or போச்சு is used for போயினது or போனது. This is elegantly போயிற்று. So ஆயினது, ஆனது or ஆயிற்று is vulg. ஆச்சுது or ஆச்சு.

(*b*) The shortened செய்யா is occasionally used in composition where செய்யாமல் (§ 121. 2) would be the full form. This is chiefly found in the phrases இல்லா விட்டால், செய்யா விட்டால், போகா விட்டால், and the like. விட்டால் = *if* (you) *leave* (§ 68). Thus, செய்யா விட்டால் will mean '*not doing, if* (you) *leave*'; இல்லா விட்டால் = '*not being, if* (you) *leave*'; போகா விட்டால் = '*not going, if* (you) *leave*.' They are equivalent to '*unless you*,' &c., '*if you do not*,' &c.

செய்யாமல் இருந்தால் is perhaps more elegant.

(*c*) For செய்தால் (§ 95. *a*) you will often hear செய்தாக்கா = *if you do*, போனாக்கா = *if* (you) *go*, &c. This is either from the poetical form செய்தக்கால், or from செய்தால் கால் (ல் + க் = ற்க், செய்தாற் கால்), where கால் is a poetical word for காலம், *time* = *when* (§ 97).

(*d*) Letters are often interchanged in different parts of the Tamil country. Thus, ழ் is ய் in Madras, and ள் in Tinevelly and the south.

கோழி, *a fowl*, is கோயி in Madras, and கோளி in the south.

ச and ய are also interchanged.

Thus, வியாதி, *sickness*, in the south is (often) விசாதி.

(*e*) The 3rd plural (masc. and fem.) is strangely corrupted in very vulgar conversation. Thus, செய்வார்கள் becomes செய்வாங்கோ, &c.; செய்தார்கள் is sometimes pronounced something like செய்தாவ (ÇEYTHĀWA).

(*f*) There is a common form, which the lower orders sometimes use in addressing a superior, that is puzzling to a beginner: for இல்லை they say இல்லீங்க, &c. This seems to be the honorific plural in உங்கள். This is carried to a great extent in Madras.

(*g*) We have in English a number of words which are apparently mere reduplications, such as *hurly-burly*, *topsy-turvy*, &c. In Tamil these occur much more frequently. In general any noun may be so repeated (of course, in the merest colloquial dialect). If the word does not begin with க், the reduplicated syllable generally does. Thus, விறகு, *fire-wood*, becomes விறகு கிறகு = 'fire-wood, &c.'; மேசை கீசை is 'the table and its appurtenances'; கட்டில் கிட்டில் for கட்டில், *a cot;* கொஞ்சம் கெஞ்சம் for கொஞ்சம், *a little.* [So in Telugu, *kuli-nāli.*] This is worth noting carefully. Comp. §§ 223, 273. Sometimes the alliterative, meaningless word comes first: thus தொப்புநுரை = *foam, &c.* (தொப்பு is meaningless). அக்கு அழுக்கில்லை = *it is clean* (அக்கு is meaningless). Comp. அக்கம் பக்கம்.

☞ [This whole lesson may be talked over with a munshi or other intelligent native and such forms collected. These are given as a specimen. The great matter is to know exactly what the people say! We can choose our own words and forms at leisure.]

§ 124. Vocabulary.

இன்னம் (இன்னும்), *yet.*
போ, *go*, added to intransitive words, gives the idea of completeness, as போடு does to transitives. (§§ 106. (5); 256.)
குறை (§ 56. I), *be deficient*, (§ 56. III) *diminish, lessen.*
தமிழ், *Tamil.*
பாஷை, *a language.*

Exercise 40.

§ 125. [1] அந்த வீடு கட்டப்பட்ட பின்பு, நீர் போய்ப்பார்க்க வேண்டும்; இல்லாவிட்டால், உம்முடைய குமாரன் போகவேண்டும். [2] இவர்கள் அந்தப் பணத்தைச் செலுத்தாவிட்டால் (செலுத்தாமல் போனால், செலுத்தாதே போனால்), அவர்கள் காவலில் போடப்பட (§ 68) வேண்டும். [3] இந்த வேலை செய்தாச்சு, ஐயா! [செய்து, *having done*, ஆயிற்று, *it has become = the work is finished.* Very common form.] [4] என்ன! வேலை ஆச்சா? (*What, has the work become? = well, is the work finished?*) [5] Madras cook (speaks) கோயி செத்துப் போச்சு for கோழி செத்துப் போயிற்று, *the fowl is dead.* [6] Tinevelly Shāṇān speaks: இதென்ன விசாதி என்ணு[1] தெரியாறு (every R pronounced with a whirr), for இது என்ன வியாதி என்று தெரியாது (*I don't know what disease this is*). [7] சேவகா! அந்த வேலே இன்னம் ஆகவில்லேயா? [8] நீ செய்தவேலே வெகு நன்ணுய் இருக்குது (ironical). [9] நீ இன்னம் அந்தப் பணத்தைச் செலுத்தாமல் இருக்கிறது என்ன? [10] என்னம் ஆச்சுது சொல்லு (*tell me how you got on*). [11] காரியம் முடிஞ்சுது, for முடிந்தது (*the affair is accomplished*).

[1] This work is finished. [2] If you do this evil you will perish. [3] Don't go! [4] You had better not go. [5] Put it on the table. [6] Do you understand Tamil (தமிழ் or தமிழ்ப்பாஷை)? [7] I understand it a little (red. form). [8] Unless you go you cannot obtain it. [9] If he does not send his servant for it the gentleman will not give it. [10] If you do not hear [obey] you will perish. [11] Should the little boy be so disobedient? (அடங்காமல், § 56. II.)

LESSON 42.

WORDS AND FORMS EXPRESSING UNIVERSALITY.

§ **126.** Some uses of உம், *and.* [Less. I.]

(*a*) When added to an interrogative உம் makes a universal.

1. எப்பொழுது, *when?* + உம் = எப்பொழுதும், *always.*
2. எவன், *who?* + உம் = எவனும், *everyone: quisque.*
3. எங்கு, *where?* + உம் = எங்கும், *everywhere.*
4. எப்படி, *how?* + உம் = எப்படியும், *by all means.*
5. யாவன், *who* [poet.] + உம் = யாவரும் (plur.), *all persons.*
6. யாது, *which* + உம் = யாதும், *everything.*

(*b*) உம் is also added to மேல், பின்னே, மறுபடி, and many other words used adverbially. [Latin *que.*]

மேல் (= *over*) + உம் = மேலும், *moreover.*
பின்னே (= *after*) + உம் = பின்னேயும், *besides.*
மறுபடி (= *another step*) + உம் = மறுபடியும், *again.*

§ **127.** எல்லா = *all*, சகல = *all*, அனே, *so much.*

(*a*) எல்லா as an adjective is prefixed to nouns, but requires உம் to be put after the noun.

எல்லா மனிதர்களும், *all men.*
எல்லா ஸ்திரீகளும், *all women.*
எல்லா வீடுகளும், *all houses.*

So எல்லா மனிதர்களேயும் (2nd case).

[1] ன்ற் becomes ண்ண் in common talk; thus, நன்றாய் is நண்ணுய்.

(*b*) எல்லாம் (எல்லா + உம்) is a neuter noun = *everything*. It is declined after the analogy of nouns in ம், substituting அற்று for த்து, and requires the உம் after each case. [G. 67.]

2nd case: எல்லாவற்றையும், &c.
3rd „ எல்லாவற்றோடும், &c.

(*c*) சகல is a Sanskrit word = *all*. It is used as an adjective = எல்லா. சகல மனிதர்களும், &c., *all men*, &c. It is also used as a neuter noun, சகலம், and declined regularly, like மரம் but with the addition of உம். சகலத்தையும் கண்டான், *he saw the whole*, *all*.

(*d*) அனை makes அனைத்து (sing. neut.), *so much*, and அனைய (plur. neut.), *so many*. அனைத்தும் = *the totality*, is regularly declined. These are little used except in poetry.

(*e*) எல்லா, சகல, and அனை all form nouns plural (masc. and fem.). Thus:—

எல்லாரும் (+ ர் + உம், comp. § 87),
சகலரும் (+ ர் + உம்),
அனைவரும் (+ வ் + அர் + உம்), } *all people*.

These are declined by inserting the signs of the cases between the stem and உம்: எல்லாரையும், சகலரையும், அனைவரையும், &c.

(*f*) These forms are often put after the nominative case of the noun to which they belong. Thus:

பட்டணம் எல்லாம் கலங்கிற்று (§ 70. 2), *the whole town was agitated;*

ஊரார் எல்லாரும் வந்தார்கள், *all the villagers came;*

படித்தவர்கள் அனைவரையும் கூப்பிட்டான், *he called all who had learned.*

Many of the other words in § 126 may be used in the same way.

(*g*) எல்லோரும் and அனைவோரும் are elegantly used instead of எல்லாரும் and அனைவரும்.

(*h*) முழு, adj. = *whole;* முழுமை = *the whole;* முழுவதும், முழுதும் = *the whole*. The last two are declined as the words in (*e*). முழு requires உம் to be added to the noun to which it is prefixed.

§ 128. **Vocabulary.**

கொற்றன், *a mason.*
கொல்லன், *a blacksmith.*
{ கூலி, *hire.*
{ சம்பளம், *wages.*
{ வெகுமானம், *a present.*
{ சந்தோஷம், *joy; a present.*
அபராதம், *a fine.*

உலகம், *the world.*
உள்ள, *which exists* (§ 133).
திரு, *sacred*, *holy*. [Skt. srī.]
சபை, *a congregation*, *assembly*.
திருச்சபை, *the holy Church.*
போற்று, *extol* (§ 56. II).
கொஞ்சம், *a little*, *a few*.

அரசன், இராசா, a king (with or without இ).
தீர், be removed (§ 60); act. *remove* (§ 56. III).
கால், time (for காலம்).
ஒருக்காலும், at any time whatever.

Exercise 41.

§ 129. [1] எல்லாரும் வந்தார்கள். [2] வீடெல்லாம் வெந்து போயிற்று (§§ 58. IV; 124). [3] உலகம் எங்கும் உள்ள திருச்சபை உம்மைப் போற்றும். [4] வேலைக்காரர் எல்லாருக்கும் அபராதம் போட்டேன். [5] எல்லா வேலைக் காரரிடத்திலும் அபராதம் வாங்கினார். [6] கொற்றர் யாவரும் கூலி (§ 50) வாங்கிக்கொண்டார்கள். [7] அந்த வேலைசெய்த தச்சருக்கும் கணக்கனுக்கும் சம்பளம் கொடுக்கிறபொழுது கொஞ்சம் சந்தோஷங் கொடுத்தேன். [8] சகல இராசாக்களும் குடிகளும் சாசத்தான் வேண்டும் (§§ 58. III; 108. *c*). [9] உலகத்தை எல்லாம் ஆளும் அரசன். [10] நான் யாரும் அற்ற பாவி (*I'm a destitute wretch*, § 90). [11] எவ்வுயிரும் என்னுயிர்போல் எண்ணி நான் இரங்கவேண்டும். [12] 'பாராயோ என்னை? முகம்பார்த்து ஒருகாலும் என் கவலை தீராயோ? பராபரமே!' (Poetical, but understood.) [13] தான் இல்லாத போதெல்லாம் என்னைத் தன் மந்தையைப் பார்த்துக்கொள்ளச் சொல்லுவான். [14] குடும்பக்கவலை எவ்வளவும் இல்லாமையால் (§ 154) இவ்வளவு பெலத்துடன் (§ 239) இருக்கிறான். [15] சபையாரை (§ 180) எல்லாம் கேட்டுப் பார்த்தும் (§ 100) ஒருவருஞ் சொல்லவில்லை. [16] முழுதுங் கெட்டான். [17] முழுவதுங் கொடாதே. [18] அந்த நாட்டில் அனைவரும் கூடினார்கள்.

[1] Did you see all the peons? [2] Why are all the villagers assembled together? [3] All who had committed sin feared. [4] You must learn all the lesson well. [5] He wrote and sent a letter to all the servants. [6] Why did all the carpenters leave their work? [7] Where are all the bricklayers? [8] Give all the blacksmiths their hire. [9] Have all the servants received their wages? [10] The boy who learns all the lessons well. [11] The kings who govern all the world. [12] The king who governs the whole world. [13] I will fine you. [14] He never learns. [15] I shall never see him again. [16] How many came besides?

LESSON 43.

QUALIFYING WORDS. APPOSITION.

Appositive Enlargements of Subject or Object.

§ 130. In Tamil *there are no adjectives*, strictly so called. How then are nouns qualified? (§ 74.) The past relative participle of ஆ is ஆன or ஆகிய (forms of ஆயின or ஆகின) = 'which have become.' These inserted between any two nouns will either convert the former into something answering to an adjective, or place the two in apposition.

சிவப்பான சட்டை. *a red jacket* (சிவப்பு, *redness*, சிவப்பான, *red*, or *which has become red*. You may also say சிவப்புச் சட்டை).

இராசாவாகிய தாவீது, *king David,—David the king*. You can say also தாவீது ராசா or தாவீது என்னும் இராசா (in common language என்கிற is used for என்னும்), or தாவீது என்னப்பட்ட இராசா.

ஆகும் or ஆம் is used for ஆன poetically, as is என்னும் (§ 132). Thus, வீரனாம் அரசன், *a heroic king* [*a king who will be a hero*].

§ 131. Two nouns may often be simply joined to form a compound, after the manner of *steam-ship*, *brick-house*, &c. This is constantly done in Tamil poetry, and is in accordance with the genius of the language. In fact, it may be laid down as a law that *every noun becomes an adjective by being prefixed to another*, with or without change. [The Sanskrit scholar may compare these forms with TAT-PURUSHA and KARMA-DHĀRAYA compounds.]

(*a*) Sometimes this is done without any other change than the doubling of letters; as, தீப்பொறி, *a spark of fire* (தீ, *fire*, பொறி, *a spark*); தெருத்திண்ணை, *the outside verandah* (தெரு, *a street*, திண்ணை, *elevated verandah*); ஏரிக்கரைமேலேபோனான், *he went* (along) *the top of the bank of the tank*.

(*b*) When the former noun ends in ம், that letter is elided.

[This is especially the case in Sanskrit compounds.]

Thus, மரக்கொம்பு, *branch of a tree* (மரம், *tree*, கொம்பு, *branch*); சர்வ வல்லமை, *omnipotence* (சர்வம், *all*, வல்லமை, *power*).

(*c*) Various changes may take place in the former word, of which the following are types (§ 18. *c*, *d*).

இருப்புச் சங்கிலி, *an iron chain* (இரும்பு, *iron*, சங்கிலி, *a chain*).
எருத்துக் காளை, *a young bullock* (எருது, *a bullock*, காளை, *a young male*).
ஆற்று மீன், *fish from the river* (ஆறு, *a river*, மீன், *a fish*).
ஆட்டு மந்தை, *a flock of sheep* (ஆடு, *a sheep*, மந்தை, *a flock*).
பனங் காடு, *a palmyra jungle* (பனை, *a palmyra*, காடு, *a jungle*).

☞ [1. The nasal is hardened into the surd; 2. ட் of டு, and ற் of று doubled; 3. அம் inserted.]

(*d*) இன், அத்து, அற்று are often used as connectives; and are thus used as signs of the sixth case, பசுவின் பால், *cow's milk*, இவ்விடத்து மனிதன், *a man of this place*.

☞ [The inflexional base is used in compounds.]

(*e*) Some nouns of quality ending in மை (§ 184) when prefixed to other nouns undergo certain euphonic changes. The following are chiefly to be noticed :—

(1) பெருமை, *greatness*, becomes பெரு, பெரிய, பெரும், பேர்.
(2) சிறுமை, *littleness*, becomes சிறு, சிறிய, சிறும், சிற்று, சீறு; சின், சின்ன.
(3) அருமை, *preciousness*, becomes அரு, அரிய, அரும், ஆர். [Comp. எள்.]
(4) பசுமை, *freshness*, becomes பசு, பசிய, பசும், பச்சை, பைம்.
(5) நெடுமை, *length*, becomes நெடு, நெடிய, நெடும், நீடு [√நீள்].

Comp. in Lex. the roots உரி, *pertaining to* = கிழ; மெல் (மென்), *soft*; கடு (கொடு), *hard*, *cruel*; பழ (பழை), *old*; வெ (வெம்), *hot*; கொழு, *fat*; இள (இளை), *tender*; வறு (வெறு), *bare*, *empty*; இன், *sweet*; வெள் (வெண்), *white*; கரு (கறு), *black*: THESE ARE AMONG THE OLDEST AND MOST USEFUL ROOTS OF REAL TAMIL.

Examples.

பெரு நெஞ்சு, *pride* [நெஞ்சு, *breast*].
பெரிய நன்மை, *a great benefit*.
பெரும் பாவி, *a great sinner* [before க், ச், த், ப்].
பேரின்பம், *heavenly bliss* [before a vowel].

[பெரிய may be regarded as a kind of past relative participle (§ 184). Compare அனுப்பிய (§ 74); and பெரு as the stem of a kind of verb, called குறிப்புவினை. பெரும் is a kind of future rel. part. from பெரு(கு) (§ 62), *grow great*.]

☞ [Of these the roots are undoubtedly பேர் (பர், பல்), சிற் (சில்), அர், பச்; but the *Nannūl* (Sūt. 135, 6) treats each of them as having become first an abstract noun, and as having been variously modified, when placed as the first member of a compound by the rejection of மை, the addition of இய or உம், the lengthening of the root vowel, or the reduplication of the final root consonant. Comp. Pope's G. 93, 121.]

§ **132.** என்னும் is the rel. part. fut. of என், *say*, lit. '[of whom] *one would say*.' It is thus used :

தாவீது என்னும் இராசா, *king David*.
மானம் என்னுங் காப்பு, *the defence of modesty*.
பத்தி யென்னும் ஏணி நாட்டு, *plant the ladder of piety*.

This is rather stiff and pedantic.

§ **133.** The root உள் signifies '*existence, the having within*.' To it are referred the following verbal forms:

3rd sing. for all genders and numbers. } உண்டு (உள் + து), *there is*. (§ 43.)

உள்ளது is used to signify '*it is*,' but more generally '*it is true, really so*.'

Rel. part. உள்ள, *containing, possessing within itself*. (§ 184.)

This last form added to a noun will have nearly the same effect as ஆன.

Thus, இரக்கமுள்ள தேவன் (இரக்கம், *mercy*), *a merciful God*.

Sometimes உள்ள and ஆன may be used indiscriminately:

என் பிரியமுள்ள குமாரன், } *my dear son.*
என் பிரியமான குமாரன்,

Generally, however, the difference between ஆன = *having become*, and உள்ள = *having possessed*, must be observed:

இரக்கமுள்ள பிதா (not இரக்கமான), *a merciful father.*
நீளமான கோல் (not நீளமுள்ள), *a long staff.*

The opposites to உள்ள and ஆன are அற்ற, இல்லாத, which are in the same way added to nouns:

Thus, இரக்கமற்ற = *merciless.* [அறு, *cease*, §§ 68, 74.]
பணமில்லாத = *penniless.* [இல் = *not*, § 112.]

To Sanskrit nouns ஈன (HĪNA), *destitute of*, is added:

Thus, புத்தியீன,
புத்தியீனமான, } மனிதன், *a senseless man.*
புத்தியீனமுள்ள,
or புத்தியீனன்.

[In Tamil grammar the fourth class of words consists of those called உரிச்சொல் = *quality words.* Comp. Pope's G. 118-121.
These are subdivided into பெயருரி = *noun quality*, and வினையுரி = *verb quality.*
The words included under these divisions are used to qualify nouns and verbs respectively; they may, therefore, be called *adjectives* and *adverbs.* They are, however, really nouns and participles, and it will tend greatly to aid the learner in acquiring the Tamil idiom if he steadily regard them as such.]

§ 134. **Vocabulary.**

மதுரம், *sweetness.*
கசப்பு, *bitterness.*
நவம், *newness.*
எதிர், *opposite.*
சிறு, *little.*
பழக்கம், *custom, familiarity.*
சுகம், *comfort, health.*
சருவ வல்லமை, *omnipotence.*
இராமன், *a proper name:* Rāman.
கீரை, *herb.*
பாண்டம், *a vessel.*
நாலு, *four.*
திருடன், *a thief.*
பள்ளம், *a pit.*
நடு, *middle.*
வெற்றிலை, *betel.*
கொடி, *a creeping plant.*
பலன், பலம், or பெலன், *strength.*

Exercise 42.

§ 135. 1 மதுரமான தேன் காட்டில் உண்டு. 2 கசப்பான கீரைகளைக் கொண்டுவந்தார்கள். 3 சருவவல்லமையுள்ள பிதாவாய் (§ 81) இருக்கிற பராபரன். 4 நவபாண்டங்களை வாங்கிவா. 5 அவன்சொன்னது நவமான சங்கதி. 6 எதிர்வீட்டிலே பேசிக்கொண்டிருந்தார்கள். 7 நாலுபேர் திருடர் ஒரு வீட்டிலே வந்தார்கள். 8 சிறு பிள்ளைகள் இப்படிப் பேசலாமா? 9 அவள் நடந்தசங்கதியை எல்லாம் சொன்னாள். 10 பள்ளம்உள்ள இடத்திலே தண்ணீர் நிற்கும். (Proverb.) 11 இராமன் என்கிற கடைக்

காரன் வந்தான். [12] கடு வழியிலே சிறுபிள்ளைகளைக் கண்டேன். [13] பசுவின் தயிர். [14] மனைக்கவலையே பலக்குறைவுக்குக் காரணம். [15] இது வெற்றிலைக்கொடி நடுகிறதற்கான நிலம். (ஆன = *which is suitable for.*) [16] தனக்குள்ளது உலகத்துக்கும் உண்டு தனக்கில்லது (இல் + அது = *that which is not*, § 87) உலகத்துக்கும் இல்லை என்றான். [17] அவர்கள் வாய்மொழி கேட்டார். [[18] மேகச்சாயை இளம்புல் தனம் இவைகள் வெகு நாளைக்கு நில்லா.]

[1] This is a joyful day. [2] I have come to (7th case) my merciful father. [3] This is an evil thing. [4] He is a just king. [5] This is a reasonable complaint. [6] The accountant has brought a right account to the bazaar-man. [7] Four accountants gave evidence in the court. [8] Will the watchman put the thieves in prison? [9] All my familiar friends came with me to the place of justice. [10] This is David the accountant. (3 ways.) [11] This is an affair concerning the church. [12] A new vessel. [13] Sweet Tamil. [14] Are you well? [15] This is a herb garden.

LESSON 44.

IDIOMS CONNECTED WITH THE VERB ஆ, ஆகு [§ 58].

§ 136. (*a*) நாங்கள் நாலு பெயரும் ஆக வந்தால் = *if we four persons come together.*

(*b*) ஆக is used in summing up = *all altogether:*

நான்	கொடுத்தது	நாலு,	அவர்	கொடுத்தது	ஐந்து,
That which I gave (is)		*four,*	*that which he gave* (is)		*five,*

ஆக	ஒன்பது.
making altogether	*nine.*

(*c*) பத்திரமாகப் புதைத்து வை, *bury it carefully.* Here ஆக or ஆய் = *ly*, added to a noun, converts it into an adverb (§ 40).

(*d*) அவர் என்னை வரச் சொன்னதாக நினைத்தேன், *I thought he told me to come* [சொன்னது, ஆக, *as if . . . said.* சொன்னதாய் is also used. ஆய் = *as if*].

(*e*) ஆம் for ஆகும் (§ 103) is either a finite verb = *it will become*, or a future relative adj. part. (Less. 25) = *which will be, or become.* Consider: ஓட்டாங் கிளிஞ்சல் காசாமோ? *Will a broken bit of conch-shell become money?* (It has a silvery appearance!) [ஓட்டு ஆம் கிளிஞ்சல் காசு ஆம் ஓ.]

(*f*) A curious form is found in letters: for வந்தேன் we have வரல் ஆனேன்; for செய்தோம் is used செய்யல் ஆனோம், and so throughout the past tense (§ 149).

§ 137. *a.* கணக்கன் இருக்கிறான், *an accountant is.*

b. கணக்கனாயிருக்கிறான், *he is an accountant.*

c. கணக்கன் இருக்கிறானா, *is the accountant (there)?* இல்லை, *he is not.*

d. கணக்கனாயிருக்கிறானா, *is he an accountant?* அல்ல, *he is not.*

☞ ஆய் added to a noun *shows it to be a complement of the predicate* (§ 82).

THIS IS OF THE UTMOST IMPORTANCE. Carefully consider the above examples.

§ 138. **Vocabulary.**

பட்டணம், *a town.*
கிழவன், *an old man.*
கிழவி, *an old woman.*
இறங்கு, *go down to, descend, alight* (§ 62).
திருடு, *steal* (§ 56. II).
பொது, *that which is common.*
உடைமை, *possessions.*
பொருள், *substance, wealth.*
சாமான், *goods, utensils.*
தவலை, *a large brass vessel.*
முத்திரை, *a seal.*
பத்திரம், *care.*
ஐந்து, *five.*
ஒன்பது, *nine.*
வை, *place, put* (§ 56. III).
வரை, *limit* (வரைக்கும், 4th case + உம் = *until*).
புதை, *bury* (§ 56. III).
சாப்படு, சாப்பிடு, *eat* (§ 68).

Exercise 43.

§ 139. [1] நாலு பேர் திருடர் ஒரு பட்டணத்தில் ஒரு கிழவியின் வீட்டிலே இறங்கித் தாங்கள் திருடிப் பொதுவில் (in common) வைத்திருந்த [§ 79. (2)] உடைமைகளையும் பணங்களையும் ஒரு தவலையிலே போட்டு (§ 68) மேலே முத்திரை (§ 50) இட்டு (§ 68); 'நாங்கள் நாலுபேரும் ஆக வந்து கேட்கும் போது (§ 106) இதைக் கொடு அதுவரைக்கும் பத்திரமாய்ப் புதைத்து வை' என்று கொடுத்துச் சில நாள் (§ 50) அவள் (§ 50) வீட்டிலே சாப்பட்டுக் கொண்டிருந்தார்கள் [§ 106. (4)]. [2] இராசா தான் சீக்கிரமாய் வருகிறதாகச் சொன்னார். [3] நானும் நீயுமாகப் போவோம், வா! [4] அநேகநாளாய்ச் சாமான் வரவில்லை. [5] இராசா சீக்கிரமாய் வருகிறார் என்று தூதன் சொன்னான்.

[1] Here (are) 5 and there 4; total, 9. [2] If he and you together go to the old man's house, he will give you the goods. [3] Put it carefully in the house. [4] He has great wealth which he has carefully buried in the garden. [5] At which house has he alighted? [6] When we obtained the goods which he had carefully sent by the peon we put them into the store-room. [7] Is this honey? [8] No, it is bitter. [9] Did he eat this sweet honey? [10] Is there

honey there? No. [11] Did he speak as if (*d*) the Muhammadan would come? [12] I have not seen the old man for many days (*for* = ஆக).

☞ NOTE.—The learner may feel inclined to translate 'It is bitter' by கசப்பான இருக்கிறது instead of கசப்பாய் இருக்கிறது.

But, in Tamil, an adjective (so called) is never used as a noun, or with a noun understood. In English 'bitter' = 'a bitter thing': in Tamil it is, 'this is *as bitterness*.'

To convert the adjective into a noun the terminations must be added as in § 87. We then have கசப்பானவன், -ள், -து, &c., or கசப்புள்ளவன், -ள், -து. We can then write (though it is clumsy) கசப்பானதாயிருக்கிறது.

ஆய் must be used to connect the complement with the verb of incomplete predication.

ஆய் sometimes = *of one's own accord:* thus, அவருடையகட்டளையின்படி பண்ணினோமே அல்லாமல் நாங்களாய்த் தீங்கு செய்ய வில்லை, *we did the mischief by his command and not of our own free will.*

LESSON 45.

OPTATIVE AND DESIDERATIVE FORMS. [G. 85.]

§ 140. *a.* இது குழியில் விழக் கடவது, LET *this fall into the pit.*

b. நீ வாழ்வாயாக, MAYST *thou prosper!* [WISH and COMMAND.]

c. நீர் வாழ்க, MAY *you prosper!* [BENEDICTION.]

d. போகட்டும், LET *it go!*

e. நாம் எழுதி அனுப்பின கட்டளையின்படி (§ 157) நீர் நடக்கவும், *act according to the order I have sent you.* [POLITE IMPERATIVE.]

[*f.* ஆறுவதுசினம் (§ 270), *let anger be subdued.* POET. (ஆறுவது, *that which must cool down* (§ 88) *is wrath.*)]

(*a*) The defective root கட, *ought, must,* is regularly conjugated thus:

நான் [செய்யக்] கடவேன், *I ought* or *must* [do].
நீ [செய்யக்] கடவாய், *thou oughtest* or *must* [do].

It is added to the infinitive of any verb to form a kind of optative mood.

(*b*) ஆக [like the Hebrew ָה, Nordheimer's Hebrew Grammar, §§ 204–206] added to the future of any verb forms an optative mood. The neuter participial noun future is used for the 3rd person neuter future.

செய்வேன், *I will do,* செய்வேனாக, *may I do! I much wish to do!*

செய்வான், *he will do,* செய்வானாக, *may he do! I long for him to do!*

நடப்பதாக, *may it take place.*

This seems to be merely a strong breathing, expressive of desire; but it is explained by grammarians as the inf. of ஆகு (§ 41). It is pronounced ĀHA.

(*c*) க like ஆக forms an optative mood, but is added to the root of a verb, and is the same for all numbers and persons, being chiefly used in poetry.

நான் போக, *let me go!* நீர் கேட்க, *may you hear!*

(*d*) Is an unauthorized, but very common form. It consists in the addition of அட்டும் or அட்டு to the root, inserting க்க் when the present takes க்கிற. The form is abbreviated by casting away the final vowel of the root. It is the same for both numbers and for the 1st and 3rd persons.

நான் } செய்யட்டும் { *let me do!* நான் செய்யட்டா, *may I do it?*
அவன் } { *he may do!*

This is said to be a corruption of ஒட்டும் = *permit*, from ஒட்டு.

(*e*) This is a polite imperative: add உம் to the infinitive mood.

§ 141. **Vocabulary.**

அ privative; thus—
அநியாயம், *injustice.*
புரம், *a town.*
துன் or துர், a prefix = *evil, bad.*
மார்க்கம், *a way.*
மார்க்கன், *one who walks in a way.*
புத்தி, *sense.*
புத்திசாலி, *a sensible person.* [The termination சாலி = Skt. sālin, *one who possesses*, is often used.]
மந்திரி, *a counsellor, prime minister.*
இராசரீகம், *kingly rule.*
மிகுந்த, *much, very.*
மிகு, *be abundant* (§ 56. II), past rel. part. = *which has abounded.*
மிகுதி, *abundance.*
மிகுதியான (§ 30), *abundant.*
தீர்க்கம், *length* (pronounced DĪRKKAM) *in the compounds.*
தீர்க்காயுசு, *long life* (ஆயிசு or ஆயுசு, *age, life*).
தீர்க்கதரிசி, *a prophet, a seer* (தரிசி, *one who sees*).
போல், *as* (போல, போலே). (§ 227.)
சித்தி (§ 56. III), *prosper, succeed, answer.*

Exercise 44.

§ 142. [1] அவன் அப்படிச் செய்தானே ஆனால் அழிந்து போகக் கடவான். [2] நீ மிகுந்த புத்திசாலி ஆனதால் தீர்க்காயுசுள்ளவனாகச் சுகத்தோடு வாழ்க! [3] தீர்க்கதரிசி இராசாவினிடத்தில் என் வசனத்தைக் கேட்பீராக என்றார். [4] கொலை செய்யாதிருப்பாயாக! (§ 121.) [5] இந்த அநியாயத்தீர்ப்பைப் பண்ணினவன் வாயிலே மண் விழுவது போலே (§ 227) இது குழியிலே விழக்கடவது. [6] என் உயிர் போனாலும்

போகட்டும். [7] உம்முடைய இராச்சியம் வருவதாக! [8] அநியாயபுரம் (§ 131) என்ற பட்டணத்திலே துன்மார்க்கன் என்கிற இராசா துர்ப்புத்தி என்கிற மந்திரியை வைத்துக் கொண்டு இராசரீகம் பண்ணினார். [9] புத்தியுள்ளவர்களுக்குச் (§ 185) சித்தியாததொன்றில்லை (சித்தியாதது ஒன்றும் இல்லை § 121) என்றறிக. [10] வழியே ஏகுக வழியே மீளுக [(poet.) *no by-paths*]. [11] தைரியசாலி வந்தான்.

[1] Say not so. [2] Pray do not say so. [3] I beg you to do this. [4] If I have destroyed his house may I myself perish. [5] There is much honey in the town. [6] Let the unjust man perish! [7] He who commits injustice will not prosper. [8] Although I perish I will not do injustice. [9] May I walk sensibly! [10] He is a very sensible person. [11] Let him do as his counsellors have said. [12] May my affairs prosper. [13] It won't answer. [14] Hail, O king!

LESSON 46.

WORD-BUILDING: VERBAL NOUNS IN கை.

§ **143.** By adding கை to verbal roots which take கிற in the present (WEAK forms), and க்கை to those which take க்கிற (STRONG forms), a verbal noun is formed nearly equivalent to the English verbal noun (gerundial infinitive) in -ING, expressive of the act or its result.

செய்——செய்கை, *the doing = a deed.*
நட ——நடக்கை, *the walking = a line of conduct.*

§ **144.** Some of the above are in common use as mere nouns; but more generally they are used in the 7th case, corresponding to the ablative absolute in Latin, or the gen. abs. in Greek, retaining a kind of participial power.

அவன் அதைச் சொல்லுகையில், *while he was saying it.*

Here it forms a time-phrase.

§ **145.** ஆகையால் (ஆ)=(*by the becoming:*) *therefore:* ஆனதால், ஆனபடியால்.

§ **146.** **Vocabulary.**

திண்ணை, *a pial, elevated seat in front of a house.*
இரண்டு, *two.*
எடு, *lift up, take up* (§ 76. III).
எடுத்துப்போடு, *take away* (§ 256).
ஸ்ரீதேவி, *the goddess of prosperity.*
உதை, *kick* (§ 56. III).
தள்ளு, *turn away* (§ 56. II).

சாப்பாடு, *food, a meal.*
போசனம், *food, nourishment.*
அன்னம், *food,* chiefly *boiled rice.*
ஆகாரம், *food, what is received into the body.*
அப்பம், *rice cakes, bread.*
உரொட்டி, *bread, a loaf.*
சாதம், *boiled rice.*

Exercise 45.

§ **147.** [1] ஒருநாள் (அந்தநாலுபேரும்) எதிர்வீட்டுத்திண்ணையில் (§ 131.*c*) பேசிக்கொண்டிருக்கையில். [2] அவர்கள் எல்லாரும் வழியிலே போகையில் இரண்டு திருடரைக் கண்டார்கள். [3] அதை எடுத்துப்போடலாமா என்று கேட்டேன்,—இருக்கட்டும் என்றார். [4] அநேகர் வீணாய்ப் பேசிக்கொண்டிருக்கையில் நீ பேசாமல் இருக்கக்கடவாய். [5] அவர்கள் அவன்வீட்டிலே சாதம்சாப்படுகையில் நான் வந்துவிட்டேன். [6] தானாக வந்தசிதேவியைக் காலால் உதைத்துத் தள்ளலாமா? [7] உரொட்டி இல்லையா? [8] எனக்குச் சாப்பாடில்லை. [9] எல்லாரும் கலகம்பண்ணிக்கொண்டிருக்கையால் அழிந்துபோனார்கள்.

[1] While the bazaar-man came running the thief knowing that came down from the tree. [2] Give me the loaf. [3] Give us bread. [4] While there are rice-cakes there is enough for us. [5] While the mother was gone to procure (§ 94, *note*) food the child died. [6] While the five men were sleeping in the verandah of the house, the peons came. [7] May I go while he is learning his lesson? [8] While all are working is it right for you to be idle?

LESSON 47.

WORD-BUILDING: VERBAL NOUNS IN அல், ETC.

§ **148.** Verbal nouns are also formed by adding அல் (தல், கல், குதல், or க்கல், த்தல், or க்குதல்) to the root. These are like the *gerundial* infinitive, and express the *act* merely.

(*a*) Verbs which take கிறு in the present (WEAK forms) take அல், தல்.

செய் ——செய்யல், செய்தல், *a doing*.
அடங்கு——அடங்கல், அடங்குதல், *a submitting*.

The few cases where கல் (or குதல்) is apparently added may be thus explained: there was a root in கு, now obsolete, to which அல் or தல் was added: thus,—

போ (போகு)——போகல், போதல், போகுதல்.
ஆ (ஆகு) ——ஆகல், ஆகுதல், ஆதல்.

(*b*) Verbs which take க்கிறு in the present (STRONG forms), take த்தல், க்கல், க்குதல்.

பிழை——பிழைத்தல், பிழைக்குதல், *a living*.
உதை——உதைத்தல், உதைக்குதல், *a kicking*.
நட —————— நடக்குதல், *a walking*.

§ **149.** **Vocabulary.**

மோர், *butter-milk.*
தோண்டி, *an earthen pot.*
எளிது, *that which is easy,* } § 131.*e.*
அரிது, *that which is hard,* } § 131.*e.*
படி, *measure, manner* (added to relative participles = *as*).
ஏவல், *a command* (ஏவு, *stir up*, § 56. II).

☞ அவன் ஆலோசிக்கல் ஆனான்.
He began to consider.
He fell a-thinking.

This idiom, though poetical, is sometimes heard in common conversation. Thus செய்யலானேன், *I did* (or *have done it*). In higher Tamil we find வீரன்நோக்குதலும், *as soon as the hero saw.*

Exercise 46.

§ **150.** [1]'மோர் வாங்குதற்கு (4th case = *in order to*) அந்தக்கிழவி வீட்டிலேபோய்த் தோண்டி எடுத்துக் கொண்டுவா' என்று அனுப்பினார்கள். [2]'சொல்லுதல் எல்லாருக்கும் எளிது ; சொல்லிய [§ 70. (I) for சொன்ன] படி செய்யல் அரிதாம்.' [3]'என் செயலாவது [ஆ, § 87] யாதொன்றும் [யாது + ஒன்று + உம், §§ 47, 126, 172, *any one thing whatsoever*] இல்லை ; இனித் தெய்வமே எல்லாம் உன் செயல் என்று உணர்ந்தேன்.' (Poet.) [4]அப்போது சொல்லுகிறசங்கதியும் தெரியலாம். [5]ஏறுதற்கும் இறங்குதற்கும் தடையாய் இருக்கிறது. [6]அந்தவீட்டிலே ஆடலும்பாடலுமாய் இருக்கிறது. [Comp. § 40. Any number of nouns may thus be united together by உம் ; and ஆய் added to the last converts the whole into an adverbial clause.] [7]அவன் ஏவற்படி செய்யாதே. [8]இது தங்களுக்குத் தெரியலாவதாக மனு எழுதிக் கொண்டேன்.

[1]It is easy to send the watchman to buy milk. [2]While he commanded I submitted. [3]This is the king's command. [4]It is difficult to walk thus. [5]The submitting to the command of the judge is easy. [6]The having pity is easy. [7]May you kick the earthen pot? [8]Is it hard for boys to learn their lessons? [9]Is it not easy to read a book while walking?

LESSON 48.

PARTICLES THAT EMPHASIZE OR REPLACE CASE-ENDINGS.

[COMP. §§ 233–251.]

§ **151.** (*a*) Particles used instead of, or in addition to, the proper terminations of nouns are—

ஆனவன், ஆனவள், ஆனது, ஆவது, ஆனவர், ஆனவர்கள், ஆனவை.
என்பவன், என்பவள், என்பது, என்பவர், என்பவர்கள், என்பவை.

These participial nouns from the roots ஆ and என் are sometimes used to point out, and throw emphasis on the nominative case. ஆகிறவன், என்கிறவன், &c. are also used in very common talk. (§§ 87, 88.)

These answer in some degree to the Greek article. They are not to be translated in English.

(*b*) ஆர், மார் are added to nouns honorifically.

தாய், *a mother*, but தாயார் is more respectful.
உபதேசி, *a teacher*,—உபதேசியார்.

மார் is plural, கள் may be added. [In Telugu GĀRU.]

தகப்பன்மார், *the fathers* (தகப்பன்).
குருக்கள்(ண்)மார், *the spiritual guides* (குரு).
உவாத்திமார், *the schoolmasters* (உவாத்தி, உவாத்தியார்).

(*c*) An honorific form is made by adding ஈர் to certain words; of these தேவரீர், *Thou, O God*, is common.

(*d*) உடன் (=ஓடு), *together with;* கிட்ட, *near;* அண்டை, *by the side of;* இன், signifying *connexion* (இனம்), are used as casal terminations. அண்டை is often redundant: தென் அண்டைப்பக்கம், *on the south side.* Put them on to the inflexional base, as case-endings.

(*e*) '*Trees, beasts, &c.*' = மரங்கள் மிருகங்கள் முதலியவைகள். '*Selling, buying, and other affairs*' = கொடுக்கல் வாங்கல் முதலான காரியங்கள்.

'*Call the carpenter, bricklayer, &c.*' = தச்சன் கொற்றன் முதலானவர்களைக் கூப்பிடு.

'*Food, clothes, &c.*' = அன்ன வஸ்திராதிகள். (ஆதி is the Sanskrit for முதல்.) The words are formed into a Sanskrit compound with Tamil termination கள். Distinguish carefully from § 131!

So இரதகஜதுரகபதாதிகள், *chariots, elephants, horses, foot-soldiers, &c.*

☞ முதலியவைகள், முதலானவைகள் neuter, முதலியவர்கள், முதலானவர்கள், masculine and feminine, are added to nouns in the nominative singular or plural, and are then equivalent to '&c.' முதல் = 'first.'—முதலியவைகள் as if a part. noun from root முதலு (§ 87. *b*); முதலானவைகள் (முதல் + ஆனவைகள்), *those which have become.*

முதலான followed by a noun common to all the particulars intended to be included may be used: முதலான காரியங்கள்.

முதலியவைகள், &c. (and in the last காரியங்கள், &c.) may be in any case; but the particulars enumerated remain in the nominative.

In official documents we have Arabic வகையரா (wagairā) for *&c.*

(*f*) இடத்து is used for இடத்தில் (7th case): எவ்விடத்தும் for எவ்விடத்திலும், *everywhere.*

§ 152. **Vocabulary.**

அதிக, *much, more.*
மேரு, *Mount Mēru.*
துரும்பு, *a straw.*
மனை|வி, *a house-wife.*
காப்பாற்று, *protect* (§ 56. II). [ஆற்று.]
கடவுள், *Deity.*
மகிழ் (§ 56. I), *exult.*
எட்டி, *the strychnos tree* (add மரம்).
இலவு, *the silk cotton tree* (add மரம்).
தீ, *fire.*
தீப்படு (§ 56. II), *be burned.*
சிஷன், *a disciple.*

Exercise 47.

§ 153. [1] அதிக சந்தோஷத்துடனே சீக்கிரமாய்த் தோண்டித் தவலையை எடுத்துக்கொண்டு போனான். [2] தேவரீர் மேருவைத் துரும்பாகச் செய்வீர் துரும்பை மேருவாகச் செய்வீர். (§ 136. *d.*) [3] அவன் மனைவிமார் இரண்டுபேர்மாத்திரம் அங்கே இருந்தார்கள். [4] கடவுளானவர் எவ்வளவுங் குற்றம் வராமல் என்னைக் காப்பாற்றுவார். [§ 121. (2.)] Translate, *so that it shall not come.* [5] துன்மார்க்கர்கள் கூட்டத்தில் மகிழ்ந்து சேராதே! [6] எட்டியுடன் சேர்ந்த இலவுந் தீப்பட்டது. [7] அந்தமனிதன் அந்தக்கொல்லையில் அவரை, துவரை, உழுந்து, எள்ளு, கொள்ளு, சாமை, தினை, வரகு, கம்பு, கேழ்வரகு, சோளம் முதலானவைகளைப் பயிர்செய்து வந்தான். [8] கொடுக்கல் வாங்கல் (*business in general*), முதலான காரியங்களில் தப்பக் கூடாது. [9] என்கிட்ட வராதே. [10] இதின் கருத்து என்ன? [11] கனவான்கள் தனவான்கள் முதலானோர்களும்.

[12] 'ஆசாரம் இல்லா அசடருடன் கூடிப்
பாசாங்கு பேசிப் பதிஇழந்து கெட்டேனே!'

[1] He came with his wife, children, servants, &c. [2] This is my mother. [3] Thou, O God, art our Father. [4] The spiritual guides came with their disciples. [5] Come not near me. [6] He is just in all his dealings (கொடுக்கல் வாங்கல் முதலான). [7] Come to the north side (வடவண்டைப்பக்கம்). [8] What is the name of this tree (இன்)? [9] Near Mount Mēru is a sea. [10] On the south side of the strychnos tree is a silk cotton tree. [11] The next house caught fire (அண்டைவீடு). [12] The king with his counsellors and others came to the town.

LESSON 49.

WORD-BUILDING: NEGATIVE VERBAL NOUNS IN ஆ-மை.

§ 154. A *negative verbal noun* is formed by adding ஆமை to the root (or, more precisely, by adding மை = *ness, ty* [§ 184. *a*] to the abbreviated form of the neg. verb. part. [§ 121. (4)] : செய்யா + மை). The form செய்யாமே is also found. These nouns are especially frequent in verse.

செய்|யாமை, *the not doing.*	படி|யாமை, *the not learning.*
நட|வாமை, *the not walking.*	அல்|லாமை, *the not being so.*
இல்|லாமை, *the not existing.*	சா|வாமை, *the not dying.*

[மை is added to the present (and less frequently to the past) relative participle to form an affirmative noun corresponding to this: thus, செய்கின்ற (not செய்கிற) + மை = செய்கின்றமை, *the doing*; படித்த + மை = படித்தமை, *the having learned.* This is little used.]

This noun with the 3rd case = *because . . . not* (a negative sentence of reason).

§ 155. Vocabulary.

பொறாமை, *envy* (பொறு, *endure*).	பழி, *guilt, blood-guiltiness.*
சக்களத்தி, *one of several wives, a rival.*	பூ, *flower, bloom* (§ 56. III); also, as a noun, *a flower.*
கூவு, *call out* (§ 56. II).	சத்தியம், *truth, an oath.*
நன்று, *it is good, a good thing* (நல் + து), § 184.	சிந்தை, *thought.*
	திறம், *ability, faculty.*

Exercise 48.

§ 156. [1] அவனைக்காணாமையாலே போய்விட்டார்கள். [2] அன்னம் இல்லாமையால் இவ்விடத்திற்கு வந்தேன். [3] எப்பொழுதும் தீமை செய்யாமை நன்று (rather high). [4] தன் பிள்ளையைச் சக்களத்தி பொறாமையினாலே கொன்றாள் என்று பழிபோட்டுக் கூவி அழுது கொண்டு பிரியாது செய்யப் போனாள். [5] பூத்தவில் பூவாமைநன்று. (§ 196.) [6] வேறே சாட்சி இல்லாமையால் சத்தியம் பண்ணுங்கள். [7] அவன் மனம்அறிந்து (*mind knowing = wilfully*) செய்ததல்லாமையினாலே நியாயாதிபதி அவனைத் தண்டியாமல் விட்டு விட்டார். [8] இல்லாத காரியத்தை இச்சித்துச் சிந்தைவழி (சிந்தையினுடைய வழியிலே) செல்லாமை நல்லோருடைய திறம்.

[1] Why do you envy him? [2] How can this guilt be removed? [3] They have submitted because they had no money. [4] I suffer much because I have no food. [5] Because there were no witnesses the gentleman sent the complainant away. [6] Why did the rival wife kill the little child? [7] I climbed the tree to look for grass. [8] He came down from the tree because there was no grass on it. [9] Do you think it is good not to talk? [10] You will die from not eating bread, rice, and other food.

LESSON 50.

CLAUSES AND PHRASES EXPRESSING PURPOSE.

§ 157. It will be useful to the learner to compare the variety of ways in which such an English phrase as 'man eats to live,' may be rendered in Tamil.

(*a*) மனிதன் பிழைக்கச் சாப்பிடுகிறான்: the infin. governed by the following verb. Literal, but not clear.

(*b*) மனிதன் { பிழைக்கும் படி / ——— படியாக(ச்) / ——— படிக்கு(ச்) } சாப்பிடுகிறான்.

Lit. { *as a step* / *as the step that* / *for the step that* } = *in order to, that he may.*

The use of படி, படியாக, படிக்கு added to the fut. rel. participle is perfectly idiomatic. Added to the 6th case of a noun (in இன்) it means *according to.*

(*c*) மனிதன் பிழைக்கத் தக்கதாகச் சாப்பிடுகிறான், lit. '*as a thing that is fit for him to live*' = *that he may.*

[R. தகு (§ 68), *be fitting:* defective but reg. Pret. தக்கேன், rel. part. தக்க, part. noun தக்கவன், தக்கவள், தக்கது, &c.]

This use of தக்கதாக is not inelegant.

(*d*) மனிதன் { பிழைக்கிறதற்கு(ச்) / பிழைப்பதற்கு(ச்) / பிழைக்கிறதற்காக(ச்) / பிழைப்பதற்காக(ச்) } சாப்பிடுகிறான் { The part. noun neut. sing. pres. and fut. in the 4th case.

The *future forms* are esteemed more highly than the other.

(*e*) மனிதன் பிழைக்கும் பொருட்டுச் சாப்பிடுகிறான் = *for the purpose of living* (rather high).

[பொருட்டு, from பொருள் (+ து, § 184. *h.* ள் + த் = ட்ட்), *substance* = *that which has the property of.*']

(*f*) மனிதன் பிழைக்க வேண்டும் என்று சாப்பிடுகிறான், lit. *saying, it is necessary to live* (colloquial).

(*g*) மனிதன் பிழைத்தலின் நிமித்தம் சாப்பிடுகிறான் = *for the sake of living* (somewhat stiff).

[நிமித்தம், *cause,* is used absolutely, alone or with ஆய் or ஆக added to it, in the sense of '*for the sake of.*']

(*h*) எனக்குக் குறைவு வராமல் இப்படிச் செய்தேன், *I did this that no deficiency might arise to me* (வாராதபடிக்கு).

☞ All these forms often occur in books and in common conversation. They illustrate idioms with which the learner must take great pains to familiarize himself.

§ 158. **Vocabulary.**

உள்ளே, *inside, within.*
ஓட்டம், *a rapid course.*
ஓட்டம்பிடி, *take to flight, gallop off* (பிடி, *seize*, § 56. III).
மூன்று, *three.*
நாழிகை, *a Tamil hour* = 24 minutes.
மணிநேரம், *an English hour* (மணி, *bell*; நேரம், *time*).
ஒரு தாசு, *an hour* (தாசு is *a gurry* on which hours are struck).
நியாயாதிபதி, *a judge* (நியாயம், *right*; அதிபதி, *a ruler*; a Sanskrit compound).
தீர்ப்பு, *a decision* (§ 190).
சட்டம், *regulation, rule.*
படி, *according to.*
மாத்திரம், *only.*
பிரார்த்தி (§ 56. III), *pray, beseech.*
இஷ்டம், *pleasure, desire.*
பங்கு, *a part, share.*
பஞ்சு, *cotton.*
வர்த்தகம், *traffic.*
மூட்டை, *a bundle, bale.*
எலி, *a rat.*
வளர் (§ 56. III), *bring up, educate, train.*
ருசு (§ 160) or உருசு, *proof* (Hind. ruju).
உருசுகொடு (§ 56. III), *give proof.*
உருசுவாக்கு, உருசுப்படுத்து (§ 56. II), *prove.* (Comp. § 92.)
திருஷ்டாந்தம், *an example, proof.*

Exercise 49.

§ 159. [1] அந்தஉடைமையைக் கிழவி கொடுக்கும் படியாகத்தீர்ப்புச்செய்தான். [2] உங்கள்வாக்குமூலப்படியே [properly வாக்குமூலத்தின்படியே] நீங்கள் மூன்றுபேர் மாத்திரம் கேட்டால் கொடுக்கக்கூடாது; நாலுபேருமாகவந்துகேட்டால் உங்கள் பொருளை அவள் கொடுக்கவேண்டும் என்று தீர்ப்புச்செய்வேன். [3] இதை நான் விட்டுவிடச்சொல்லாதிருக்கும்படி உம்மைப்பிரார்த்திக்கிறேன். [4] உன் இஷ்டப்படி செய் (இஷ்டத்தின்படி). [5] ஊர் எல்லாம் அறியும்படியாகக் கூவினாள். [6] நாலுபேர் பங்காகப் (§ 136) பஞ்சுவர்த்தகம் பண்ணினார்கள். [7] பஞ்சு மூட்டைகளை எலிகள் கடியாதிருக்கும்பொருட்டு அவர்கள் ஒரு பூனையை வளர்த்தார்கள். [8] இது என்னுடைய மாடு என்று உருசு கொடுக்கிறதற்கு ஒரு திருஷ்டாந்தஞ் சொல்லுகிறேன். [9] தன் பெண்சாதியை அழைத்துக்கொண்டு வருகிறநிமித்தம் மாமியார் வீட்டுக்குப் போனான். [10] என்வல்லமையை அறிதற்பொருட்டு இப்படிச் செய்தார். [11] அண்ணே! நான் கன்றுக்குட்டிக்குப் புல்லுப் பிடுங்க ஏறினேன் என்றான்.

[1] How can you prove this? [2] What example have you to afford evidence that this house is yours? [3] He went to fetch his wife. [4] I beseech you to do me justice. [5] He traffics to obtain profit. [6] He gives an example to prove his case. [7] You must act only according to rule. [8] Do as you please. [9] I will

give you a reason why you should learn diligently. [10] Prove clearly before the magistrate that this house is your father's. [11] From the absence of proof and examples the house will be taken from you and given to the merchant. [12] The cat runs to catch the rat. [13] Will not the rat run to escape the cat? [14] What is this for? [15] I obtained this money by his means. (§ 242.)

LESSON 51.

CAUSAL AND TRANSITIVE VERBS IN GENERAL.

160. *From primitive verbs how are causal verbs to be formed?* The following examples will render explanations and rules unnecessary. These are generally to be found in the dictionary, and may be divided into two main classes:

I. Those indicating that *a person causes another to perform the action of the verb.* Thus—

(*a*) From அழை, *call* (§ 56. III, where the present takes க்கிற), is formed அழைப்பி, *cause to call* (§ 56. III). Here பி is added and ப் doubled.

அரசன் என்னை அழைப்பித்துக் கேட்டார்=*the king sent for me and asked.*

(*b*) From செய், *do* (§ 56. I, where the present has கிற), is formed செய்வி, *cause to do* (§ 56. III). Here வி is added to form the causal root.

ஒரு கப்பலைக்கட்டச் செய்வித்தான்=*he caused a ship to be built.*

(*c*) From root என், *say* (§ 82), is formed என்|பி (§ 56. III), *cause to say, prove;* root காண், *see* (§ 70), காண்பி=காட்டு (காண் + து), *cause to see, show.*

உண், *eat* [§ 56. (III)], gives உண்பி, *feed;* and கல், *learn* (§ 70), கற்பி, *teach.*

Here பி is added. There are many other forms of this kind in common use with euphonic variations.

II. Simple transitives formed from intransitive roots.

(*d*) From நட, *walk* (§ 57. I), is formed நடத்து, *cause to walk, lead* (§ 56. II). There are few of these, and chiefly from roots in அ and உ.

[The root நட has also a causal நடப்பி, according to (*a*). (§ 56. III.)]

(*e*) From ஏறு, *ascend* (§ 56. II), we have ஏற்று, *cause to ascend, lift* (§ 56. II). To ஏற்று and other transitive forms வி may be added to form a causal.

☞ [In this and the following forms the causal strengthens the root by doubling the consonant, or by hardening a nasal.]

(*f*) From ஓடு, *run* (§ 56. II), is formed ஓட்டு, *cause to run, drive* (§ 56. II), (com.)

[In Lexicon, Part I, comp. சாடு, சாட்டு; வாடு, வாட்டு, &c. &c.]

(*g*) From root அகல், *recede, be removed* (§ 70), is formed அகற்று, *remove, put away* (§ 62); and from உருளு, *be rolling* [§ 56. (III)], உருட்டு, *roll over* (§ 62).

(*h*) From அடங்கு, *submit* (§ 56. II), we find அடக்கு, *put under, cause to submit* (§ 56. II).

[Comp. நீங்கு, நீக்கு.]

(*i*) From பெருகு, *grow, increase* (§ 62), is formed பெருக்கு (§ 62), *multiply*.

[In Lex. comp. ஆகு, ஆக்கு; சறுகு, சறுக்கு, &c. &c.]

(*j*) From root திரும்பு, *turn one's self* (§ 56. II), comes திருப்பு, *turn another, cause to turn* (§ 56. II).

[In Lex. comp. கிளம்பு, கிளப்பு; நிரம்பு, நிரப்பு; எழும்பு, எழுப்பு; குழம்பு, குழப்பு; கூம்பு, கூப்பு, &c. &c.]

(*k*) From காய், *become dry* (§ 56. I), is formed காய்ச்சு, *boil, make dry by heat* (§ 56. II). There are very few of these forms.

(*l*) Many roots may follow § 56. I, and are then intransitive; or § 56. III, and are then transitive. (Compare § 15. *g*.)

[தொங்கிறது, தொங்கிக்கிறது; கிழிகிறது, கிழிக்கிறது, &c. &c.]

☞ [An intransitive verb in the நன்னூல் is called தன்-வினை = *own-action*, and a transitive verb பிற-வினை = *another-action*. These terms are taken from the *parasmai-padam* and *ātmane-padam* of the Sanskrit; but the classes of verbs are far from corresponding. Comp. Pope's II. G. 100-106.]

§ 161. **Vocabulary.**

கிட, *lie down*, § 56. (I).
கிடத்து, *lay down, place in a recumbent position.*
படு[1], *suffer*, § 56. (II).
படுத்து[1], *inflict upon, cause to suffer.*
செல்(லு), *go, pass* (§ 56. III).
செலுத்து (§ 56. II), *cause to go, pay, discharge.*
இரு, *be* (§ 60. II).
இருத்து (§ 56. II), *place, cause to be.*
குழந்தை, *an infant.*
ஆச்சரியம், *astonishment.*
சமீபம், *nearness.*
மாறு, *other, different.*
வேஷம், *disguise, appearance.*
அறிவி, *make known, inform.*

[See II. G. 103.]

[1] These two verbs are added to nouns to form intransitive and transitive verbs respectively: thus, சந்தோஷம், *joy*; சந்தோஷப்படு, *rejoice*; சந்தோஷப்படுத்து, *make glad*. For படு in somewhat higher idiom we find உறு (§ 68), and for படுத்து—உறுத்து: விசனமுற்றேன், *I suffered grief*; பயமுறுத்தினான், *he threatened—inspired fear*.

Exercise 50.

§ 162. [1] அவன் சிறுகுழந்தையைக் கொண்டுவந்து என்பக்கத்திலே கிடத்தி விட்டுப் போனான். [2] அவனுடைய தகப்பன் தனக்குள்ளே ஆச்சரியப் பட்டு மாறுவேஷங் கொண்டு நியாயஸ்தலத்துக்குச்சமீபத்திலே வந்திருந்தான். [3] எழுத்தறிவித்தவன் இறைவன் ஆகும் (ஆகும் = ஆவான். Poet.). [4] நான்சொன்னபடி கேட்டுக்கொண்டிருந்தால் உனக்கேபட்டமுங்கட்டுவித்து விவாகமுஞ் செய்விக்கிறேன். [5] பால்காய்ச்சு. [6] எழும்பு நீ! [7] அவனை எழுப்பு. [8] அந்தக்கல்லை உருட்டிப்போடு (§ 256).

[9] 'பசுவின்பாலை வற்றக் காய்ச்சினாலும் தன்சுவை குறைபடாது.'

[1] They brought a little infant and laid it before me. [2] The physician led the mother to the house. [3] The gentleman caused the watchman to be called. [4] Why have you caused the merchant to be sent for? [5] Turn the bandy round. [6] Put that man down. [7] Lift that bundle. [8] Put that bundle upon the bandy. [9] Boil that conjee for the infant. [10] Drive the bullocks. [11] They lifted up the child upon the horse. [12] The rats are astonished to see the cats. [13] The cats rejoice to see the rats. [14] Did you boil the milk? [15] Will you lift the cotton-bales? [16] Don't drive the bandy.

LESSON 52.

VERBS FORMED FROM NOUNS.

§ 163. (*a*) Verbs are formed from nouns of Sanskrit derivation ending in அம் by changing அம் into இ. They follow § 56. III. These are not very common, and should be used sparingly.

பிரகாசம், *splendour*; பிரகாசி, *shine*; பிரகாசிக்கிறேன், *I shine.*

(*b*) From Tamil nouns in அம் by rejecting ம் and adding க்கிறது we obtain verbs (strong form):

திணம் makes திணக்க, *grow fat.*
மணம் „ மணக்க, *diffuse fragrance.*
கனம் „ கனக்க, *grow weighty.*
மரம் „ மரக்க, *be turned into wood* (poetical).
எமம் „ எமாக்க, *be haughty* (§ 66).
பயம் „ பயக்க, *fear* (§ 66).
பயன் „ பயக்க, *bear fruit* (§ 66).

(*c*) Some nouns in அல் form verbs in அற்று. These are quasi-causals (§ 160):

நிழல் — நிழற்ற, *overshadow* (நிழலு, நிழல்செய், நிழலிடு).
குயில் — குயிற்ற, *enchase.*

(*d*) Some adjectives form verbs:

புது, *new*, makes புதுக்குகிறது, *renew, make new.*
சிறு, *small*, „ சிறுகுகிறது, *grow small.*
பெரு, *great*, „ பெருகுகிறது, *increase*, and
பெருக்குகிறது, *make great.*

§ **164.** Many nouns are also verbal roots, as in English.

களி, *exceeding joy*; களி, *rejoice* (§ 56. III); களிக்கிறேன், *I rejoice*, &c.
துதி, *praise*; துதி, *praise* (§ 56. III); துதிக்கிறேன், *I praise.*
So பூ, காய், புளி, &c.

§ **165.** பண்ணு, *make, perform*; செய், *do*; ஆ, *become*; ஆக்கு, *make, cause to become*, are often added to nouns. Thus:

சுத்தம், *purity*; சுத்தம்பண்ணு, *purify* (§ 56. II).
சுத்தமா, *become pure* (§ 56. II).
சுத்தமாக்கு, *cleanse* (§ 56. II).
விசாரணை, *investigation*; விசாரணைசெய், *investigate* (§ 56. I), [or விசாரி.]

☞ [These forms may be divided into two kinds, in one of which there is a manifest ellipsis of the 2nd case; in the other the noun or particle forms with the verb one compound idea. The former are explained in § 50, and in them க், ச், த், ப் at the beginning of the added verb are not doubled generally. In the latter case they are. Thus, நிலை = *stability, a standing-place*, and நிலைபெறு (ப் not doubled), (§ 56. II) = நிலையைப்பெறு. But நிலைப்படு (§ 161) is a compound = *become settled, fixed* (ப் is doubled). They are in constant use.]

§ **166.** **Vocabulary.**

ஏற்படுத்து, *appoint, establish* (§ 56. II). ஏற் for ஏற from ஏறு.
ஆனை, *an elephant.*
தேர், *a chariot.*
காலாள், *a foot-soldier* (கால், *foot*; ஆள், *person*).
ஸ்திரீ, *a woman* = பெண்.
தங்கம், *pure gold.*
பாரம், *a load, weight* = சுமை.
பிரகாரம், *manner* = வகை.
வாரம், *a week* = கிழமை.
தெய்வம், *the divinity, providence, fate.*
உள்ளம், *the mind, the inner man.*
கள்ளம், *falsehood, guile.*
தொந்தரவு, *trouble.*
குழை (§ 56. I), *become soft, dissolve away.*

{அன்று, *that day.*
{இன்று, *this day.*
{என்று, *what day? when?*

[These three words form their 4th case irregularly: அன்றைக்கு, இன்றைக்கு, *to-day*; என்றைக்கும், *for ever*. என்று is doubled generally in the last form: என்றென்றைக்கும், *for ever and ever.* Comp. § 25.]

ஆர (infin. of ஆர், *be full*, § 56. I) is used idiomatically; thus,
கண்ணார, *clearly, face to face.*
மனதார, *willingly, knowingly.*
காதார, *clearly, distinctly.*

Exercise 51.

§ **167.** [1] அதைக்கேட்டு இராசா சந்தோஷித்து அவனை நியாயாதிபதியாக ஏற்படுத்திச் சகல வெகுமானமுஞ் செய்து தன்னிடத்தில் வைத்துக் கொண்டார். [2] இன்றைக்கு உன்னைப் பெரியவன்ஆக்குவேன். [Here பெரியவன் ஆக்கு is a compound.] [3] ஒரு வாரத்துக்குள்ளாக நான் நன்றாய் விசாரணைபண்ணுவேன். [4] காதாரக்கேட்டுச் சந்தோஷத்தை அடைந்தேன் (சந்தோஷித்தேன், சந்தோஷமானேன்). [5] நெஞ்சாரப் (= *wilfully*) பொய்சொல்லக்கூடாது. [6] தங்கம் தரையில்தான் கிடந்தால் என்ன? [7] எந்தப்பிரகாரமாகச் சுத்தம்பண்ணுவீர்கள்? [8] மனங் குழைந்து தோத்திரஞ் செலுத்தினார்கள். [9] என்றென்றைக்கும் அவரைத் துதிசெய்வார்கள் (or துதிப்பார்கள்). [10] கண்ணாரக்கண்டு களித்தேன். [11] இன்றைக்கோ என்றைக்கோ தெரியாது.

[1] The king came with elephants, chariots, and foot-soldiers. [2] Although you saw it with your eyes, do not speak of it to any one. [3] He will perish for ever. [4] That king's foot-soldiers carried burdens of gold. [5] We all rejoiced and praised the king. [6] They purified the chariots that day for the women. [7] If you sin wilfully how can you escape? [8] I heard distinctly. [9] To-day I shall have much trouble. [10] Pray examine this well, my father! [11] Will not the judge do justice to the villagers? [12] The gentlemen will punish the watchman.

LESSON 53.

THE INFINITIVE MOOD. [II. G. 140.]

§ **168.** The verbal form obtained by adding அ to the roots of (weak) verbs with present கிற, and க்க to the remainder, has been called *the infinitive mood*, because it in many respects answers to that part of the English verb (§ 41). The learner must beware of supposing, however, that wherever the English has the infinitive mood this Tamil form can be used, or *vice versâ*. The following examples require attention :—

(*a*) வரச்சொன்னார், *he told* (me) TO *come*. The English and Tamil idioms correspond. [PURPOSE.]

(*b*) சிலர் போய் அரசனிடத்தில் சொல்ல அரசனவர் அழைப்பித்தார், WHEN *some went and told the king, the king called* (him). [TIME.] So, போ எனப்போ = *go when you are told*.

(*c*) நீர்சொல்ல or சொல்லவும், *please to say*. [COURTEOUS IMPERATIVE, § 140.]

(*d*) செய்யக்கூடாது, (you) *must not do* (it). [PROLATIVE.]
அடிக்கப்பட்டேன், *I was beaten.*

(*e*) கேட்கப் பண்ணினார், *he made me hear.* [A dubious way of forming a causal. Comp. § 160.]

§ **169**. The use of the infinitive in (*b*) answers to the Latin ablative absolute, and is very concise and elegant; but sometimes not very clear. It is essentially poetical.

☞ நான் அப்படிச் சொல்ல அவர் வந்தார் = நான் அப்படிச் சொல்லும்பொழுது அவர் வந்தார், or நான் அப்படிச் சொல்லுகையில் அவர் வந்தார்.

The verbal noun that in English often has *to* before it, and looks like an infinitive mood, and is equivalent to a participial noun in *-ing*, must be rendered into Tamil by one of the forms in §§ 87, 88. But it is necessary to have regard to idiom!

1. Thus, '*To see is to believe*' = '*seeing is believing.*' Here காண்பது நம்புவது would scarcely give any meaning: தான்கண்ணினாலே கண்டதைமனிதன் (மெய்யென்று) நம்புவான், or some such paraphrase is needed.

2. '*To err is human, to forgive divine.*' Here the infinitives are subjective noun-phrases: தப்புவது மனிதருக்கு இயல்பு; பொறுப்பதோதேவர் இலட்சணம்.

So, '*It is not right to do so*' (= *to do so is not right*), அப்படிச்செய்வது சரியல்ல.

§ **170**. Several infinitives are used as adverbs, prepositions, or conjunctions:—

Infinitive.	*Verb-Root.*	*Examples.*
அற, *without* .	அறு, *cease.*	எல்லாப்பாவமும் அறச்சுத்தமானான், *he became clean* FROM *all sin.*
⎧ ஒருப்பட, *together.*	ஒருப்படு, *coalesce.*	ஒருப்பட வேண்டாம் என்றார்கள், *they* UNANIMOUSLY *said they did not want it.*
⎩ ஒருமிக்க . .	ஒருமி, *unite.*	எல்லாரும் ஒருமிக்கச் சேர்ந்தார்கள், *they all came* TOGETHER.
ஒழிய, *besides, but.*	ஒழி, *fail.*	இதொழிய வேறேவகை இல்லை, *there is no way* BESIDES *this.*
கிட்ட, *near* .	கிட்டு, *draw near.*	பட்டணத்துக்குக்கிட்ட வருகையில், *when they came* NEAR *the town.*
கூட, *with, together*, § 239.	கூடு, *join.*	என்னோடு கூட என் மகனும் வந்தான், *my son came* WITH *me.*
சூழ, *round about.*	சூழ், *surround.*	அவரைச் சூழ நின்றார்கள், *they stood* ROUND *him.*
தவிர, *except* .	தவிர், *remove.*	இவனைத் தவிரமற்ற எல்லாரும் சந்தோஷப்பட்டார்கள், *they all rejoiced* BUT *he.*

Infinitive.	*Verb-Root.*	*Examples.*
பலக்க, *loudly, clearly.*	பல, *grow strong.*	பலக்கப் பேச, *speak* OUT *loud.*
போல, *as* . .	போலு, *resemble.*	இதுபோல அதுவும், *that also* (is) LIKE *this.*
முடுக, கடுக, *quickly.*	முடுகு, கடுகு, *make haste.*	கடுக(முடுக)ச் சொன்னான், *he spoke* QUICKLY.
மெல்ல, *slowly*	(மெல்லு, *chew.*)	மெல்ல மெல்லச் செய், *do it* SLOWLY.
வரவர, *gradually.*	வா, *come.*	பூ வரவரக்காய்ந்துபோகிறது, *the flower is* GRADUALLY *drying up.*
வலிய, *spontaneously.*	வலி, *be impelled.*	வலியப் பத்துப்பணத்தைக்கொடுத்தார், *he* FREELY *gave* 10 *fanams.*
விலக, *off*.. .	விலகு, *get out of the way.*	விலகப்போ, *get* OUT *of the way.*

The expressions அது நிற்க, '*that standing so*'; இப்படி இருக்க, *this being so;* அப்படி இருக்கக்கொள்ள, *that being so* (=*moreover*), seem to be inelegant, though not absolutely incorrect.

Exercise 52.

§ **171.** (**Vocabulary**, § 166.)

1 கடவுள் அறிய நான் இதைச் செய்யவில்லை. 2 பாதிச்சேறுகூடப் போகவில்லை (*not even half the mud was removed.* கூட=*even*). 3 நீ ரெம்பச் சாப்பிடுகிறாய் [ரெம்ப vulgarly for நிரம்ப, *to be full,* inf. of நிரம்பு. § 56. II]. 4 எனக்கு ரெம்பவும் தொந்தரவு பண்ணுகிறான். (Sometimes ரொம்பவும் [vulg.].) 5 ஒருவனுக்கு மழைவெள்ளத்திலே தலைமயிர்நீரில்அலையக் கீழேவெள்ளம்ஓடக் கல்லுகள்உடம்பிலேஉறுத்த நித்திரை பிடிக்குமா?

6 'உள்ளங் குழைய உடல் குழைய உள்ளிருந்த
கள்ளங் குழைய என்று காண்பேன்?'[1]

7 இன்னும் ஒரு பரீட்சை பெரிதாகச் செய்தால் ஒழிய எனக்குச் சந்தேகந் தீராது. 8 அன்று முதலாக வரவர நோய் அதிகரிக்கிறதுபோல்

[1] Inf. of consequence.

(அதிகரிக்கிறதுபோல) பாசாங்குபண்ணிக்கொண்டிருந்தான். [9] அதைச் சற்றே எட்ட வைத்துவிடு. [10] முதிர்ந்திருந்த பழம் ஒழியக் காற்றினால் நல்ல காய்களும் விழுவதுண்டு. [11] வா என வருவான். [[12] சிந்தையின் மகிழ்ச்சிபொங்க இருந்தபின் செப்பலுற்றான்.]

[1] Unless you pay the money you will not be allowed to go. [2] Unless a man eats he will not live. [3] I did not obtain even that. [4] When shall I obtain knowledge so that my ignorance shall depart, my doubts remove, and my heart rejoice? [5] He gave the money spontaneously to all who asked him, so that their hearts rejoiced. [6] My servant goes and comes when I tell him. [7] By conversation the way will seem short. (§ 244.) [8] You must not speak or think so. [9] He gave much.

LESSON 54.

§ 172. NUMERALS: CARDINALS.

(1) Simple Forms: 1–10.

Cardinals.		*Tamil Signs.*	*Adjective Forms.*	*Derived Nouns.*
ஒன்று, *one* (vulg. ஒண்ணு).	1	௧	ஒரு, ஓர் [ஒரு மனிதன், ஓர் அரசன்][2].	ஒருவன் (m.) (or ஒருத்தன்), ஒருத்தி (f.), *a certain person.*
இரண்டு, *two* (vulg. ரெண்டு).	2	௨	இரு, ஈர், இரண்டு.	இருவர், *two persons.*
மூன்று, *three* (vulg. மூணு).	3	௩	மு, மூ, மூன்று.	மூவர், *three persons.*
நாலு, நான்கு, *four*	4	௪	நால், நான்கு, நான்.	நால்வர், *four persons.* (POET.)
ஐந்து, *five* (vulg. அஞ்சு).	5	௫	ஐ, ஐம், ஐந்து.	ஐவர், *five persons.*
ஆறு, *six* . . .	6	௬	அறு, ஆறு.	
ஏழு, *seven* . . .	7	௭	எழு, ஏழு.	
எட்டு, *eight* . .	8	௮	எண், எட்டு.	
ஒன்பது, *nine*[1] . .	9	௯		
பத்து, *ten* . . .	10	௰	பது, பதின்.	பதின்மர், *ten persons.*

[1] This seems to be = *one from ten.* Compare the Roman numeral ix, where the idea is the same. Skt. ŪNA: *ūna-viṅçati:* xix.

[2] ஒரு before a consonant, ஓர் before a vowel; and so with the other numbers.

(2) Compound Forms: பத்து changed into பது + இன், or into பன், or unchanged: 11-19.

Cardinals.		*Tamil Signs.*	*Derived Nouns.*
பதினொன்று . . .	11	௰௧	பதினொரு [பெயர்], *eleven persons.*
பன்னிரண்டு . . .	12	௰௨	பன்னிருவர் = *twelve persons.*
பதின்மூன்று . . .	13	௰௩	
பதினாலு, பதினான்கு, &c.	14	௰௪	
பத்தொன்பது . . .	19	௰௯	

(3) The Adjective Forms of numbers 1 to 8 prefixed to பது, the shortened form of பத்து: 20–199.

இருபது	20	௨௰	The adjective forms of all the following are similar to this: பத்து is changed into பது or வது.
இருபத்தொன்று, &c.	21	௨௰௧	
முப்பது	30	௩௰	
நாற்பது	40	௪௰	
ஐம்பது	50	௫௰	
அறுபது	60	௬௰	
எழுபது	70	௭௰	
எண்பது	80	௮௰	
தொண்ணூறு . . .	90	௯௰	Probably from தொள் (= *defect*) and நூறு.
நூறு	100	௱	The adjective form is நூற்று throughout.
நூற்றொன்று . . .	101	௱௧	Vulg. நூற்றி ஒன்று, &c.

(4) The Adjective Forms of 1 to 8 prefixed to நூறு: 200-1000, &c.

இருநூறு	200	௨௱	
முந்நூறு	300	௩௱	
நானூறு	400	௪௱	
ஐந்நூறு	500	௫௱	
அறுநூறு	600	௬௱	
எழுநூறு	700	௭௱	
எண்ணூறு . . .	800	௮௱	
தொள்ளாயிரம் . .	900	௯௱	

(5) Miscellaneous.

Cardinals.		*Tamil Signs.*	
ஆயிரம்	1000	௲	ஆயிரம் is Skt. ÇAHASRAM. Its sign is ஸஹ, hence ௲.
ஆயிரத்தொன்று . .	1001	௲௧	The adjective form of ஆயிரம் is ஆயிரத்து.
100,000 is இலட்சம், *a lac.* *A million* is பத்து இலட்சம். கோடி is used for 10 *millions.* கோடா கோடி for 10 *million times a* கோடி.			

Exercise 53.

§ 173. (Vocabulary, § 166.)

[1] ஆனை ஒன்று குதிரை மூன்று தேர் ஏழு காலாள் ஒன்பது ஸ்திரீகள் நாலு தங்கம் ஒருபாரம் இந்தப்பிரகாரங் கொடுக்கவேண்டும்[1]. [2] ஒரு ஆனையையும் மூன்று குதிரைகளையும் ஏழு தேர்களையும் ஒன்பது காலாள்களையும், நாலு ஸ்திரீகளையும், தங்கத்தில் ஒரு பாரத்தையும் கொடுக்க வேண்டும். [3] ஆயிரத்து எண்ணூற்று ஐம்பத்தைந்தாம் (§ 175) வருஷத்திலே அது நடந்தது (vulg. ஆயிரத்தி எண்ணூற்றி). [4] சாட்சிக்காரராகிய (§ 130) பதினைந்துபேர் கூடவந்தார்கள். [5] எத்தனை மணி? [6] எத்தனை மணிநேரம்? [7] எத்தனை மணி ஆயிற்று? (ஆச்சு). [8] பதினைந்து நாழிகை ஆயிற்று (the Tamil way of saying, *It is noon*). [9] இருவருமாக வந்தார்கள் (§ 136. *a*). [10] தான் ஒன்று நினைக்கத் தெய்வம் ஒன்று நினைக்கும். [11] ஒன்பதினாயிரம் வராகனை இந்தப் பிள்ளைக்குக் கொடு. [12] அந்த மூன்றையும் ஒன்றாய்க் (§ 40) கலந்து (§ 66) சமையல் (§ 148) பண்ணினான் (§ 165). [13] மூன்று பெண்டுகளுக்குள் ஒருத்தி காலுங் கழியும் ஒன்றடி (§ 194) என்றம்; மற்றொருத்தி இறகும் இலையும்

[1] Observe the ellipsis of the plural sign கள், the noun put before the numeral, உம் omitted, and all summed up by இந்தப் பிரகாரம். Compare the following, where the same is expressed more precisely, but less idiomatically. The placing of the noun of number *after the noun it belongs to* is often elegant.

ஒன்றடி என்றும்; பின்னொருத்தி வாயுங் கனியும் ஒன்றடி என்றும் பேசிக்கொண்டு போனார்கள் (*its leg is like a stick*, &c., *is one with it*, அடி, familiarly = '*my friend*'—sometimes in contempt). [14] மாணிக்கம் ஒன்று வெகுமானமாகப் பெற்றுக்கொண்டு போனான்.

[1] Fifty persons came. [2] The whole fifty persons came. [3] This happened in the year one thousand four hundred and twenty-seven (§ 175). [4] There are 60 nāṛigai in one day. [5] There are seven days in a week, and 52 weeks in a year. [6] How many peons are there in the court (§ 37)? [7] What o'clock is it? (How many bells?) [8] They came, ten together. [9] Give the boy 10,000 pagodas. [10] Has the complainant one eye or two? [11] He brought ten fanams to the bazaar. [12] You may buy two rice-cakes for a pie. [13] The Hindus say there are six sects. [14] Give the servant three rupees, five annas, six pice. [15] Five times five.

LESSON 55.

NUMERALS: ORDINALS.

§ **174**. The Tamil people did not ordinarily use the decimal notation; it is now introduced into schools. In Tamil ௫௲௮௱௰௫ = 5815. This should, of course, be written ௫௮௧௫. The Arabic notation has been introduced in all Government offices.

§ **175**. *Ordinals* are formed from the above by adding to the *cardinals* ஆம் or ஆவது (3rd pers. neut. fut. and part. noun fut. of ஆ), (§§ 72, 88). But ஒன்று, *one*, makes முதல், முதலாம், or முதலாவது, *first;* and in compounds ஒன்று becomes ஓர் (taking the adj. form): பதிஞோராம், &c.

Ex. இரண்டாந் தேதி	நாலாவது மந்திரி
the second day of the month.	*the fourth minister.*
(Lit. *two-which will become.*)	(Lit. *four-which will become.*)

§ **176**. The former is used as an adjective only; the latter is either an adjective or an adverb:

அவன் முதலாவது வந்தான், *he came first.*

§ **177**. Some of these numbers are repeated in a peculiar way to form distributives: *one by one*, &c. &c. Thus,

ஒவ்வொன்று (the first letter only of ஒன்று is taken), *one by one.*
இவ்விரண்டு (the first letter of இரண்டு, இ), *two by two, in twos.*
மும்மூன்று (the first syllable of மூன்று shortened, மு), *by threes.*
நன்னாலு (நன்னான்கு), ஐயைந்து (ஐவ்வைந்து), அவ்வாறு, எவ்வேழு, எவ்வெட்டு.
பப்பத்து (பவ்வத்து). None is formed from ஒன்பது.

☞ [How are we to express 1853 in Tamil?

It may be written according to the Arabic notation (i.e. the ordinary English notation) or the almost obsolete Tamil notation; thus—

௧௮௫௩ or ௧௲௮௱௫௰௩.

When expressing this in Tamil words there will be *one*, *thousand*, *eight*, *hundred*, *five*, *ten*, and *three*, i.e. seven words:—

ஒன்று, ஆயிரம், எட்டு, நூறு, ஐந்து, பத்து, மூன்று.

All of these, but the last, must be written in one of the abbreviated forms given in the table. We are at liberty to select, where a choice is given, the most euphonic, but any of them will be intelligible. The result will be as follows:—

ஓர் ஆயிரத்து எண் நூற்று ஐம் பத்து (or பதின்) மூன்று
(ஓராயிரத்தெண்ணூற்றைம்பத்துமூன்று).

The point to be kept before the mind is that IN EVERY CASE BUT THE LAST, THE ADJECTIVE FORM (inflexional base, or shortened form) ALONE CAN BE USED—the whole forming, in fact, one compound word—the number in the unit's place having all that precedes it as adjective enlargements. This will be quite simple if steadily carried out.

If 'year' is added the cardinal *three* will become the ordinal *third*: மூன்றாம் வருஷம்.]

§ 178. Vocabulary.

அதிகாரம், *chapter*.
ஏறக்குறைய, *more or less* (ஏற, *to ascend*; குறைய, *to decrease*), § 168.
உத்தேசம், *about, more or less*.
சராசரி, *on an average*.
சந்தேகம், *doubt*.
குருடன், *a blind man*.
கூனன், *a hunchback*.
இகழ்|ச்சி, *contempt* (p. 140).
பார்|வை, *vision, sight*.
முதுகு, *a back*.
மூட்டை, *a bundle*.
மற்று, *other*.

Exercise 54.

§ 179. 1 தேவிக்குத் தொளாயிரத்துத் தொண்ணூற்றொன்பது இராசாக்களின் தலைகளைப் பலிகொடுத்தான். 2 ஒவ்வொன்றாய் வந்து கேட்டார்கள். 3 இவ்விருவர் சொல்லையுங் கேட்டு சந்தேகப்பட்டு இதற்குச் சாட்சி உண்டா என்று கேட்டான் (obs. the two uses of கேள், § 70). 4 ஒரு கண்குருடன் வரும்போது அவனைக்கண்ட கூனன் இகழ்ச்சியாக: 'வாரும்[1] ஐயா ஒருகண்பார்வைக்காரரே!' (§ 182). என்றான். குருடன் கூனனுக்குச் சொல்லுகிறான்: 'மெய்தான்[2] ஐயா முதுகு மூட்டைக்காரரே! நான் ஒருவரை ஒரு கண்ணும் மற்றொருவரை ஒரு கண்ணுமாய்ப் பார்க்கிறதில்லை; யாவரையும் ஒரு கண்ணாகப் பார்ப்பேன்' என்றான். 5 முப்பத்து முக்கோடி தேவர்களும் நாற்பத் தெண்ணாயிரம் முனிவர்களும் சூழும்படி கோடாகோடி சூரியர்கள் உதயமானாற்போல் விளங்கினார். 6 இரண்டொரு மாதத்தில் இறந்து போவாய். 7 பரிசுத்தமத்

[1] வாரும், வாராய் = *marry come up!*

[2] மெய்தான், *quite true!*

தேயுஎன்பவர் எழுதின சுவிசேஷம் பத்தாம்அதிகாரம் நாலாம்வசனத்தில் எழுதியிருக்கிறதாவது[1]. [8]என்தகப்பனார் இறந்தபொழுது நான் ஐந்து மாதத்துக்குழந்தையாயிருந்தேன்.

[1]In the fourth chapter. [2]A man blind of one eye. [3]One was deformed, and the other had but one eye. [4]They must come one by one. [5]Place these bundles by threes. [6]The children are arranged five in a class. [7]This is the fiftieth time I have walked round the temple. [8]On an average he comes every fifth month. [9]On the second day of last month. [10]Ten witnesses, more or less, proved the complainant's statement. [11]The fourth person had a bundle on his back. [12]Come for your wages on the first of the month. [13]I will pay you the money on the twentieth in the evening.

LESSON 56.

DERIVATIVE NOUNS.

§ **180.** From primitive stems are derived what are sometimes called appellative nouns. These are in constant use.

From nouns in ம் they are formed by changing ம் into அத்து (§ 18. *e*) and adding ஆன் for the sing. masculine, ஆள் for the sing. feminine (அது for the sing. neuter), ஆர் or ஆர்கள் for the epicene plural, and அவை for the neuter plural. Many other nouns simply add these terminations; thus—

கோத்திரம், *a tribe;* கோத்திரத்தான், *a man of a tribe.*
கோத்திரத்தாள், *a woman of a tribe.*
கோத்திரத்தார்,—கள், *people of a tribe.*

ஊர், *a village;* ஊரான், ஊராள், ஊரார்.
ஊரது, ஊரவை[2].

☞ There are many exceptions to this, since Sanskrit words introduced into Tamil mostly follow the rules of their own language.

Thus, புண்ணியம், *virtue*, has புண்ணியவான் (the Sanskrit for *a virtuous man*); so பாவம், *sin*, makes பாவி, *a sinner;* and வியாபாரம் gives வியாபாரி, *a merchant*. The dictionary must be consulted for these forms. நாடு makes நாட்டார், *the country people* (§ 18. *c*), but also நாடான், *a landholder, a head man among certain tribes;* வைத்தியம், *medical treatment*, forms வைத்தியன் or வைத்தியக்காரன்.

[1] ஆவது = *as follows:* lit. *that which will become.*
[2] These two are not so frequently used.

§ 181. காரன் (m.), காரி (f.). [S. *a maker, doer.*]
ஆளி (m. and f.): or (m.) ஆளன், (f.) ஆட்டி. [ஆள், *manage affairs* + இ.]
சாலி (m. and f.). [S. *a possessor.*]

These suffixes are added to the inflexional base of nouns (§ 131) to make derivatives of *agency, possession*, or *relation:* but their use varies much.

From கடன், *a debt*, we have கடனாளி, *a debtor*, கடன்காரன் (m.), *a debtor*, கடன்காரி (f.). From ஆடு, *a sheep*, we have ஆட்டுக்காரன், *a sheep-man*, ஆட்டுக்காரி (f.); புத்தி, *sense*, புத்திசாலி, *a sensible person;* தோட்டம், *a garden*, தோட்டக்காரன், *a gardener;* மணம், *marriage*, மணவாளன் or மணாளன், *a bridegroom*, and மணவாளி, மணவாட்டி, *a bride*.

§ 182. **Vocabulary.**

திறம், *a part, ability* (a man of parts).
இனம், *kind, family*.
பாக்கியம், *happiness, luck, wealth*.
பாக்கியவான் (m.), *a happy man*.
பாக்கியவதி (f.), *a happy* or *blessed woman*.
சந்ததி, *a race*.
சாதி, *caste*.
வமிசம், *family*.
பாட்டாளி (பாடு, *suffering*), *a laborious man*.
கூட்டாளி, *a partner*.
மருளாளி (மருள், *bewilderment*), *one under the influence of a demon*.
குற்றவாளி, *a criminal*.
அயலார், *near neighbours* (அயல்).
கப்பற்காரர், *sailors*.
தூண்டிற்காரன், *a fisherman* (தூண்டில், *a hook*).
மிதப்பு, *a float used by fishermen* (மித).
மூத்தோர், *elders* (மூ, *become old*).

Exercise 55.

§ 183. 1 இரு திறத்தாரையுங் கூப்பிடு (§§ 173, 181, both parties). 2 மூத்திறத்தாரிடத்திலும் விசாரணை செய்தான். 3 நீதியின்படி நடக்கிறவன் பாக்கியவான். 4 'எல்லாச் சந்ததியாரும் என்னைப் பாக்கியவதி என்பார்கள்.' 5 தன் கூட்டாளிகள் ஐந்து பெயரோடுங் கூட வந்தான். 6 அந்த நாட்டார் எல்லாருங் கூடி இருக்கிறார்கள். 7 உன் வீட்டாரிடத்தில் விசாரி. 8 இவன் வெகு பாட்டாளி. 9 எங்கள் கோவிலுக்கு அநேகம் மருளாளிகள் உண்டு. 10 நியாயாதிபதி சிலகுற்றவாளிகளை விட்டுவிட்டார். 11 அயலாரைவிசாரித்தால் தெரியும். 12 'தூண்டிற்காரனுக்கு மிதப்பின் மேலே கண்.' [Prov.] 13 'ஞானிக்கல்ல இன்பமுந் துன்பமும்.' (Poet.) 14 மூத்தோர் சொன்ன வார்த்தை அமிர்தம். 15 இவன் பாக்கியசாலி அவன் பத்திசாலி.

[1] All the villagers stood near. [2] My people. [3] The people of my tribe. [4] All the people of the world will be astonished. [5] All the people of the inhabited country and those who dwell in the wilderness (நாடு, காடு). [6] The inhabitants of all lands praised that brave person. [7] They are all of one caste and family. [8] The watchman is a very hard-working man. [9] You must inquire from the neighbours of the criminal. [10] Many foolish people go about as if possessed by a demon. [11] All the sailors left the ship. [12] The fisherman sits on the bank of the river.

LESSON 57.

DERIVATIVES. [G. 93.]

§ 184. We have seen (§ 180) that from some primitive roots used as adjectives derivative nouns are formed, which are both common and elegant.

(*a*) By adding மை many of these stems become abstract nouns of quality [மை என்பது தன்மைப்பொருளை உணர்த்தி வரும்]:—
நல், *good* [or *that which is good*]; நன்மை, *goodness* (ல் + ம் = ன்ம்). (So ஆண்மை, பெண்மை.) § 131. *e*.

(*b*) Nouns are formed from these by adding the suffixes (comp. § 31):—

அன், அவன், ஆன், ஒன், sing. masc. rational. (Comp. § 30, *note*.)
அள், அவள், ஆள், sing. fem. rational.
அர், அவர், ஆர், ஓர், plural masc. and fem. rational.
அது, து, sing. com. irrational.
[1] அ, அன, அவை, plural com. irrational.

These terminations may be added to most nouns. இன் is often inserted.

☞ Final உ generally becomes இ before these terminations. Those given here are colloquial forms.

நல், *good*, makes—
நல்லவன், *a good man*.
நல்லவள், *a good woman*.
நல்லவர்கள், *good people*.
(நல்லோர், நல்லர்.)
நல்லது, *good thing*: நன்று.
நல்ல, நல்லவைகள், *good things*.

சிறு, *small*, makes—
சிறியவன், *a little person* (m.).
சிறியவள், *a little person* (f.).
சிறியோர், *little persons* (m. & f.).
சிறியது, *that which is little*.
சிறிய, சிறியவைகள், *those which are little* (n.).

[1] Comp. this with the rule in Latin that the nom. and acc. of neuter plurals always end in *a*.

(*c*) The above belong to the 3rd person. But such nouns may be formed for the 1st and 2nd persons also, though not much used in the common dialect; thus—

அடி, *foot*, makes அடியேன், *I a servant* (ஏன் being the verbal personal term. of 1st singular. § 31).

When a person wishes to be very humble in his address he says:

அடியேன் தங்களிடத்தில் வந்தேன் for நான், &c.
I a slave to themselves am come.

Even நாயேன், *I a dog*, and other disgusting expressions of the same kind, are sometimes used.
And கொடு, *cruel*, makes கொடியாய் = *thou a cruel person.*

(*d*) Personal nouns are formed from a few roots (chiefly in poetry) by adding ஞன் (pl. ஞர்):
அறிஞன், *one who knows.*

[Tamil grammarians consider these to be a species of verb. An ordinary verb is called தெரிநிலை வினை = [understanding-position-verb], a *verb which implies an action, a time, an object*, or *an instrument*. But these forms are called குறிப்பு வினை = *sign verb*, (i.e.) they can only *inferentially* express time, &c.

They have been called 'conjugated nouns,' 'verbal appellatives,' and 'appellative verbs.' (*Nannûl*, Sût. 321.) They are formed in poetry in great abundance from nominal roots, which are divided, for this purpose, into six classes; viz.—

(1) Nouns expressive of thing possessed (பொருள்): குழை, *an earring.*
(2) Nouns of place (இடம்): புறம், *outside.*
(3) Nouns of time (காலம்): மாசம், *a month.*
(4) Nouns expressive of some member, or part (சினை): கண், *an eye.*
(5) Nouns of quality, outward or inward (குணம்): உண்மை, *fidelity.*
(6) Nouns expressive of something done (தொழில்): சொல், *a word.*

RULE.—*Prepare the noun for the reception of the casal signs* (§ 18), *then add the personal terminations as in* §§ 31, 87. The nouns thus formed for all persons and numbers may be regularly declined. Comp. Pope's II. G. 93.]

§ 185. Vocabulary.

From உடை, *belonging to*, are derived—

உடைய, a sign of the 6th case.
உடையவன், *he who possesses, the owner.*
உடையவள், *she who possesses.*
உடையது, *that which possesses.*
உடையவை, *those which possess.*
உடையவைகள், " "
உடையவர்கள், *they who possess:* உடையார்.
உடைத்தானவன், &c., are also used.

[Here உடைத்து is used for உடையது. For ஆனவன், &c., see §§ 58, 87, 151.]

உள் (§ 133) உள்ளவன் (உள்ளோன்) = *he to whom there is, who has.*
உள்ளவள் = *she to whom there is, who has.*
உள்ளது = *it to which there is, which has.*
உள்ளர் { உள்ளவர் (உள்ளோர்) = *they to whom*, &c. (m. & f.).
உள்ளவர்கள் " " "
உள்ளவை-கள் = *they to which*, &c.

☞ The above are regarded by Tamilians as finite verbs; but the plural neuter nouns, as உடைய, உள்ள, இல, பெரிய, are capable also of being used in every respect as relative participles, and are sometimes so considered.

Exercise 56.

§ 186. [1] பாக்கியமுடையவர்கள் ஒருவரும் இல்லை. [2] நல்லோர் யாவரும் அவரைப் புகழுவார்கள். [3] அதிசூரன் என்னும் பெயரையுடைய ஒரு மல்லகஜெட்டி (here உடைய governs the 2nd case). [4] சிறியோரையும் பெரியோரையும் அழைத்துக் கொண்டு வா. [5] இது நல்லது தான். [6] பெரியோர் வார்த்தையைத் தட்டாமல் நட. [7] மனையாள் இல்லாதவீடு பாழ். [8] எனக்கு அந்தக் கொடியனாலே உண்டான தொந்தரவு சிறியதல்ல. [9] பாவியேன் பட்டபாடு மெத்த. [10] தங்களுடைய ஆசீர்வாதத்தினாலே அடியேன் சுகமே (எ = ஆய்) இருக்கிறேன். [11] 'சிறியோர் செய்த சிறு பிழை எல்லாம் பெரியோர் ஆனவர் பொறுப்பது கடனே.' [12] உயிருள்ளவன். [13] உயிருள்ளோர் எல்லாரும். [14] முயற்சியுடையார் இகழ்ச்சி அடையார். [15] இல்லோர் இரப்பதும் இயல்பே, இரந்தோர்க்கீவதும் உடையோர் கடனே [see § 87].

[1] There are none who are always happy. [2] The great have said so. [3] He is a man of great wealth. [4] Well. [5] Cruel people give trouble to the poor. [6] All, both small and great, will be there. [7] What shall I, a sinner, do? [8] Three of his partners are great people. [9] The inhabitants of that village are little people. [10] He is a man of mercy. [11] Your humble servant is well by your blessing! [12] Help your servant who is but as a dog. [13] All generations shall call me blessed (f.). [14] Little people must be humble.

LESSON 58.

FOREIGN WORDS.

§ 187. Many words of *foreign origin* are in use in Tamil.

(*a*) Some of these are English; thus, சிக்கு, *sick*, a word of universal use; கோர்ட்டு, *Court;* கலம், *column of a MS.;* பீஸ், *fees*, &c.

(*b*) Some have come through the Hindī. These are of most frequent occurrence in official documents. To express these, certain doubtful experiments in orthography have to be made. Notably, the sign ஜ (p. 13. vii) is often used for Z: ☞ in Sanskrit words ஜ = J; but in Arabic or Persian it more often becomes Z.

(*c*) Many are of Portuguese origin: குசினி, *kitchen*, &c.

(*d*) Some are derived from Mahratta, Telugu, Canarese, Malayāḷim, &c.

(*e*) Sanskrit words can hardly be spoken of as foreign to the Tamil.

☞ [These words cannot be altogether dispensed with. However we may dislike intermingling words of foreign origin with what we call pure Tamil, these are in universal use and must be learnt. Again, since many of these are names of things brought into the country by foreigners, there can be no reason why they should not bring in the names as well as the things. It is mere pedantry to refuse to use மேசை for *table*, and make the compound போசனப் பலகை (*food-board*). On the other hand, if there is a good Tamil word for a thing, why should a foreign one be introduced? Why say சீக்கு when வியாதி, *sickness*, is well known? Most of these words will be found in these Lessons (or in Lex.) and the equivalent Tamil words where any exist.]

§ 188. **Vocabulary** (as specimens).

மயில், *a mile.*
ஜட்ஜி, *judge.*
ஆஸ்பத்திரி, *hospital.*
நம்பர், *number.*
நபர் (Arab.), *a person.*
சப்பாத்து (sabot), *shoes.*

லாந்தர், *a lantern* (also ராந்தல்).
மோஜா (Hind.), *boots.*
கைதி (Arab.), *a prisoner.*
தோம்தர, *musquito-curtains*, is Tel. DÔMA TERA = musquito-veil, திரை.

Exercise 57.

§ 189. [1] அவன் சீக்காய்க் கிடக்கிறான். [2] இவன் நின்ற இடத்திற்கும் அவன் போன இடத்துக்கும் ஒருமயில் தூரம் இருக்கும். [3] ஜட்ஜிதுரை வருகிறார். [4] அந்த மனிதன் ஆஸ்பத்திரிக்குப் போக வேண்டும். [5] மேசை போடு. [6] சேவல் கோர்ட்டிலே பிராது பண்ணினான். [7] கேட்டல் கொண்டுவா. [8] இண்டாஸ் பண்ணி அனுப்பி இருக்கிறார். [9] கலெக்டர் சாயிபு வந்திருக்கிறார். [10] பாதிரிதுரை எங்கே இருக்கிறார். [11] கைதி ஆஜீர் பண்ணு. [12] இந்தப்பிரதிவாதி அப்பீலுக்குப் போனான்.

[1] Bring my shoes. [2] Let down the musquito-curtains. [3] How many miles is it to the town? [4] Has he laid the table? [5] Bring the kettle. [6] Have they made a complaint in the court? [7] Has the collector arrived? [8] Where is the clergyman?

[Obs. There are peculiar ways of expressing foreign words in Tamil which must be noticed! No native would understand சிக் = *sick*, but all recognize சீக்கு.]

LESSON 59.

NOUNS DERIVED FROM VERB-STEMS.

§ **190.** (*a*) Some verbal derivatives have been noticed in §§ 87, 88, 143, 148. Besides these, many nouns are formed from verb-stems by adding வு or ப்பு according to the analogy of the future: அறிவு, படிப்பு. Some miscellaneous stems take பு or ம்பு. Among these are—

இரும்பு, *iron;* கரும்பு, *sugar-cane;*
அம்பு, *an arrow;* அன்பு, *love;*
பாம்பு, *a snake;* நட்பு, *friendship.*

Stems of verbs which have வ் in the future take வு; those which have ப் or ப்ப் take ப்பு.

The nouns treated of in this Lesson differ from those in §§ 87, 88, 148 in having no governing power. Those are in every sense parts of the verb; these are *nouns formed from verb-stems.*

(*b*) *Passive nouns* are formed chiefly from roots in உ by changing உ into ஐ:

தொடை, *a garland* (that which is strung), from தொடு, *string together* (poet.).
உடை, *a garment* (that which is put on), from உடு, *put on* (உடுப்பு).
சுமை, *a burden* (that which is carried), from சும, *carry.*

Compare உடுக்கை, வகை, பகை, பொறை, பெடை, பெட்டை, படை, மடை, விடை, அறை, நகை, நடை, இடை, அளவை, பிழை, &c.

☞ Sanskrit nouns in Ā generally change ஆ into ஐ when they are brought into Tamil: so SĪTĀ = சீதை; SABHĀ, *a congregation,* is சபை.

(*c*) அம் is added to some verb-roots to form nouns:

ஆக்கம், *wealth* (what is made or acquired), from ஆக்கு, *make;*
ஆட்டம், *a motion* (what is moved), from ஆட்டு, *move.*

So தோன்று, *appear,* makes தோற்றம், *appearance.*
குன்று, *grow small,* „ குற்றம், *fault.*
ஏறு, *ascend,* „ ஏற்றம், *flowing tide.*
ஊன்று, *rest on,* „ ஊற்றம், *prop.*

☞ [In some cases the consonant of the root is doubled or hardened before the addition of அம்; as தோட்டம் from தோண்டு, &c. There is, however, a form தோட்டு. தூங்கு makes தூக்கம்.]

(*d*) Many roots consisting of one short syllable (final உ does not really belong to the root) lengthen this in order to form nouns:

பெறு, *bring forth, obtain,* makes பேறு, *that which is gained or brought forth.*

பொரு, *meet, fight,* makes போர், *a heap, battle.*
இடு, *give,* makes ஈடு, *what is given as an equivalent* or *pledge.*

☞ [Tamil rarely violates the principle, that through every modification in inflexion and conjugation, the ROOT (*stem, crude form, base*) is unchanged. Of course final உ does not belong to the root. But compare § 131.]

(*e*) Some roots in று, ழு, டு (not short monosyllables) double the final consonant. [Comp. §§ 18. *c. d*, 131. *c.*]

Thus, எழுத்து, *a letter* (எழுது, *write,* § 62); பாட்டு, *a song* (பாடு, *sing,* § 62); கீற்று, *a line* (கீறு, *a scratch, split*).

(*f*) வி is added to some (verbal) roots:

கேள், *hear, ask;* கேள்-வி, *a question, report.*
தோல், *be defeated;* தோல்-வி, *defeat.*
பிறவி, *birth.*

(*g*) இ is added to some roots, chiefly of middle form (§ 62): தூற்றி, *a sweeper* (தூற்று, § 56. II). These nouns then indicate the doer of the action. From ஆடு comes ஆடி, and from அட்டு, அட்டி.

(*h*) தி is added to some roots:

கெடு-தி, *ruin* (கெடு); மற-தி, *forgetfulness* (மற).
அறுதி, *cessation;* உண்டி, *food* (உண் + தி).

(*i*) சி or ச்சி is added to some roots:

மகிழ்-ச்சி, இகழ்-ச்சி (மகிழ், *rejoice;* இகழ், *despise*).
ஆட்சி (ஆள்), *dominion.*

(*j*) மை is added to the present and past relative participles (§ 154). Thus, செய்-கின்ற-மை, செய்-த-மை. But this is by no means common, and is strictly a verbal form.

(*k*) In many cases the root of the verb is itself used as a noun. [Comp. § 164.] Thus,

வெட்டு, *a cut,* or *cut,* § 62; கட்டு, *a tie,* or *tie,* § 62.

(*l*) Some nouns are formed by adding உள் = *existence* to the verbal root. Thus,

செய்யுள், *poetry* (from செய், as the Greek ποίησις from ποιέω, *I make*); பொருள், *substance* (from பொரு, *come together*).

(*m*) A few nouns end in பம், ப்பம்:

அடைப்பம், *pouch* (அடை); துடைப்பம், *broom* (துடை); இன்பம், துன்பம், நட்பம் (நண்).

191. Vocabulary.

கல்வி, *learning* (கல், *learn,* § 70).
பிறன், *a neighbour* (பிற, *other*).
பறவை, *a bird* (பற, *fly*).
வீண், *vain* (வீணிலே = *in vain*).
மீது, *on* (மீதில், 7th case = மேலே).

எய் (§§ 56. I, 58), *send* (as a missile, *arrow*).
கோவில்கூட்டி (கூட்டு, *sweep*, § 46. II), *a church-sweeper*.
நோக்கம், *intention* (நோக்கு, *look*, § 56. II).
கேடு, *destruction* (கெடு, *destroy*).
கூட்டம், *a congregation* (கூட்டு, *collect*).
பாடு, *suffering* (படு, *suffer*).
நடை, *walk*, *conduct* (நட, *walk*).
அச்சம், *fear* (அஞ்சு) : பயம்.
{கருத்து, *intention* (கருது, *think*).
{அர்த்தம், *meaning* : பொருள்.

Exercise 58.

§ **192.** [1] கல்லை வீணிற் பறவைகள் மீதில் எறியாதே! [2] வாழ்வுந் தாழ்வும். [3] போரிலே அம்புகளை எய்தார்கள். [4] மகன் பிறந்தான் என்று மகிழ்ச்சியாய் இருக்கிறார். [5] தலைச்சுமை தாங்கக்கூடாமல் இறக்கிவிட்டான். [6] ஆடை [from ஆடு] ஆபரணங்களைத் தரித்துக் கொண்டு வந்தான். [7] உடைமையும் வறுமையும் ஒரு வழி நில்லாது. [8] 'அச்சமும் நாணமும் அறிவில்லார்க்கில்லை.' [9] கல்வியுடைமை பொருளுடைமை என்றிரண்டு செல்வமும் செல்வம் என்னப்படும். [10] பிறர் தாழும்படிக்கு நீ தாழ்வு பண்ணாதே! [11] அவனுடையநோக்கம் என்ன? [12] அவன்கொண்ட கருத்து வேறே. [13] இது ஆருடையகையெழுத்து? [14] அதின் பாடு. [15] அவனவன்பாடு வனவனுக்கு. [16] வந்ததேவரைக் கண்டு அரிச்சந்திரன் மகிழ்ந்தார்.

[1] Do not rejoice too much in prosperity, nor grieve too much in adversity. [2] Call the church-sweeper. [3] Neither praise nor blame affects the dead (இறந்தவர்களுக்கு இல்லை). [4] The household are much delighted because a son is born. [5] They all fought in the jungle. [6] Do not neglect learning. [7] The young (சிறுவர், § 185) should not kill birds. [8] What is the intention of this verse? [9] What is the meaning of this word? [10] What is the substance of this sentence? [11] What is the purport of the letter he has written? [12] This is a fatal affair. [13] He is a very forgetful person. [14] So I hear!

LESSON 60.

INTERJECTIONS.

§ **193.** The following are used as *interjections*.

(*a*) ஆஅ, *oh!* ஓஓ, ஓகோ, *oho!* இதோ, *here*, *behold!* அந்தா, *there*, *see!* இந்தா, *here*, *see!* ஐயோ, *alas!* ஓய், *hallo! oh!* ஐயையோ, *oh! alas!* அகோ, *hallo!*

These are used at the beginning of a sentence: ஐயோ பாவம், *what a pity!*

அன்றோ? அல்லவா? அல்லவோ (corrupted into அல்லோ)? *is it not? eh?* ஆக்கும், *I suppose, forsooth! certainly.*

(*b*) ஆக்கும் is put at the end when it signifies *forsooth*, and after the emphatic word when it indicates *certainty*:

> அவன் நல்லவன் ஆக்கும், *he must be reckoned a good man, I suppose.*
>
> அவனாக்கும் நல்லவன், *he is indeed a good man.* (This is not classical.)

(*c*) அன்றோ (rather high), அல்லவோ, அல்லவா, அல்லோ (vulgar) are put at the end of a sentence, or after the emphatic word = *is it not?*

(*d*) காண், காணும் (imperative of காண், *see*) are in constant use in much the same sense as we use the word *now*: என்ன காணும்? *well, what now?*

§ 194. Vocabulary.

மதி, *discretion.*
மோசம், *detriment, danger, deceit.*
மதிமோசம், *loss of sense;* with போ (§ 58), *lose one's senses.*
சூட்சமம், *subtility, nicety.*
எளிது, *easy* (§ 131. *e*).
சற்று, சற்றே, *a little.*
பிசகு, *mistake* (§ 56. II).
விளை, *grow up* (§ 55. I).
மிக, *much* (generally used with உம், மிகவும்).
சோதி (S.), *brightness.*
அடா (masc.), *you fellow!*
அடி (fem.), *my good woman!*
பாட்டி, *grandmother!*
அப்பா, *father!*
பயல், *a worthless fellow!*
வாராய், *marry come up! well!*
தாய் and தகப்பன் are used as words of respect. தாயே! தகப்பனே!
ஆயி, *mother* (= தாய்).
அம்மை, அம்ம, *mother!*

Exercise 59.

§ 195. [1] ஓகோ பிள்ளாய்! (§ 21. *h*, ஐ is changed into அய்) என்னகாரியஞ் செய்தாய்? [2] இப்படி மதிமோசம் போகலாமா? [3] நியாய சூட்சமம்அறிகிறது தேவர்களுக்கும் எளிதல்லவே (§§ 184–186). [4] சற்றே பிசகினால் அதிகபாவம் விளையுமே. [5] ஓய் நியாயாதிபதியே இவள் மிகவும் மோசக்காரி (§ 182). [6] இவன்அல்லோ அப்படிச் சொன்னவன்? [7] அது தான் காரியம்! [8] 'எங்கும் நிறைந்தே இருக்கின்ற சோதி.' [9] என் பாட்டி அழுகிறாய்? [10] எண்டா அப்படிச் செய்கிறாய்? (vulg. for

என் + அடா). 11 நீ யார் அடா என்று கேட்டான். 12 இதென்ன அதிசயம்! 13 இதோ தெரியப்படுத்துகிறேன். 14 என் அப்பா இந்நேரம்? 15 அவன் ஐயையோ என்று கூவி அழுதான். 16 சீ இவ்வளவுதானா? 17 இதோ தங்களிடத்தில் வந்திருக்கிறாரே வித்துவான். (Observe the inversion, which is very idiomatic.)

1 Well, is it not ten o'clock? 2 Alas, I am deceived, what shall I do! 3 My mother. 4 Which is the way to Tanjore (தஞ்சாவூர்)? 5 This boy is the clever fellow! 6 So this is the learned man you mentioned. 7 Here is a rupee for you. 8 I will come myself. 9 Hallo, gardener, come here. 10 I suppose that physician was your father. 11 Stop a bit, you fellow! 12 He's a great scamp. 13 Alas, nothing has grown in my field.

LESSON 61.

COMPARATIVE AND SUPERLATIVE DEGREES.

§ 196. From § 130 to § 133 it appears that there are no adjectives, *properly so called*, in Tamil.

The noun, used as an adjective, does not, of course, admit of changes expressive of the degrees of comparison. How then can we express in Tamil, '*this is better than that*,' and '*that is the best of all?*'

I. 'This is better than that.'

(*a*) அதற்கு இது நல்லது. The dative of that which has less of the quality spoken of: '*To that, this is good.*'

(*b*) அதிலும் இது நல்லது. The 5th case with உம் (denoting completeness): '*From that altogether, this is good.*' This is to be preferred to the former. If this be regarded as the 7th case, in opposition to native grammarians, the sense will be '*In all that, this is good.*'

(*c*) அதில் (அதிலே) இது நல்லது. The 5th case: '*From that, this is good.*' (ஏ should be added.)

These three are elegant.

(*d*) அதைப் பார்க்கிலும் இது நல்லது (பார்க்கிலும், from பார், § 56. III, *although* (*you*) *see*, § 100. (2))='*Although* (*you*) *see that, this is good.*'

(*e*) அதைப் பார்க்க இது நல்லது (பார்க்க, the infin. of பார், § 169): '*That while* (*you*) *see, this is good.*'

These are common and quite correct, though not very elegant forms.

(*f*) அதற்கு இது அதிக நல்லது (அதிக, *more*, may be prefixed to நல்லது in all the above; but is not needed).

(*g*) அதைவிட இது நல்லது (விட, *to leave*): '*That to leave, this is good.*'

This is colloquial.

(*h*) அதைக் காட்டிலும் இது நல்லது (காட்டிலும், from காட்டு, *show*, § 56. II, *although you show*) = '*Although you show that, this is good.*' This is decidedly a vulgar form.

II. 'That is the best of all.'

(*a*) அது எல்லாவற்றிலும் (எல்லாத்திலும்) நல்லது. The 5th case with உம் and a word denoting universality: '*From all—this is good.*'

(*b*) அது எல்லாவற்றிற்கும் (எல்லாத்துக்கும்) நல்லது (§ 127). The 4th case with உம்: '*To all—this is good.*'

(*c*) அதுவே உத்தமம் (சிரேட்டம்). These two words are Sanskrit, and signify *best, most excellent.*

(*d*) செல்வத்துள் செல்வம், *the greatest, highest degree of prosperity* (good).

§ 197. Vocabulary.

மென்மேலும், *more and more* (மேல + மேல் + உம், the first syllable shortened for the sake of euphony), § 107.
முந்து, *go before*, § 56. II.
முந்தி (verb. and part.), *before.*
முந்த (infin.) முந்த முந்த, *first of all.* (Com.)
So பிந்து, பிந்தி, பிந்த, *come after.*
இராஜோபசாரங்கள் (இராஜ, *kingly*, உபசாரம், *observance*. அ + உ = ஓ in Sanskrit compounds), *kingly honours.*
இடையன், *a man of the shepherd caste.*
மணங்கு (மடங்கு), *a weight, maund, time, -fold.*
மிக்க = பார்க்கிலும், *than* (மிகு, *exceed*).

Exercise 60.

§ 198. [1] இராஜோபசாரங்கள் தனக்கு நடந்து வருகிறதிலும் அவ்விடையனுக்கு நாளுக்கு நாள் [from day to day] அதிகமாக நடந்து வரும்படியாகத் (§ 157) திட்டஞ் (§ 165) செய்தான். [2] சுவாமீ! அடியேனுக்கு அதை விடப் பெரிதான காரியம் ஒன்றும் இல்லை. [3] இவன்தான் இருக்கிறவர்களுக்குள்ளே பரமயோக்கியன். [[4] 'ஓதலினன்றே (ன் + ந = ன், p. 22) வேதியர்க் கொழுக்கம்' (poet.).] = பிராமணருக்கு ஆசாரமானது வேதத்தைப் படிக்கிறதிலும் நன்மை ஆம். [5] உன்னிலும் பதின் (§ 173)

மணங்கு (மடங்கு) அதிகமாகக் காப்பாற்றுவேன். [6] 'தந்தை சொல் மிக்க மந்திரம் இல்லை.' (Poet.) [7] தாயில் சிறந்த ஒரு கோயிலும் இல்லை. [8] எல்லா மிருகங்களைப் பார்க்கிலும் ஆனை பெரியது; ஆனையைப் பார்க்கிலும் சிங்கம் வலியது. [9] தங்களிலுந் தங்கள் பிள்ளைகள் அறிவுடையவர்களாய் இருப்பது எல்லாருக்கும் மகிழ்ச்சியைத் தரும். [10] பொய்பேசுகிறதைப் பார்க்கிலுஞ் சாகிறது (§ 164) ஆகிலும் நல்லது.

[1] You must learn more and more in the school. [2] In the school you must get the first of all. [3] He is the most stupid of all the shepherds. [4] This minister is greater than the king. [5] It is better to work than to beg. [6] There is no wealth more precious than learning. [7] She is the best of all the women in the village. [8] The mother rejoices when her son is said to be wiser than others. [9] The elephant is greater than the tiger, but the tiger is more cruel. [10] This is the heaviest burden. [11] The son is better than the father. [12] This is greater than that. [13] This is sweeter than honey.

LESSON 62.

SO, THUS, SUCH, AS.

§ **199.** (*a*) இப்படிச் செய்யலாமா? *May* (we) *do thus?* (§ 103.)

இவ்விதமாக, இவ்வகையாய், இவ்வண்ணமாக, இந்த விதமாய், &c. &c., might be used instead of இப்படி.

(*b*) இப்பேர்ப்பட்ட காரியத்தைச் செய்யக் கூடுமோ? *Is it right to do such a thing?* (பேர், *name;* படு, *suffer.* Common,—not elegant.)

(*c*) இப்படிப்பட்ட மானக்கேடான காரியத்தைச் செய்யலாமா?
Is it right to do such a dishonourable action?

So அப்படிப்பட்ட and எப்படிப்பட்ட.

(*d*) இப்படிக்கொத்தவன் என்னத்துக்கு?
What is such a (fellow) good for?

[ஒ, *agree, be like,* § 56. III.]

(*e*) இதிலே, எவ்வளவு கெட்டிக்காரனோ, அதிலே, அவ்வளவு
In this, how-much-soever he is clever, in that, so much

மூடனாயிருப்பான். (எவ்வளவு with ஓ and அவ்வளவு.)
a blockhead he will be. He is *as* stupid in that *as* he is clever in this.

(*f*) தகப்பன் எப்படியோ பிள்ளை அப்படித்தான்.
As is the father, so is the child.

This may be also thus expressed: தகப்பனைப் போலப் பிள்ளை இருக்கும்.

[It can hardly be necessary to remind the learner that in rendering *as* into Tamil, he must consider its exact meaning. If *as* = *when*, the sentence must be changed. Thus:

(1) As *I was going* = நான் போகையில்,
or நான் போகிறவழியில்,
or நான் போகிற வேளையில் (பொழுது),
or நான் வழியில் நடந்துபோகிற சமயத்தில், &c. &c.

(2) *This is* AS *large* AS *that* = இதுவும் அதுவுஞ் சரி,
or இது அதற்குச் சரி,
or இது அதைப்போலப் பெரிது, (?)
or இதினுடைய அளவு பார்க்கிறபொழுது அதற்குச் சரியாய் இருக்கும், &c. &c.]

§ **200.** **Vocabulary.**

கண்டுபிடி, *find out* (§ 56. III) (கண்டு, *having seen*; பிடி, *seize upon*).
எங்கணும், *everywhere* (for எங்கும்).
சிசு, *an infant*: குழந்தை.
சிசுவத்தி, *infanticide* (அத்தி, ஹத்தி, *murder*, Skt.).
அலை, *wander* (§ 56. I).

Exercise 61.

§ **201.** [1] எப்படிப்பட்ட நியாய சூட்சுமத்தையும் கண்டுபிடிக்கத்தக்க புத்தியைக் கொடுப்பார். [2] குழந்தையைக் கொன்றுபோட்டவனை அழைப்பித்து, நீ ஏன் இப்படிப்பட்ட சிசுவத்தி செய்தாய் என்று கேட்டான். [3] 'எங்கணும் நீர் என்றால் இருந்தபடி உம்மை அடையாமல் நான் அங்கும் இங்கும் என்றும் அலையலாமோ!' (Poet.) [4] அவன் எப்படிப்பட்டவனோ? [5] அவனைப் பார்க்க எனக்கு இச்சை உண்டு. [6] எப்படிஆகிலும் (at any rate) இவன் சம்மதித்ததே பெரியகாரியம். [7] அப்படிக்குப் பிள்ளை பிறந்திருக்கிறது. (*Such a child*, com.) [8] பழைய படியே ஓடிப்போனான். [9] அப்படித் தான். [10] வழக்கப்படி சும்மா திரிகிறாயே. [11] தங்களுடைய இஷ்டத்தின்படி ஆகட்டும்.

[1] Did you ever see such a boy? [2] What is this dog good for? [3] The more he wanders in the streets, the more will he learn evil things. [4] What kind of people are there in the village? [5] Why did you commit such great folly? [6] How can I do such an evil? [7] He has gone as he was wont. [8] At any rate I have seized the thief. [9] What are such boys good for? [10] They are talking just as they used to talk. [11] May we do such a thing? [12] What kind of things may we do? [13] Oho! is he such a fool? [14] Such an one came.

LESSON 63.

BESIDES, EXCEPT, BUT.

§ **202.** *அல்லாமல், அன்றி* (from *அல்*, which denies a QUALITY), and இல்லாமல், இன்றி (from இல், which denies EXISTENCE, § 43) are in constant use.

அல்லாமல் and இல்லாமல் are neg. verb. part., § 121. (2).

அல்லாது and இல்லாது are also used, generally with ஏ: இல்லாதே, அல்லாதே.

அன்றி and இன்றி are irreg. verb. part. from the unused past tenses அன்றேன், இன்றேன், § 77. Comp. § 56. (III).

(*a*) இல்லாமல் and இன்றி are both used for *without*, ABSOLUTELY DENYING the existence of that to which they are attached.

மழை இல்லாமல் குடிகள் வருத்தப் படுகிறார்கள், *the inhabitants suffer from the absence of rain.*

யாதொரு உதவியும் இன்றி வருத்தப் பட்டான், *he suffered without any aid whatsoever.*

These, obviously, govern no case.

(*b*) அல்லாமல், அன்றி are used for *besides*, *except*, *but*, AFFIRMING the existence of the thing to which they are attached.

அல்லாமல் being thus a *preposition*, and having the meaning of *excepting*, *excluding*, governs the 2nd case: என்னையல்லாமல் = *besides me.*

கல்தூண் பெரிய பாரத்தைத் தாங்கினால் பிளந்து அழிவதல்லாமல் தளர்ந்து வளையுமோ? வளையாது, *if you put a heavy burden on a stone pillar it will break, but not bend.*

(*c*) அல்லாமலும் and அன்றியும் also signify *moreover*. The உம் may be added to the previous word thus: இதுவும் அல்லாமல், இதுவும் அன்றி.

(*d*) Compare also § 170. Many particles have an exceptive force, especially தவிர and ஒழிய.

§ **203.** **Vocabulary.**

யாதொரு . . . உம், *any whatsoever* (யாது, *which*; ஒரு, *one* . . . உம், *even*, § 126).

வருத்தம், *trouble.*

வருத்தப்படு, *be troubled* (§ 162).

வேண்டு, *desire* (§ 56. II).

சிவம், *the supreme Blessedness* (used chiefly by worshippers of சிவன்).

வித்து, *seed* (also விதை, விரை).

Exercise 62.

§ **204.** [1] என் கண்களே அல்லாமல் வேறே சாட்சி இல்லை. [2] சிவம் அன்றி வேறே வேண்டாதே[1]! [3] அதல்லாமல் இன்னம் வேறே உண்டா? [4] சோதிக்கும் பொருட்டு உனக்குச் சொன்னதே அல்லாமல் வேறில்லை. [5] உனக்கு வேண்டுவதைக் கேள். [6] அதை யாதொரு தடையும் இல்லாமற் கொடுப்பேன் என்றார். [7] அதுவும் அன்றி (vulg. அன்னியில்) அவனுடைய தாயாரையும் அழைப்பித்தார். [8] என் விதியை நான் தொலைக்க வேண்டுமே அல்லாமல் உமக்குக் காரியம் என்ன? [9] உன்னையல்லாமல் யார் வந்தார்கள்? [10] ஒரு பிரயாசமுமின்றி உனக்குக் கிடைக்கும்.

[1] This child is the only witness; there is no other. [2] Will anything grow without water? [3] This seed will grow, but not that stone. [4] Are there any besides this? [5] Will they come without it? [6] He must learn his lessons: what else? [7] He troubles me without any cause whatever. [8] I have told you one thing: besides that, there is another which no one knows but myself. [9] The people are suffering from the lack of true wisdom. [10] They are wandering about without any light. [11] It is hard to live without sin. [12] Come without delay. [13] If there should be no water.

LESSON 64.

ALTERNATIVES: ஆவது, ஆகிலும்.

§ **205.** '*Either* this *or* that must be true.'

a. இது ஆவது (இதாவது)[2], அது ஆவது (அதாவது) மெய்யாய் இருக்கும்.

b. இதானாலும் (ஆகிலும்), அதானாலும் (ஆகிலும்) மெய்யாயிருக்கும் (§ 100. (2)) = *and if it be this, and if it be that.*

c. இது மெய்யாயிருக்கும்; அல்ல என்றால், அது மெய்யாய் இருக்கும்.

d. இது அல்லது அது மெய்யாய் இருக்கும்.

e. இது மெய்; இல்லாவிட்டால், அது மெய் (§ 123. *b*).

f. ஒன்றில் இது, ஒன்றில் அது மெய்யாய் இருக்கும்.

☞ Observe the use of the future in the above = *must be acknowledged to be, must be, you must confess that it is.* ஏ may be added . . . மெய்யாய் இருக்குமே.

[1] Compare these two: வித்தன்றியாதும் விளைவது உண்டோ? *Will anything besides that which is sown be produced?*

வித்தின்றியாதும் விளைவது உண்டோ? *Will anything grow without seed?*

[2] Here the correlative conjunctions, *either . . . or*, must be rendered by ஆவது . . . ஆவது, or by ஆகிலும் . . . ஆகிலும், or by ஆனாலும் . . . ஆனாலும், appended to the alternative subjects. The other examples are not literal.

(*a*) ஆவது is the part. noun, neut. fut. of ஆ, *that which will be* or *become*=*either* . . . *or*. It must be repeated after each of the things disjoined. [Lesson 29.]

It is used for (1) *at least*, இதாவது மெய்யாய் இருக்குமே, *this, at least, you will grant to be true*; (2) *at all*, யாருக்காவது, *to any one at all*; (3) *even if*, உன்னை என்முதுகில் கொண்டாவது போவேன், *I will go even if I carry you on my back.*

(*c*) அல்ல என்றால் (அல்லவென்றால்), *if you say it is not, then.*

(*d*) அல்லது, neut. part. noun of அல், *that which is not so*, is used for *or*. It has some authority, but it seems a doubtful use of the word.

(*f*) ஒன்றில், 7th case of ஒன்று, *one*=*in one* (*case* understood) *this, in one* (*case*) *that is true.* This is not a classical form, but expresses the dilemma very exactly, and is quite intelligible.

§ 206. Vocabulary.

பதில், பதிலாக, *in place of.*
ஆகஸ்மீகமாக, *without any apparent reason, suddenly, by the visitation of God.*
தெய்வீகமாக, *by divine appointment.*
நாள், *a day.* நாளை, நாளைக்கு, நாளையத்தினம் (அ, *that*; தினம் *day*), *to-morrow.*
நாளையின் அன்றைக்கு (comp. § 166) (pron. நாளின்னிக்கு or நாளண்ணைக்கு), *the day after to-morrow* (அன்று, 4th case).

Exercise 63.

§ 207. [1] உங்களில் யாருக்காவது சாட்சி உண்டோ? [2] உன்னுடைய யானை ஆகஸ்மீகமாகச் செத்துப்போச்சுது [போயிற்று]. [3] அதற்கு விலையானாலும் பதிலாக யானையானாலும் உனக்குக் கொடுக்கிறேன் (pres. for fut.). [4] தெய்வீகமாக நேரிட்டபடியால் (§ 239) பதிலாக யானையானாலும் வாங்கிக்கொள், அல்லது விலையானாலும் வாங்கிக்கொள். [5] நீங்கள் நாளையத்தினமாவது நாளையின் அன்றைக்காவது வாருங்கள். [6] 'இல்லறம் அல்லது, நல்லறம் அல்ல.' [7] பரிகாசமாக விளையாடினோம், அல்லது இரத்தினம் விழுங்கினதில்லை. [8] வருகிறையோ (வருகிறாயோ) இல்லையோ? [9] இவன் திருடனாயிருப்பான், அல்ல வென்றால், இப்படி வருவானா?

[1] Either this or that must be true. [2] Either he is guilty or the witness is speaking falsely (*e.* or *f.*). [3] Come to-morrow, or else I will punish you. [4] Bring me either a horse, or a bandy, or an elephant. [5] Give it to some one or other. [6] Put some

one in your place, or I must fine you. [7] This, at least, you will acknowledge. [8] They either suffer from the absence of rain, or from some other cause. [9] I am a learned man and not a merchant.

LESSON 65.

NEITHER . . . NOR.

§ 208. 'Neither this nor that is true.'

(*a*) இதுவும் மெய் அல்ல, அதுவும் மெய் அல்ல, *this is not true, and that is not true.*

இது மெய் அல்ல, அதுவும் மெய் அல்ல, *this is not true, that also is not true.*

(*b*) இதாவது, அதாவது மெய்யாய் இராது. (Neg. of § 205. *a.*)

(*c*) இது ஆகிலும் (ஆனாலும்) அது ஆகிலும் (ஆனாலும்) மெய்யாய் இராது, § 100. (2), = *and if it be this, and if it be that—it is not true.*

§ 209. **Vocabulary.**

மஞ்சள், *saffron-yellow.*
நிறம், *colour.*
இடி, *thunder.*
ஒதுங்கு (§ 56. II), *give way, recede.*
செலவு, *expenditure* (செல், *go*).

Exercise 64.

§ 210. [1] நான் இவனிடத்தில் கடன் வாங்கினதும் இல்லை, சீட்டைக் கிழித்ததும் இல்லை. [2] நான் அந்தக்காரியத்தைச் சொன்னவனும் அல்ல, செய்தவனும் அல்ல. [3] அந்தப்பூ சிவப்பும் அல்ல, மஞ்சள் நிறமும் அல்ல. [4] அவர் ஞானியும் அல்ல, மந்திரியும் அல்ல. [5] அதுவும் வரவில்லை இதுவும் போகவில்லை. [6] பலபெயரிடத்தில் விசாரிக்கும்பொழுது, இவன் சொன்னது நிசம் என்று தோன்றவும் இல்லை, அவன் மனம் அறிந்து பொய் பேசினான் என்று தோன்றவும் இல்லை. [7] நீ ஆவது அவன் ஆவது இரண்டுபேரில் ஒருவன் ஒதுங்கிப் போகவேண்டும். [8] மழை அல்ல, இடி அல்ல எப்படியும் போக வேண்டியது. [9] ஆறல்ல, நூறல்ல, எவ்வளவு செலவானாலும் ஆகட்டும். [10] இதுவுமில்லை, அதுவுமில்லை, இரண்டுமில்லை. [11] 'அரிசி உண்டானால் வரிசையுமுண்டு.' (Proverb.) [12] அரிசியுமில்லை வரிசையும் இல்லை.

[1] Neither the king nor any one of his counsellors was present. [2] This was known to neither the watchman of the village nor to the inhabitants. [3] The book is neither here nor there. [4] Neither of these is sweet. [5] Neither has the physician come, nor has he sent his servant. [6] He has neither friends nor relations in the village. [7] Neither of these will yield to the other. [8] I cannot quite believe what either the plaintiff, or the defendant, or the witnesses, or the peons say. [Compare and go over Lessons 12, 38.]

LESSON 66.

WORDS SIGNIFYING EXTENT.

§ 211. The word மட்டு means *extent* (probably a corruption of வட்டம், *a circle*).

வரை, *boundary* (வரை, *write*);
பரியந்தம், *term, limit;*
அளவு, *measure.*

These words are used to express *extent*, *duration*, &c., and are equivalent to '*as far as*,' '*until*,' '*unto*,' '*to*,' &c.

a. இந்நாள் மட்டும், *until to-day, up to to-day* (not necessarily including the day spoken of).

இவ்விடம் மட்டும், *to this place, as far as this.*
உன்னால் ஆனமட்டும் படி, *learn as much as you can.*
மட்டுக்கும் (4th with உம்) is also used, but is not elegant. It should follow the nominative or the relative participle.
இம்மட்டும், *thus much;* அம்மட்டும், *so much;* எம்மட்டும், *how much*, are also used. மட்டோடிரு, *keep within bounds.*

b. இந்நாள் வரையும்,
இந்நாள் வரைக்கும், } *to this day.*
இந்நாள் வரையிலும்,
கழுத்து வரைக்கும், *up to the neck.*
நீ இப்படிச் செய்கிறவரைக்கும், *as long as you do this.*

உம் is elegantly added to denote completeness (§ 126).
வரை follows the nominative or the relative participle.

c. பரியந்தம் should only be used in combination with a Sanskrit noun. மரணபரியந்தம், *till death*, is elegant, and is a regular Sanskrit compound.

d. சீவன் உள்ளளவும். *as long as I live* (உள், *existence*, used absolutely, and ள் doubled). (நான் உயிரோடிருக்கிற மட்டும்; எனக்கு உயிருள்ளளவும்.

நான் பிழைத்திருக்கும் அளவும், *as long as I survive* (பிழை, § 56. III, *live*).

நான் வரும் அளவும் (வரும் வரைக்கும், வருகிற வரைக்கும், வரும் மட்டும்), *until I come*.

இவ்வளவு, அவ்வளவு, எவ்வளவு, *thus much, so much, how much* (§ 25).

எவ்வளவாகிலும், *how much soever* (§§ 100. (2), 208. *c*).

e. என்னால் கூடியமாத்திரஞ் சொல்லுகிறேன், *I* (will) *tell you as much as I can*.

[மாத்திரம் (used colloquially for மட்டும்) = *the whole extent*.]

§ **212.** **Vocabulary.**

மட்டு, as an adj. *scanty*.
ஆத்திரக்காரன், *a rash, hasty person*.
தனை denotes *measure* and *number*, and is only used in comp., thus:
இத்தனை, *thus much*.
அத்தனை, *so much*.
எத்தனை, *how much* or *many?* (§ 25.)

சாதம், *boiled rice*.
எலுமிச்சு, *lemon tree*.
காய், *unripe fruit*.
எலுமிச்சங்காய் (§ 131. *c*).
தர்க்கம், *disputation*.
தர்க்கசாஸ்திரம், *logic*.
அது முதல் (முதலாக or முதற்கொண்டு) இதுவரைக்கும் = *from that to this*.

Exercise 65.

§ **213.** 1 கூடினமட்டும் பிரயாசப்படு (com.). 2 இதுகளை நான் வரும் அளவும் காப்பாற்றி வை. 3 என்னால் ஆகிற வரைக்கும். 4 'ஆத்திரக்காரனுக்குப் புத்தி மட்டு.' 5 எலுமிச்சங்காய் அத்தனை சாதம் போட்டாள். 6 நெல்லையாகிலும் கொடு, இல்லாவிட்டால் ஒருமாதம் வரைக்கும் அவன் போடுகிற சாதத்தை ஆகிலும் சாப்பிட்டுக் கொண்டிரு. 7 போகக் கூடாதென்று வேண்டிய மட்டுக்கும் சொன்னாள். 8 நான் எவ்வளவு? 9 இப் பஞ்சையின் மேல் இப்படியாக வரலாமா? 10 பத்து வயது முதலாக முப்பது வரைக்கும் தர்க்கசாஸ்திரம் ஒன்றையே கற்றுக்கொண்டான். 11 அந்தமட்டுக்கும் ஏற்றம் நிற்குமோ எப்படி? என்றான். 12 அந்தமட்டும் நான் வழி மிதிக்கிறேன் என்றார். 13 தாய் வரும் அளவும் பேச்சிழுத்தாள். 14 அதற்களவில்லை. 15 இவ்வளவென்றில்லை. 16 நேற்றை அளவிலே செய்தி இப்படி. 17 இற்றைவரைக்கும்.

1 As long as we all live we must labour patiently and diligently. 2 I will not yield a jot of what I claim. 3 He was up to the chin in water. 4 Thus much I have borne. 5 At least take up this little burden. 6 Be thou faithful unto death! 7 It

is as large as a lime. [8] I will wait till to-morrow. [9] I will do what I can. [10] From the time the learned man came until now I have been thinking about the matter. [11] His wisdom is immeasurable. [12] Until to-day.

LESSON 67.

IDIOMS CONNECTED WITH என்=*why?* [§ 47.]

§ **214.** என்? *why?*

என்ன? *what?* (Less. 13.) Poet. என்னே?

a. என் வந்தாய்? *Why did you come?* [vulg. எங்கே வந்தாய்?]

These words are sometimes used in a manner that may perplex the learner.

b. இப்படிச் செய்வானேன்? *Why does he* (any one) *do this?*

இப்படிச் செய்வதேன்? *Why do this?*

c. அதேனெனில, அதேனென்றால் [அது, என், என்றால்], *if you say why=wherefore.*

(Many similar forms are in use.)

d. நீ இப்படிச் செய்கிறதென்ன? *Why do you do thus?*

e. எனும்=*soever.* [This may be என்+உம் or a corruption of ஆயினும்.] It is equivalent to ஆகிலும் in such forms as எவ்வளவேனும் (எ, அளவு, எனும்), *how much soever.* (§ 212. *d.*)

f. இருந்தென்ன? போயென்ன? = இருந்தால் என்ன? போனால் என்ன? *What matters it whether (they) remain or go? live or die?* This is common, and yet strictly classical.

g. என்பேரில் இரங்கும் என்! *Pray have mercy upon me!*

Here என்=*pray do*, is either for எ emphatic, or from என்=*why not?*

§ **215.** **Vocabulary.**

ஓய், *cease* (§ 56. I).
நிந்தி, *revile* (§ 56. III).
சதி, *deceit.*
சாஸ்திரம், *science.*
ஆராய், *search into* (§ 56. I).
அண்டு, *draw near* (§ 56. II).
ஆநந்தம், *felicity.*
வெள்ளம், *a flood.*
பாய், *rush* (§ 56. I).
வண்டி or வண்டில், *a bandy.*
மச்சான் (மைத்துனன், மச்சுனன்), *a brother-in-law.*
உறவு, *relationship.*
உறவாடு, *claim relationship* (§ 56. II).
காளை, *a bullock.*
அக்காள், *an elder sister.*

Exercise 66.

§ **216.** [1] ஓயாமற் பொய் சொல்லுகிறவர்களும், நல்லோரை (§ 184) நிந்திக்கிறவர்களும், பெற்ற தாயாரை வைகிறவர்களும், ஆயிரஞ் சதிகளைச் செய்பவர்களும், சாஸ்திரங்களை ஆராயாதவர்களும், பிறர்க்கு உபகாரஞ் செய்யாதவர்களும், தங்களை அண்டினவர்களுக்கு ஒன்றும் கொடாதவர்களும் இருந்தென்ன, போயென்ன? [2] 'ஓயாதோ என் கவலை? உள்ளே ஆநந்தவெள்ளம் பாயாதோ?' [3] ஏனோ தானோ என்றிருக்கிறான். [4] அதின் அழகு என்னென்று சொல்லுவேன்? [5] அதென்னவோ? [6] நீங்கள் வேட்டை ஆடி இளைத்துக் களைத்துப் போவானேன்? [7] நீ என்துக்கிக்கிறாய்? [8] உனக்கென்ன குறைபாடு? [9] உனக்கவன் என்னவேண்டும்? [10] ஆறு சுவையோடு உண்டால் என்ன? அற்பமாம் கூழைக் குடித்தால் என்ன? [11] எல்லாந் தெரிந்தவர்களுக்குச் சொல்வானேன்? [12] என் மரத்தின் மேல் என் ஏறினாய்? [13] என் என்பாரில்லை.

[14] Ques. வண்டில் ஓடுவதேன்?
மச்சான் உறவாடுவதேன்?

Ans. அக்காளைக் கொண்டு.

[This is a specimen of a kind of riddle very common among Tamilians.
'The bandy runs—why?
The brother-in-law claims relationship—why?'

By means of the [கொண்டு, § 239.] { *bullock* (அக்காளை = அந்தக் காளை, § 25).
elder sister (அக்காள், marriage with whom constitutes him a மச்சான்).]

[1] Why do you do this? [2] He will not give because he has no money. [3] He will not give even a grain of rape seed. [4] Give me a little water, at least. [5] You must examine those who claim relationship; for they seem to be deceivers. [6] It rushes on without ceasing. [7] Draw near to the Giver of blessedness. [8] What is all this noise about? [9] What matters it whether such people come or go? [10] Please give me the money.

LESSON 68.

WHETHER, SOEVER, ALTHOUGH.

§ **217.** *a.* அவனிடத்தில் பத்தி இருக்கிறதோ இல்லையோ என்றுசோதிக்கும் பொருட்டுச் சொன்னேன்[1], *I said so to try whether there was devotion in him or not.*

b. இப்படிச் செய்கிறவன் யாரோ அவன் கள்ளன்.
Whoever does thus, he is a robber.

[1] The ஓ is the proper interrogative particle, where doubt is expressed (§ 46).

c. எங்கே ஆகிலும் கறுப்புநாய் வெள்ளைநாய் ஆகுமா? (§ 100.)
In any place soever[1] *will a black dog become a white dog?*

d. சிறிய பாம்பாகிலும் பெரியதடிகொண்டடிக்க வேண்டும்.
Although it be a small snake you must strike it with a big stick.

e. யார் ஆகட்டும் (§ 140) (= *let him be who he may* [ஆக, ஒட்டும்]) = *whosoever.*

§ 218. **Vocabulary.**

பகரு (§ 60. III), *speak* [poet.].
மலர், *a flower.*
மலர்க்கால், *flowery foot.*
சென்னி, *a head* [poet.].
மிசை, *upon* [poet.].
மூலை, *a corner.*
ஒளி, *hide* (§ 64).
சூது, *gaming.*
சூதாடு, *gamble* (§ 56. II).
கீழோர், *low persons* (கீழ், § 184).
உரை, *speak* [poet.].
நெறி (§ 64), *stiffen, erect.*

Exercise 67.

§ 219. [1] எங்கே ஆகிலும் கண்டதுண்டோ? [2] அந்த ஊராரைக் காத்தவன் எவனோ, அவனை நாம் அண்டிக்கொள்ள வேண்டும். [3] பால் ஆகிலும் தயிர் ஆகிலும் கொடு. [4] மண் ஆயினும் மனை ஆயினும் காப்பாற்றினவனுக்கு உண்டு. [5] பிணியைத் தீர்ப்பது எதுவோ அதுவே மருந்து. [6] அவரைக் கண்டது எப்போதோ அப்போதே தெரியும் அவருடைய செய்தி. (Observe the order. This is very idiomatic.) [7] ஆண் ஆகிலும் பெண் ஆகிலும் பொய்சொல்லுகிறவர்களை நம்பக் கூடாது. [8] யாராகட்டும் சூதாடுகிறவன் கெடுவான். [9] 'கீழோர் ஆயினும் தாழ உரை.' [10] எப்போது அது காதுகளை நெறித்துக்கொண்டு, வாலைத் தூக்குமோ, அப்போது கொல்ல நினைத்தது. [11] என் மந்தையிலே ஓர் ஆட்டுக்கு இந்தவலி வந்து கோணக்கோண இழுத்து எதினாலேயும் பிழையாமற் செத்துப் போச்சு. (Observe the confusion of subjects. The sheep died, and not the spasm.)

[12] பாராயோ என்றுயரம் எல்லாம்? ஐயா!
Dost thou not see (§§ 46, 110) *my sorrow* (§ 50) *all? O Lord!*

பகருமுன்னே தெரியாதோ? பாவியேன்முன்
Before (*I*) *speak is it not known? Before sinful me* (§ 185. *c*)

வாராயோ? இன்னம் ஒருகாலம் ஆனாலும்
wilt thou not come? Yet at any time whatever

மலர்க்கால் என் சென்னி மிசை வைத்திடாயோ?
thy flowery foot (§ 131) *my head upon* (§ 251) *wilt thou not place?* (263.)

[1] 'Soever' is expressed by *an interrogative* + ஓ.

NOTE (1) In poetry த் after ன் is changed into ற் (p. 22).
(2) When ம் follows ம் one of them is often elided.
(3) Honorifics are not used in Tamil poetry generally.

[1] Have you seen my elder sister anywhere? [2] I will run away somewhere or other. [3] He is hidden in some corner or other (ஒளித்திருக்கிறான் = he is, having hidden). [4] Whoever teaches well (he) is a munshi. [5] Whether he be rich or poor a liar will be despised. [6] Can a murderer escape anywhere? [7] Can you tell me whether the price is what he says or not? [8] Although he is a young man he is a great physician. [9] I asked him those questions to try whether he had learnt the lesson or not.

LESSON 69.

CERTAIN NEGATIVE FORMS.

§ **220**. In § 121 we saw that the negative relative participle ended in ஆத, and that the form in ஆ was chiefly used in poetry. The negative participial noun ends in ஆதது. Note the following forms:—

a. நீ இங்கே வரா முன்னே, *before you came here* (வராததுக்குமுன்னே, வரும் முன்னே). வருகிறதற்கு or வருவதற்கு is probably better Tamil.

b. நான் அங்கே போகாததற்கு முன்னே (4th case of neg. part. noun), *before I went there.*

c. இவன் ஒன்றையுஞ் செய்யாதபடிக்கு வீணாய்த் திரிகிறான், *he wanders about idly doing nothing* (very common, but not very elegant).

நீ இப்படிச் செய்யாதபடி கற்பித்தேன், *I ordered you not to do it.* [More elegantly இப்படிச் செய்யக்கூடாது என்று சொன்னேன்.]

§ 221. Vocabulary.

பிழை, *a fault* : குற்றம்.
கசி, *yield moisture, ooze, weep* (with அழு), (§ 56. I).
உருகு, *melt* (§ 56. II, உருக்கு, act.).
கருது, *regard, think of* (§ 56. II).
நினை, *think, remember* (§ 56. III).
பொறு (§ 56. III), *bear with, forgive.*
அருளு, *vouchsafe* (§ 62).

Exercise 68.

§ **222**. [1] 'கல்லாப் பிழையுங், கருதாப் பிழையுங், கசிந்துருகி நில்லாப் பிழையும், நினையாப் பிழையுந், துதியாப் பிழையுந், தொழாப் பிழையும்,

எல்லாப் பிழையும், பொறுத்தருள்வாய்[1].' ²காணா முன் நிச்சயப்படக் கூடாது. ³அதைக் கேளா முன் நடுக்கம்வந்து விட்டது. ⁴சூரியன் தோன்றாததற்கு முன்னே (தோன்றுதற்கு முன்னே, தோன்றும் முன்னே) வேலைக்காரர் வந்தார்கள். ⁵அவன் வராததற்குத் தடை என்ன? ⁶அந்தப் பையன் பாடம் ஒன்றையும் படியாதபடிக்குத் திரிகிறான். ⁷அஞ்சும் மூன்றும் உண்டானால் அறியாப் பெண்ணுங் கறி சமைப்பாள்.

¹ Pardon my fault in not thinking of it. ² He goes about without speaking a word. ³ Before the sun set he went to sleep. ⁴ Before I thought of that I wept. ⁵ Why does the boy go about learning no lessons? ⁶ Should any one go about doing nothing? ⁷ He is a blockhead that understands nothing.

LESSON 70.

ADJECTIVE FORMS.

§ 223. **Vocabulary.**

கன்னங்கரிய, *very black* (கன்னங் கறுத்த).
தன்னந்தனியே, *quite alone* (தன்னந் தனித்த).
சின்னஞ்சிறிய, *very little* (சின்னஞ் சிறுத்த).
பென்னம்பெரிய, *very great* (பென்னம் பெருத்த).

☞ These and similar forms are in constant use. No rule can be laid down for their formation. Either the ADJECTIVAL FORM is used as கரிய, or the பெயர் எச்சம் (§ 76) as கறுத்த.

மணல், *sand*.
தயங்கு (§ 56. II), *to languish*.
காமம், *lust*.
காமாதி, *lust, &c.* (§ 151).
ராக்ஷசன், *a demon*.
இலக்கு, *a butt to be aimed at*.

நிறம், *a colour*.
பேய், *a devil*.
செக்கச்சிவந்த, *red*.
பச்சைப்பசத்த, *green*.
புத்தப்புதிய, *new*.
இடை, *the waist, middle*.

Exercise 69.

§ 224. ¹சின்னஞ் சிறியர்கள் செய்த மணற் சோற்றை ஒக்கும். ²சின்னஞ்சிறுத்த இடை. ³கன்னங்கறுத்த முகமுள்ளவன் வந்தான். ⁴பென்னம்பெருத்த புயத்தோடிருக்கிறான். ⁵சின்னஞ்சிறியேன் என்னசெய்வேன்! ⁶தன்னந்தனியே இருந்து தயங்கினாள். ⁷செக்கச்சிவந்தவளாய் இருக்கிறாள். ⁸அந்தவயல் பச்சைப்பசத்த நிறமாய் இருக்கிறது. ⁹புத்தப்புதிய நெய்கொண்டு வந்திருக்கிறான்.

¹ POET. IDIOMS:—(1) The sign of the second case omitted—பிழையையும்; (2) கல்லா, &c., for கல்லாத; (3) அருள்வாய், future for imperative or optative.

10 '*கன்னங்கரிய நிறக் காமாதி ராக்ஷசப் பேய்க்*
Jet black in hue—lust and other diabolical demons unto
கென்னை இலக்காக வைத்த தென்னே? (§ 215.) *பராபரமே!*'
me a butt why hast (thou) left? O Godhead!

[பேய்க்கு + என்னை = பேய்க்கென்னை. நிறக் காமாதி (§ 151. *c*) ராக்ஷசப் பேய்க்கு = நிறத்தை உடைய காமம் முதலான இராட்சதராகிய பேய்களுக்கு.]

[1] The demon's face was jet black, and he had great broad shoulders. [2] She went all alone in the desert. [3] He has a very little dog. [4] A very black cloud hid the sun. [5] Must I languish all alone? [6] The corn is quite green in the fields. [7] That cow is entirely red.

LESSON 71.

BEFORE, AFTER.

முன், பின். (**Vocabulary**, § 84.)

§ **225**. (1) முன், *before*, in place or time; பின், *after*, in place or time.

Both these words, which are in fact *nouns*, are used in the formation of innumerable compounds of very common and idiomatic use. They require the fourth case or the sixth.

For முன் are used also—

(2) முன்னே, emphatic;
முன்பு, sometimes with ஆய் and ஆக;
முன்னம், முன்னமே, generally relating to time;
முன்னற, vulgar; முன்னர், poetical;
முன்னாக, and முன்னாலே.

(3) முன் and பின் form compounds thus: முற்காலம், பிற்காலம், *the before-time* and *the after-time*. Here ன் becomes ற் before க்.

(4) பின்னே, பின்பு, பின்னர், poetical, பிற்பாடு (பாடு = *a state*), பின்னாலே, பிறகு (Skt. Prāk.) are also used.

(5) பின்னே is used for *moreover*.

(6) The verbs முந்து and பிந்து (§ 56. II) are also used for *go before* and *come after;* of these the verb. part. முந்தி and பிந்தி are idiomatically employed.

(7) முன் and பின் (with other particles) are used in composition with many verbs. Thus:

முன்னிடு, *put before.*
முன்னில்லு, *stand before, protect.*
பின்னிடு, *put after.*
பின்பற்று, *imitate, follow after.*
பின்வாங்கு, *draw back* (§ 251).

Exercise 70.

§ **226.** [1] ஆற்றிலே புருஷன் முன்னும் பெண்சாதி பின்னுமாகப் (§ 136) போகிற பொழுது மற்றொருவன் இவர்கள் பின்னாலே இறங்கி வந்தான். [2] அவர்கள் வருகிறதற்குமுன்னே. [3] சிலநாள் போன பிற்பாடு. [4] அவனுக்குப் பின்னாலே திரும்பிவந்தார்கள். [5] சற்றிடந் தாண்டின பிற்பாடு. [6] என் பின்னே நீங்கள் எல்லாரும் வாருங்கள் (com.). [7] 'வெள்ளம் வரும் முன்னே அணை போட வேண்டும்.' (Prov.) [8] முன் பின் செய்கிறபடி செய்! [9] நான் முந்திப் போகிறேன், நீ பிந்திவரலாம். [10] முந்தாதே. [11] பின்வாங்காதே. [12] முன்னிட்ட காலைப் பின்னிட்டுத் திரும்பினான். [13] அவன் முன்னுக்கு வரமாட்டான். [14] இதற்கு முன்னேதானே நீ சேர்த்துக்கொள்ளல் ஆகாதா?

[1] The brother went before and the sister came after. [2] Dig your garden before the rain comes; for afterwards there will be no time. [3] Afterwards I heard them say so. [4] Compare the context (sentences before and after). [5] I knew this before. [6] The criminal stood speechless before the judge. [7] There were upright judges both before and after him. [8] Look well both before and behind. [9] Could you not have written the letter before this?

LESSON 72.

போல், போல, AS.

§ **227.** Of *போலு* (§ 56. [III]), *resemble, be like,* the root *போல்*, the infin. *போல*, the 3rd neut. fut. *போலும்*, and the past rel. part. *போன்ற* (rarely) are in use, and signify *like, as.*

In the higher dialect *ஒப்ப* and many other such particles are used. [Pope's II. G. 109.]

(1) All these govern the second case.

(2) But, as in other examples, the nom. may be put for the acc.

(3) *ஏ* may be added: *போலே, போலவே, போலுமே.*

(4) Sometimes *போல், போல* are added to the subjunctive in *ஆல்* (§ 95. *a*). Thus, *செய்தால் போல்*=*as if one should do.*

They are often added to the verbal noun in *து*: *செய்கிறதுபோல* (§ 87)=*like the doing.*

(5) The forms *செய்கிறாப்போலே* and *செய்தாப்போலே*=*as soon as* (you) *do* or *did*, are in VERY common use, being pronounced

in a very hurried way so as to sound like செய்றாப்பலே and செய்தாப்பலே. They are probably corruptions of செய்கிற ஆ போல=*like the way of doing* (ஆ in old Tamil means *way*, *manner*). செய்யுமாப் போல, which also frequently occurs, is a correct form (செய்யும் ஆ போல்), *as if (he) would do.*

§ **228.** **Vocabulary.**

தளர் (§ 56. I), *totter*, *grow feeble*.
குமிழி, *a bubble*.
நீர்க்குமிழி, *a bubble on the water* (§ 131).
உடல், *a body* (உடம்பு).
கிளி, *parrot*.
விலை, *price*.
விலை உயர்ந்த, *very valuable* (உயர், § 56. I, *be high*).
விலை ஏறப்பெற்ற, *precious* (ஏற, *to ascend;* பெற்ற, *which has obtained;* பெறு, *obtain*, § 56. (II)).
முத்து, *a pearl*.
அருமை, *costliness* (§ 131. *e*).
அருமையான, *costly*.
இரத்தினம், *a gem*.
இரத்தினக்கல், *a jewel* (§ 131).
வண்ணான், *a washerman*.
அம்பட்டன், *a barber*.
குயவன், *a potter*.
துவை (§ 56. III), *beat clothes on a stone*.
தீட்டு (§ 56. II), *sharpen*.
தீட்டுக்கல், *a hone* (சாணை).
பிடி (§ 56. III), *seize*.
பிடிகல், *a potter's stone*.
மாதிரி, *manner*, *fashion*.

Exercise 71.

§ **229.** [1] 'தாய் இருந்தும் பிள்ளை தளர்ந்தாற் போல் (ல் before ப் into ற்) எவ்விடத்தும் நீர் இருந்தும் நான் தளர்ந்து நின்றேன்.' [2] கேட்டதையே சொல்லுங் கிளி போல (கிளியைப்போல). [3] விலையுயர்ந்த இரத்தினக் கல்லைப் போலப் பிரகாசித்தது. [4] அப்படி அனுப்பியது போல் தோன்றுகிறது. [5] மற்றவர்களைப் போல என்னை நினைக்காதே (for நினையாதே)! [6] நித்தியம் ஒன்றில்லாத நீர்க்குமிழி போன்ற உடல். [7] அந்தச் சாட்சிக்காரர் மூன்று பேருக்குள்ளே வண்ணான் துவைக்கிற கல்லைப் போலவும், அம்பட்டன் தீட்டுக்கல்லைப் போலவும், குயவன் பிடிகல்லைப் போலவும், வேறு வேறு மாதிரியாகச் செய்து கொண்டு வந்தார்கள். [8] உன்னைப் போலும் விவேகமுள்ள மந்திரி எந்தத் தேசத்திலுங் கிடைப்பது மிகவும் அரிது. [9] அக்கனியைப் போலவே இக்கனி இருக்கின்றதே. [10] 'கல்லார் ஒருவருக்குச் செய்த உபகாரங் கல்மேல் எழுத்துப் போற் காணுமே!' [11] இருந்தாப்போலிருந்து (suddenly) வாயு வருகிறதுண்டு.

[1] Is there any one like him? [2] As you sent me, so I will send him. [3] In colour it is like saffron, in shape like the moon. [4] It would be hard to find a man as sensible as the shopkeeper is. [5] In fashion that garment is like the mother's. [6] Don't think of

him as of others. [7] Suddenly the messengers came to fetch him. [8] Is a black rock equal in value to a precious stone? [9] Are there any counsellors as valuable as these? [10] Youth is like a bubble on the water. [11] It would be very hard to find a friend as faithful as he is. [12] So in this case also you may judge.

LESSON 73.

CONCERNING. ABOUT. THE 'OF' OF REFERENCE. TO.

§ **230.** 1. குறித்து is the adverb. part. of குறி (§ 56. III) = *having pointed out.*

2. பற்றி is the adverb. part. of பற்று (§ 56. II) = *having laid hold of.*

3. தொட்டு is the adverb. part. of தொடு [§ 56. (II)] = *having touched.*

These are used for *concerning*, *regarding*, *about*, *touching*. குறித்து is correct and elegant; பற்றி is correct, but not elegant; the use of தொட்டு appears to be a foreign idiom.

அந்தக்காரியத்தைக் குறித்துப்பேசினார், அதைப் பற்றிப் பேசினார், அதைத் தொட்டுப் பேசினார்,	*he spoke of* (or *about*) *that affair.*

4. In very common talk இட்டு (from இடு, §§ 68, 263) is used in the same way:

அதை இட்டு வெகு பாடுபட்டேன், *I suffered much* FROM (*on account of*) *that.*

5. பேரில் or பெயரில் (seventh case of பேர் or பெயர், *name*) = *about*, *upon.* Thus,

ஒரு வித்துவான் இராயர்பேரில் ஒருபிரபந்தம்பண்ணிக்கொண்டான்.
A learned man about the king a work composed.

6. *About* is commonly expressed by the fourth case also (§ 242). Thus, *There is no doubt about (of) it* = அதற்குச் சமுசயம் (சந்தேகம், பிசகு) இல்லை.

Ambiguities are very apt to creep in!

7. நோக்கி, adverb. part. of நோக்கு (§ 56. II) = *having looked at.*

8. பார்த்து, adverb. part. of பார், *see* (§ 56. III) = *having seen.*

These are used as equivalent to *to* in such sentences as, *he said thus* TO *him.*

அவனை நோக்கி இப்படிச் சொன்னான்;
அவனைப் பார்த்து இப்படிச் சொன்னான்;
அவனிடத்தில் இப்படிச் சொன்னான் (this is better than either of the preceding);
அவனுடனே இப்படிச் சொன்னான் (this is not very good, but common).

☞ Adverbial participles are often elegantly and idiomatically used in Tamil for particles. This requires much attention. Comp. § 77.

§ 231. Vocabulary.

சிபாரிசு (Pers.), *recommendation.*
மூடன், *a fool.*
குந்தகம், *a hindrance* (குந்தக்கேடு is also used).
ஓசரம், *cause.*
பாடு, *part.*
பாட்டுக்கு = *on account of*, from படு.
சிறுமை, *disgrace* (சிறு + மை, § 184).
கனம், *weight.*
கன, adj. *much.*
சும்மா, *idle, without reason.*
கலியாணம், *a wedding.*
வேண்டு (§ 56. II), *desire, seek for.*

Exercise 72.

§ 232. 1 அவனைப்பார்த்து இனிமேல் அப்படிச் செய்யாதே என்றான். 2 ஒரு மூடனைக்குறித்துச் சிபாரிசு செய்தான். 3 அந்தராசா தன்பிள்ளைகள் படியாமல் மூடர்களாய் இருக்கிறதைக்கண்டு வெகுவிசனத்தோடே ஆலோசித்தான். 4 நீ அங்கே போய் எதைக்குறித்துப் பேசுவாய்? 5 சத்தத்தினாலே மாத்திரம் பயப்படல் ஆகாது (சத்தத்தைக்குறித்து might be used). 6 கலியாணத்தைக்குறித்துக் கடன்பட்டேன். 7 அவனுக்கோசரம் அதிக [அதிக] சிறுமைப்பட்டேன் (ஓசரம் for குறித்து). 8 அவனைஇட்டுக் காரியம் எல்லாம் குந்தகமாய்ப்போய்விட்டது. 9 விருதாவாய் வல்லை; ஒரு காரியத்தைவேண்டி வருகிறான் (வல்லை = வரவில்லை!). 10 வயிற்றுப் பாட்டுக்கு வருத்தப்படுகிறான். 11 கல்வியைப்பற்றிக் கன பாடுபட்டேன். 12 ஒருமுகாந்திரத்தைப்பற்றித் தங்களிடத்தில் வருவார்களேஅல்லாமல் சும்மா வரமாட்டார்கள்.

1 I have inquired concerning it. 2 He talked about the affairs of the village a long time. 3 I told you before all about it. 4 What will you talk about to the mother? 5 It is said concerning this in the third chapter. 6 He has some end in view in coming to you. 7 What are the villagers saying about the matter? 8 He addressed the king and his counsellors concerning the affairs of the country. 9 He has composed a poem about the king. 10 The man is very much troubled about the means of subsistence. 11 The teacher said to him, learn this lesson carefully.

LESSON 74.

§ 233. IDIOMATIC USES OF THE FIRST CASE. [COMPARE LESSON 48.]

☞ ELLIPSIS IS THE KEY TO ALMOST EVERY TAMIL IDIOM: so the first case often stands for the other cases (§ 50).

(1) பட்டணமே (§ 193) போனான், *he went to the town* (1st for 4th with emphatic ஏ).

(2) திரும்பி அவன் இடம் போ, *go to him again* (1st for 7th: இடம் for இடத்தில்).

(3) சுதரிசனன் என்னும் (§ 132) அரசன் ஒருவன் (§ 172) இருந்தான், *there was a king called Su-darçana.* [Apposition.]

(4) காலையும் மாலையும் நான்கு வேதம் ஓதாத அந்தணர் என்பவர்கள் அனைவரும் (§ 127) பதரே (nom. for 7th and 2nd), *all those so-called Brāhmans who do not recite the four Vēdas in the morning and in the evening are chaff.*

(5) அழுத (§ 50) கண்ணும் சிந்திய மூக்கும் ஆகக் (§ 136) கலங்கி நின்றான், *with weeping eyes he stood, snivelling and confounded.*

[Here ஆக with the nom. case is used for the first case in ஒடு, or there is an ellipsis of உள்ளவன் (§§ 133, 184) after the nom.]

(6) ஒருநாள் ஒருபிராமணன்வீட்டில் இருவரும் விலாப்புறம் வீங்கச் (§ 168) சாப்பிட்டார்கள், *one day in a Brāhman's house they both ate till their ribs were well lined.* [பிராமணன் is sixth case; நாள் is used adverbially.]

(7) அநேகநாளாய் வாழ்ந்துகொண்டிருந்தார்கள், *they lived prosperously for many days.*

[Here there is an ellipsis of கள். ஆய் = ஆக.]

§ 234. Vocabulary.

தேசாந்தரம், *a foreign country*: DĒÇA + ANTARA.
இடறு (§ 56. II), *stumble, trip.*
நொண்டி, *lame.*
பசை, *moisture.*

வெள்ளெலும்பு (வெள், *white*), *a well-picked bone.*
கௌவு (§ 56. II), *snatch at*: கவ்வு.

Exercise 73.

§ 235. [1] தேசாந்தரம் போனான்; போகும் போது [§ 106. (2)] ஒரு நாள் அந்த எருது கால்இடறி விழுந்து நொண்டி ஆயிற்று (§ 123. *a*). [2] தாகம் எடுத்துத் தண்ணீர் குடிக்கப் போனான். [3] நாய் பசைஇல்லாத

வெள்ளெலும்பைக் கௌவிக் கடித்துப் பல்லசைத்தும் (§ 100) பசி தீராமல் சந்தோஷத்தை அடைகிறது. [4] அரசரும் நெருப்பும் பாம்புஞ் சரி. [5] ஊரது தூரமாய் இருக்கிறது (அது is redundant). [6] அதைப் பார்த்து மனம் பொறுமல் பேசினன். [7] பாவஞ்செய்த யாவரும் ஆக்கினை அடைவார்கள். [8] கல்லெறி தூரம். [9] ஒருநாளிராத்திரி. [10] என் சம்பளத்தில் மாசம் மாசம் சேர்த்துக் கொடுப்பேன். [11] இதில் எடுத்துப் பட்டணத்திற்குப் புறத்திலே வந்து மூன்றுநாள் இருந்தான்.

LESSON 75.

§ 236. IDIOMATIC USES OF THE SECOND CASE. [§ 18.]

(1) அவனை மொட்டை அடித்தான், *he shaved him bare.*

(2) ஊரைப்போய்ச் சேர்ந்தான், *he went to the town.* [For ஊருக்கு (§ 50).]

(3) அதைப் பாசாங்கென்று அறியாமலிருந்தான், *he did not know that it was mere pretence—(it, that it was).*

(4) உயர்திணை என்று மனிதரைச் சொன்னார்; அஃறிணை என்று மற்றவைகளைச் சொன்னார், *he called men 'high caste'; and other things 'low caste.'* (§ 30.)

[The sign of the second case in Tamil is ஐ. In Malayāḷam E; in Telugu NU or NI, in which the real suffix is probably N; in ancient Kanarese it is AM; in modern Kanarese A or ANNU; and in all the languages of the Indo-European family M or N is, for the most part, found in the accusative.

The origin of the Tamil suffix ஐ seems to be this: the nasal was dropt (the Tamil people often pronounce அவன் AVE'), and final அ (retained in Kan. and lengthened into E in Mal.) became ஐ (as தலை is the Tamil for the Kanarese TALA). Bopp, 149.]

§ 237. Vocabulary.

பாழ்ங் கிணறு, *an old well.* பாழ் (allied to பழைய), *forsaken, decayed.* பாழ் + அம் + கிணறு and அ elided. § 131.
நொண்டு (§ 56. III), *be lame.*
கிட்டு (§ 56. II), *draw near.*
மொட்டை, *baldness.*
மொட்டை அடி, *make bald* (*strike bald*, lit.).
கோடாலி, *an axe.*
குணக்கு, *crookedness.*

NOTE ON SECOND CASE.

[Comp. III. G. 58; *Nannūl*, 296.]

The Tamil term for the *direct object* is செயப்படுபொருள் = *the thing which is done.* [II. G. 129*.]

A verb may have two accusatives: பசுவினைப் பாலைக் கறந்தான், *he milked the cow;* ஆசிரியனைப் பொருளை வினவினன், *he asked the professor the meaning.*

It is the case of the *nearer object:* ஆதியைத் தொழுது, *worship the* FIRST.

The *Nannūl* Sūtram runs thus: 'Of the second case the increment is ஐ alone. Its meaning is (that the noun which receives it is the object of a word denoting) *making, destroying, obtaining, removing, comparing possession*, &c.' Examples:—

குடத்தை, *a vessel.*
1. வனைந்தான், *he fashioned.*
2. உடைத்தான், *he broke.*
3. சேர்ந்தான், *he approached.*
4. இழந்தான், *he lost.*
5. ஒத்தான், *he resembled.*
6. உடையான், *he was owner of.*

Exercise 74.

§ 238. [1] என்னமோ பிள்ளை காலை நொண்டுகிறது. [2] அந்தச் சிங்கத்தைச் சிநேகம்பண்ணிக்கொள்ளுகிறேன். [3] மூடவன் கொம்புத் தேனுக்கு ஆசைப்பட்டால் கிட்டுமோ (not தேனை)? [4] சேறும் நீரும்மிகுந்த ஒருபாழ்ங்கிணற்றை இதில்இருக்கிறதென்று காட்டினான். [5] எய்தவனை நோகாமல் அம்பை நோகலாமா? [6] நாயின் வாலைக் குணக்கெடுக்கலாமா? [7] ஆறு கரைபுரண்டு போகிறது. [8] எலி வளை தோண்டக் கண்டேன். [9] பல்விளக்கிக்கொண்டிருந்தான். [10] என்னை அப்படி நினைக்க வேண்டாம். [11] என்னை இப்படிச் சொல்லலாமோ? [12] எங்களுக்கு ஒருதண்டனையும் இல்லாமற் காப்பாற்ற வேண்டும். [13] அவனை இருமாதே என்று சொன்னேன். [14] இது நான் காடு வெட்டுங் கோடாலி. [15] இராசன் கலகக்காரரைச் சிறைச்சாலையை அடைவித்தார். (Two accusatives.)

LESSON 76.

THE THIRD CASE: WITH.

§ 239. Other[1] particles connected with the regular terminations of the third case are—

உடன் = *together with*; கொண்டு = *by means of, through.* (§ 259.)

(1) நீங்கள் ஒருவரைஒருவர் முழுப் பூசணிக்காயைச் சோற்றோடே
You one each other a whole melon with rice

[1] This is in reality two cases, but the idea of CONNEXION OF ASSOCIATION is predominant. The English particle WITH expresses both notions. When two nouns are connected as agent and instrument, the *instrumental* form of the case is used; when merely association is implied it has a much wider scope, taking the form of the case which implies connexion in general. The following sentence combines the two:

The king came *with* his soldiers and killed his enemies *with* a sword.
அரசன் போர்வீரரோடுவந்து பகைவரை வாளால் வெட்டினர்.

மறைக்கிறது போல மோசஞ் செய்கிறது நியாயத்துக்கு விரோதம்
hiding like, deceit to make to right (is) *opposed*
என்று கண்டித்தான்.
thus he reproved.

(2) அவள் சீக்கிரத்திலே ஓடி இலையோடே அந்தச் சாதத்தை எடுத்து வந்தாள், *she ran with haste and brought the rice in the leaf.*

(3) என்புருஷனை என்னோடே கூடச் சேர்க்க வேண்டும், ஐயா! *Sir, unite me to my husband!* (§ 170.)

(4) பாலோடு தேன் கலந்திருக்கிறது, *there is honey mixed with milk.*

(5) அந்தப் பிள்ளையை மார்போடணைத்து முத்தங் கொடுத்தான், *he embraced the child and kissed it.*

(6) அவனை ஆதியோடந்தமாகக் கேட்டுக்கொள்ளுங்கள், *hear him from the beginning to the end.*

(7) இவ்விருவர்கள் ஒரே ரூபமாயிருக்கிற படியால், *since these two are both of one shape.* [படி + ஆல் (often written படியினால், படியினாலே) = *by the step that, since.*]

(8) என்பேச்சைத் தள்ளி இருமினான், அதினாலே வெட்டிப்போட்டேன் என்றான், *he coughed when I told him not, therefore, I stabbed him.*

(9) ஜன்னலாலே தெருவைப் பார்த்துக்கொண்டு நின்றாள், *she stood looking out of the window.*

(10) அவன் வாய்ச்சொல்லைக் கொண்டே இதை அறிந்தேன், *his mouth-word by means of, indeed, this I have known.*

(11) அரண்மனைவேலைக்காரி தன்புருஷனோடு சொன்னாள், *the palace servant-maid told her husband.*

(12) மணலின்(ல்)முழுகி மறைந்து கிடக்கும் தவளையுந் தன்வாயாற் கெடும், *even the frog wholly hidden in the sand will perish by its voice.*

§ 240. FURTHER NOTE ON THIRD CASE.

There are several significant particles which are used as signs (so to speak) of the third case, besides கொண்டு (§ 56 = *having taken*) and உடன் = *together;* such as மூலமாய் = *by means of,* நிமித்தம் = *sake:* அவர் மூலமாய்ப் பெற்றுக் கொண்டேன், *I obtained it by his means;* என்னிமித்தம் (என் நிமித்தம்) இப்படிச் செய், *do so for my sake.*

Of these உடன், which is evidently a cognate form of ஒடு, ஓடு, is classical. Thus,

(1) பிணியொடு மூப்பும் வரும், *together with disease old age will come.*

(2) மனத்தொடு வாய்மை பேசினால், *if you speak truth* from your heart.

(3) பொன்னோடு இரும்பைப் போலிருக்கிறார்கள் உம்மோடு மற்றவர்கள், *others when compared with you are like iron when compared with gold.*

(4) காலால் முடம், *lameness of foot.*

[Comp. II. G. 59; *Naṉṉūl,* Sūt. 297.]

It is necessary to observe that a Tamilian would not always use this case where we use *by* and *with.* Thus, *He did it* WITH *difficulty:* அந்த வேலையை வருத்தத்

தோடு செய்தான் is not quite so good as அவனுக்கு அந்த வேலை வருத்தமாயிருந்தது, or அந்த வேலை செய்கிறது வருத்தமாயிருந்தது, or அவனால் அந்த வேலை முடிந்தது வருத்தம். *With*, in adverbial phrases, often requires a peculiar idiom: *With much pleasure* = *மெத்த சந்தோஷம்!*

Exercise 75.

§ **241.** [1] வெகு விசனத்தோடே ஆலோசிக்கத் தொடங்கினான். [2] இன்னும் சம்பாதிக்க வேண்டும் என்கிற ஆசையினாலே ஆலோசிக்கலானான். [3] ஆயுசு பலத்தினாலே பிழைத்திருக்கிறது. [4] புல்லு முதலாகிய மேய்ச்சலாலே மிகவும் பெருத்துக் கொழுத்து அந்தக் காட்டிலே திரிந்துகொண்டிருந்தது. [5] அவன் வாயைக்கொண்டே நிசத்தை வெளிப்படுத்தினேன்.

[6] 'கன இருளில், அடர்மழையில்[1] கதறுகின்ற தவளைகள் போல்,
Like frogs croaking in gross darkness [and] in thick rain,
தனை உணராச் சாத்திரத்தால் தர்க்கம் இட்டால் (§ 263) பலிப்பதென்ன?'
What will result if you engage in disputations by means of science which does not understand itself?

[7] பாலோடு கலந்த நீர் பால் ஆகும், அல்லாது நீராய் நிறந் தெரியாது. [8] அதை விசாரிக்கிறதினால் நமக்காவதென்ன? [9] யார் புகழோடு சீவிக்கிறார்களோ அவர்களே பாக்கியவான்கள். [10] 'சிறு குழிகள் கொஞ்சத் தண்ணீரால் நிறையும்.' [11] பெருமையுடனே சீவிக்கிறதே நல்லது. [12] அவர் காலால் இட்டவேலையை நான் தலையாற் செய்து கொள்ளுவேன். [13] எங்களாற் செய்வதென்னென எண்ணினார். [14] குடும்பத்தோடு கூடவிருந்த ஒருவன்.

LESSON 77.

THE FOURTH (OR DATIVE) CASE.

§ **242**. This is the case of the remoter object, or recipient; and often of DETERMINATE place or time.

The particles connected with the fourth case are—

(I) ஆக = *for* (vulg.); (II) என்று, § 82 (இவனுக்கென்று கொடுத்தேன், *I gave (it) saying 'for him'*); (III) நிமித்தமாக, மூலமாக, பொருட்டு = *for the sake of, by means of*, § 157. These are used without கு, இன் being optionally inserted.

This case should be studied in II. G. 60, and நன்னூல், 298. The Sûtram is as follows :—

'For the fourth case கு alone is the sign.

'Its meanings are (1) gift, (2) opposition, (3) purpose, (4) adaptation, (5) becoming, (6) reason, (7) relation and others.' Among the 'others' are ennumerated 'connexion,' 'limit of time or place,' 'excess or defect,' and 'comparison.'

[1] அடர் for அடர்ந்த, a poet. form, § 270 (5).

Examples are—

(1) இரப்போர்க்கீந்தான், *he gave* TO *beggars.* [Dat. of recipient.]

(2) பிணிக்கு மருந்து, *medicine* FOR *a disease:* [*against.*]

(3) விளக்கினுக்கு எண்ணெய், *oil* FOR *the lamp:* [USE *of.*]

(4) அரசருக்கே உரியது, *it appertains* TO *kings only:* [*fitness.*]

(5) அவலுக்கு நெல், *paddy* FOR *parched rice:* [*which will become, material.*]

(6) கூழுக்குக் குற்றேவல் செய்தான், *he did petty jobs* FOR *food:* [*reason.*]

(7) சாத்தனுக்கு மகன், *Çāttan's son.*

(8) அவனுக்கும் அவளுக்கும் பொருத்தம் இல்லை, *there is no harmony between him and her.*

(9) அவ்வூர்க்கும் இவ்வூர்க்குங் காதம், *there is ten miles between the villages.*

(10) இன்றைக்கு வரும், *it will come to-day.*

(11) அவனுக்குச்சிறந்தவன் (தாழ்ந்தவன்) இவன், *this man is superior (inferior) to that.*

(12) மனைக்கு விளக்கு மனையாட்டி, *the housewife is the lamp of the house.*

(1) யானைக்கும் பானைக்கும் சரியாய்ப் போயிற்று (போச்சு), *the elephant and the pot are equivalent* (in the account): *Put one against the other.*

(2) எனக்கு இருபது பசுக்கள் உண்டு.
To me twenty cows there are.

The Latin idiom: a dative with the verb *to be = have.* (§ 43.)

(3) மூவரும் வந்து உனக்கெனக்கென்று வியாச்சியப் பட்டார்கள், *all the three persons came and disputed about it, each claiming it.*

(4) ஒருத்தி ஒருகாசுக்கு மீன்வாங்கி வந்து வைத்தாள், *a certain woman* FOR *a cash bought some fish, brought it and kept it* (in the house).

(5) அந்தப் பட்டணத்துக்குக் காதவழி தூரத்திலே இறங்கினார், *he alighted a kātham from that town.*

(6) உன் தாயாரையும் உன் தகப்பனையும் நான்கண்டு (கண்டதற்கு) நெடுநாள் ஆயிற்று, *it is a long time* SINCE *I saw your father and mother.*

(7) நீஅவர்களுக்கு நான் சொன்னதாகச் சொல்லவேண்டியதென்னவென்றால், *you must tell them from me that, &c.*

(8) பேருக்கு ஒவ்வொரு செம்புநீர் கொடுக்கச்சொன்னான், *he commanded to give to each one a vessel of water.*

(9) அவன் என்பிள்ளை எங்கே என்று கேட்டதற்கு இங்கே இல்லை,
To him asking, 'Where is my child?' 'Not here,'
என்றார்கள். So, இதற்குப் பிசகில்லை = *no doubt* OF *it.*
they said.

(10) அவன் கௌவின திரவியத்தை வித்துவானுக்கு வாங்கிக்கொ
He which had grasped the wealth to the scholar having taken,

கொடுத்துத் *he gave,* திருடனுக்குச் *and to the thief* சாஸ்திரப்படி *according to the law* தண்டனையுஞ் *punishment* செய்தான். *he awarded.*

(11) வீட்டுக்குள்ளே இருக்கிறான், *he is within the house.*

[Here கு is the sign of the fourth case, to which is added உள்ளே, a sign of the seventh. *This accumulation of inflexional particles is frequent in Tamil and in the other S. Indian dialects.*

So, IN-TO, WITH-IN, &c., combine two prepositions.]

(12) இம்மைக்கும் மறுமைக்குஞ் சுகங்கொடுக்கிற புத்திரன், *a son who imparts present and future bliss.*

(13) ஆனைக்கு அறுபதுமுழம் அறக்குள்ளனுக்கு எழுபதுமுழம், *for an elephant* 60 *cubits, for a downright dwarf* 70 *cubits.* [Either, 'get away so far,' the dwarf being much the more dangerous of the two; or, 'the less a man has, the greater his pretensions often are.']

§ **243.** **Vocabulary.**

உரி, *possession;* whence உரிமை, *possession* (§ 131).

உரியவன், ள், து, *he, she, it, to whom or which* (it) *belongs* (governing a dative of the thing).

துவரை, *a leguminous plant.*

போஷி (§ 64), *feed, nourish.*

பருப்பு, துவரம்பருப்பு, *peas* (§ 131. *c*).

தாளம், *time in music.*

ஒ, *agree with* (§ 56. III), ஒத்து வருகிறது, &c.

அடிக்கடி (அடிக்கு, *to a step*), அடிக்கொருதரம், *often.* The latter is vulgar.

Exercise 76.

§ **244.** [1] ஓர் அறைக்குள்ளே. [2] அதற்குத் தகுந்தஅபராதம் வாங்கிக் கோழிக்காரிக்குக் கோழிபதிலுக்குக் கொடுக்கும்படி உத்தரவுசெய்தான். [3] அந்தவேளைக்கு (வேளையிலே) துவரம்பருப்பு எங்கும் அகப்படவில்லை. [4] எவ்வளவு தொகைக்கு வாங்கினாலும் இதுதான் எனக்குச் செலவுக்கு வேண்டும். [5] என்னை இவன் என்ன செய்யலாம்? (for 4th). [6] எனக்குக் கோபம் வந்தது உனக்கு எப்படித் தெரியும்? [7] இதற்கு என்ன செய்யலாம்? [8] நீ இதற்கு என்ன சொல்லுகிறாய்? [9] நாளைக்காலமே ஊருக்கு அப்புறம் கொல்லைமேட்டில் இருப்பேன். [10] பணத்திற்குரியவனிடத்தே பணஞ் சேர்ந்தது (இடத்து elegantly for இடத்தில்). [11] இவனுக்கு யாதொரு கவலைக்கும் இடம் வையாமல் போஷித்துக்கொண்டுவருகிறேன். [12] அது பின்னடிக்கு வருத்தத்துக்கு ஏதுவாய் இருக்கும்.

[13] அது தாளத்துக்கு ஒத்துவரவில்லை. [14] வெளிக்கு நல்லதென்றார்கள். [15] ஆண்டவருடைய வாக்குக்கு எதிர்வாக்கிராது. [16] இரண்டுக்கும் பெரிய சண்டை விளைந்தது. [17] நமக்கு வழிதொலைய வேண்டும். [18] அதற்கு ஒரு கதையைச் சொல்லுகிறேன். [19] இராசாவரைக்கும் தெரியப்படுத்தினான்.

LESSON 78.

THE FIFTH CASE: REMOTION. FROM.

§ **245.** இல் really = IN; here it represents FROM, OF, OUT OF, and THAN (§ 196). This is a locative case and originally one with the seventh (§ 251).

Where ambiguity might arise, use the compound forms; as வீட்டிலிருந்து, which cannot be confounded with வீட்டினிடத்தில்.

(1) அந்த நீரிலே பாதியினாலே கால்களைச் செவ்வையாய்க்
OF *that water with the half* (my) *feet* *well*

கழுவிக்கொண்டேன்.
I washed.

[Comp. இதிலிருந்த குரங்குகளில் ஒன்று, *one* OF *the monkeys that were in it.*]

(2) பாதிச்சேறு ஆயினும் உன் காலிலே போகவில்லை.
(Even half the mud FROM your feet has not gone.)
You have not half cleaned your feet of the mud.

(3) இவ்விருவர்களிலே உன் புருஷன்
'*Of* [from, out of] *these two* [is] *thy husband which?*'

யார் என்று கேட்டான்.
he asked.

[Comp. கூடவருகிற சிலபெயரைப் பார்த்து இது எப்படி என்றான், *he asked some of those who came with him how it was.*]

(4) இவைகளிலே எதைப்போல் இருக்கின்றவன் உத்தமன்? *the best is he who resembles which of these?*

(5) வரன்முறையாக அவரவர்கள் கையிலிருந்து மாம்பழம் வந்த வகை தெரியும், [*I*] *have found out the way in which the mango-fruit passed in order from hand to hand.*

(6) அங்கிருந்து யாராவது வருகிறபேர் உண்டா? *is any one coming from that place?* (அங்கு, *that place*, used as a noun, and இருந்து used as the sign of the fifth case.)

(7) கல்விப்பொருளிலுஞ் செல்வப்பொருளிலுங் குறையில்லாதவர்கள், *those who abound in the wealth of learning, and in the wealth of earthly good.* [? Seventh case.]

(8) என்னிடத்திலிருந்து, *from me,* = என்னிலிருந்து.

[Here the sign of the seventh case is put between the root and the sign of the fifth case. Lit. = *having been in the place of me.*]

(9) மரத்துக்காரன் சத்தம் அறிந்து வீட்டிலிருந்து அதட்டிக் கொண்டே ஓடிவருகையில், திருடன் அதை அறிந்து மரத்தில் இறங்கி வந்தான், *the owner of the tree hearing the noise came running from his house, scolding all the way. The thief hearing that came down from the tree.*

§ 246. Vocabulary.

செவ்வையாய் for செம்மையாய், *rightly, well.*
வரன்முறை (வரல், *the coming;* முறை, *order*), *in order.*
ஒப்பி (§ 56. III), *deliver up to.* [ஒ.]
வசம், *charge, care.*
குரங்கு, *a monkey.*
இதாகிதம் (Skt. HITA + AHITA, *proper and improper*), *good and evil, right and wrong.*
சீவனம், *a livelihood.*
ஏற்க, *suitably* (infinitive of ஏல்).

Exercise 77.

§ 247. [1] தன்பிள்ளைகளை அவன் வசத்திலே ஒப்பித்தான். [2] அப்படி இருக்கையில். [3] சிங்கமானது தன்பராக்கிரமத்தால் சம்பாதிக்கப்பட்ட இராச்சியத்தைச் சுகமாக அநுபவித்துக்கொண்டிருக்கையில் அந்தக் குரங்குகளில் ஒன்று வந்தது. [4] இராசாவுக்குஅடுத்திருக்கையில் வெகுசனங்களுக்கு நன்மைசெய்யலாம். [5] இதாகிதம் தெரியாமற் கொஞ்சத்திற் சீவனம்பண்ணுவான். [6] மலை உச்சியில் ஒருபெருங்கல்லை ஏற்றுதல் அரிது; அங்கிருந்து அதைத் தள்ளுதல் எளிது. [7] நல்ல மழை பெய்திருக்கையில் எப்படி விதையினின்று முளைகள் புறப்படுமோ அப்படி ராசாவின் கேள்விக்கேற்க என் வாக்கினின்றும் உத்தரவு புறப்படும். [8] மணியினின்று ஒளி பிரிக்கப்படுமோ?

The Tamil grammars give இல் and இன் as signs of the fifth case, and say that it expresses நீங்கல் (= *removal*), ஒப்பு (= *comparison*), எல்லை (= *limit*), and ஏது (= *cause*).

Examples—

(1) தலையில்(ன்) இழிந்த மயிர், *hair fallen from the head.*

(2) அரசரில் பெரியர் கற்றோர், *learned persons are greater than kings.*

(3) அதனில்(ற்) பெரிது இது, *this is greater than that.*
பஞ்சியில் மெல்லிது, *softer than cotton.*

(4) மதுரையில்(ன்) வடக்குச் சிதம்பரம், *Çithambaram* (is) *north of* (= from) *Madura.*

(5) கல்வியிற் பெரியவன் கம்பன், *Kamban* (was) *great in* (= from) *learning.*

The participials நின்று and இருந்து can be separated from இல்:

துன்பத்திலும் வறுமையிலும் நின்று நீங்கினான், *he was freed* (from) *affliction and poverty.*

Comp. II. G. 61.

LESSON 79.

EXAMPLES OF THE SIXTH CASE: THE GENITIVE OR POSSESSIVE CASE.

§ **248**. What is called the *genitive relation* (II. G. 62) is expressed in Tamil by—

(i) *Composition:* *தாய்வீடு, ஆட்டுத்தோல்:* the inflexional base is used for the genitive.

(ii) The use of இன் (or *அன்*), a particle signifying connexion: சொல்லின் *அர்த்தம்.*

The beginner should avoid this form. It is a ready expedient when the speaker will not take the trouble to expand the idea. The English OF expresses many relations, and foreigners often think that OF = இன் always! But periphrasis is often needed. Take the following:—

(1) *I have no knowledge of it,* அது எனக்குச்சுத்தமாய்த்தெரியாது.

(2) *Have you any recollection of it?* அது உமக்குஞாபகமா?

(iii) The inflexional particle *அது*. [In high Tamil ஆது is used, and அ when the governing noun is plural.]

(iv) The significant particle உடைய, and the dative + உரிய.

All these are *classical*. Thus in Kamban's Rāmāyaṇam we have அம்பின் மாரி, *a shower* OF *arrows;* நிலையுடைக் கவிநீத்தம், *the torrent* OF *monkeys of firm array* (உடைய is not found); பாற்கடல், *the sea of milk.* We have too, ஆறன் உருபு, *the sign* OF *the sixth* (case). Another poetical form is இரவிதன் குலம், *the race of the sun* (§ 108).

Ex. (1) தன் வீட்டுத் தோட்டத்து வழியாக வந்தான், *he came by the way of his house-garden.*

☞ வீட்டு, தோட்டத்து: ellipses of the casal sign, the nouns வீடு and தோட்டம் being prepared for its reception according to § 18. This has been termed the 'oblique case,' or the oblique form of the sixth case. It is very common, and at the same time elegant. (§ 131.)

தகப்பன் உத்தரவில்லாமல் நீ வரக்கூடாது, *you must not come without* (your) *father's consent.* Here also there is ellipsis of the sign. (§ 50.)

நெய்க்குடத்தில் எறும்பு மொய்க்கும், *ants will swarm round the ghī-pot.*

(2) பொன்னின்குடம் உடைந்தாற் பொன்னாகும்; மண்ணின்குடம் உடைந்தக்கால் என்னாகும்? *When a vessel of gold is broken—it is gold; when a vessel of earth is broken—what is it?*

[இன் used as the sign of the sixth case, § 18. பொன்னாலாகிய குடம் would be better—'*a vessel made of gold,*' § 130.]

(3) யாரது என்றான் (for யாருடையது), *whose is it?*

[The form யாரது is poetical, அது being a termination of the sixth case in the higher dialect.]

(4) நம்முட (for நம்முடைய), *our*. [VULGAR.]

(5) மரத்துக்காரன், *the owner of the tree*; வீட்டுக்காரன், *the householder*. [மரம் + காரன்—the particle அத்து being inserted. § 18.]

(6) தன்மனையாளைத் தாய்வீட்டுக்கு அனுப்பிப் பின்பு அவளைப்பேணாத பேதை பதர், *the blockhead who sends his wife to her mother's house and does not afterwards support her is chaff*. [தாய் = தாயினுடைய.]

(7) வித்துவான் கற்ற (§ 70) கல்வி (§ 190).
The scholar's learning.
Lit. 'the learning which the scholar has learnt.'

☞ It is very elegant and idiomatic in cases like this to use an adjective participle instead of the sixth case.

(8) அவளுக்குரிய குணலட்சணங்கள், *her qualities and excellences*.

☞ உரிய added to the dative is often used for the English possessive case.

(9) நடுக்கடலில் திசைதப்பிமயங்கின மாலுமி, *a pilot bewildered, who has lost his course, in the middle* OF *the sea* [= in mid-ocean].

NOTE ON SIXTH CASE.

1. The *genitive of quality* (e.g. *a boy* OF *great beauty*) must be expressed by the aid of உள்ள, § 133. Thus, அதிக அழகுள்ள பையன்.

2. The *distributive genitive* requires the dative with உள் or the fifth case: thus, *he sent four* OF *his friends*, தன் சிநேகிதரில் நாலு பேரை அனுப்பினார்; *the elephant is the largest* OF *animals*, மிருகங்களுக்குள் ஆனைபெரியது.

3. The *objective genitive* requires a periphrasis generally. Much unintelligible Tamil has been expended in trying to put such constructions literally. Thus, *the love of knowledge* must be அறிவு வேண்டும் என்கிற ஆசை and not by any means அறிவின் அன்பு! பொருளாசை is *covetousness*. Many specific compounds like this exist. *He is eagerly desirous* OF *honour*, கனத்தை மிகவும் நாடுகிறான்.

4. For the determinative *of* in 'the great city of Benares,' see § 13; காசி என்னும் பெரியநகரம் or காசிமாநகரம்.

5. Europeans use the genitive with இன் too much! I have heard *the fear of punishment* put into தண்டனையின் பயம்; it should be தண்டனை வரும் என்கிற பயம். Thus, *he is tormented with the fear of punishment* = தண்டனை வரும் என்று பயந்து மிகவும்வாதிக்கப்படுகிறான்.

Tamil grammarians tell us that the form of the sixth case differs according to the class (§ 30) of the governing noun. If this is a noun of the உயர்திணை (a personal noun), (1) the governed word or its inflexional base must be simply prefixed, or (2) the word உடைய (§ 185) used to connect the governing and the governed words, or (3) the fourth case must be used. Thus, அவன் தகப்பன், *his father*; நாட்டு ராசன், *the king of the country*; அவனுடைய மனைவி, *his wife*; அவனுக்கு மகன், *his son*. [Thus *pater mihi*.]

If, however, the governing noun is அஃறிணை (impersonal) the governed noun takes the case-ending அது (sometimes in old poetry ஆது) or அ; the former when the governing noun is singular (ஒன்றன்பால்) and the latter when it is plural. These are the classical forms—எனதுகை, *my hand*; என கைகள், *my hands*.

A comparison of this with § 184 will show that here the 'genitive case' is really a derivative noun in apposition to கை and கைகள். எனது = *that thing which is mine;* என = *those things which are mine.*

The following table from the commentary on the *Nannūl* illustrates the native idea of the use of the sixth case. The meaning conveyed by it is called கிழமைப் பொருள், where கிழமை is equivalent to உரிமை, *property;* சம்பந்தம், *connexion;* or சொந்தம், *that which is one's own.*

கிழமை, PROPERTY.

I. தற்கிழமை, *intrinsic property.* [தன்.]

1. பண்பு, connected with quality.
   Ex. நிலத்தது அகலம், *the breadth of the land.*
2. உறுப்பு, connexion of members.
   Ex. அரசனது கண், *the king's eye.*
3. ஒன்று பல கூடிய ஒன்றன் கூட்டம், combination of many individuals of one species.
   Ex. நெல்லினது குப்பை, *a heap of paddy.*
4. வேறுபல கூடிய பலவின் ஈட்டம், combination of many of different species.
   Ex. விலங்கினது கூட்டம், *an assemblage of* (various) *beasts.*
5. திரிபின் ஆக்கம், transformation.
   Ex. நெல்லினது பொரி, *parched grains of paddy.*

II. பிறிதின் கிழமை, *extrinsic property.* [Gen. auctoris v. possessoris.]

1. பொருள், possession.
   Ex. சாத்தனதுவில், *Çāttan's bow.*
2. இடம், place.
   Ex. இராயனது தோட்டம், *the king's garden.*
3. காலம், time.
   Ex. குமாரனது வாழ்நாள், *the life-time of the son.*

§ 249. Vocabulary.

எலும்பு, *bone.* [என்பு.]
ரெட்டி, *a Reddy, a caste of cultivators.*
வாய்க்கால், *a watercourse.*
சிஷன், *a disciple.*
சண்டி, *an obstinate fellow.*

Exercise 78.

§ 250. [1] தண்ணீர் குடிக்க ஆற்றங்[1] கரைக்குப் போனான். [2] சுவாமி காரியஞ் செய்யாமல் இரைதேடுகிறதையே பெரிதாக நினைக்கலாமா? [3] அவன் பக்கத்திலே உட்கார்ந்தேன். [4] கன்றெலும்பிருக்க அதை ரெட்டி எலும்பென்று நிச்சயித்துக்கொண்டார்கள். [5] அந்தத்தண்ணீர் வாய்க்கால் வழியாய் ஓடிற்று. [6] குருமொழி கேளாதசிஷன். [7] தாய்வார்த்தை கேளாத சண்டி. [8] மனக்கவலை மாற்றுகிறது அரிது. [9] தாய்வீட்டுக்குப் போனாள். [10] அந்த இராசாவுக்குரிய மாட்சிமையும் அதிகாரமும். [11] அத்தேசத்து மனிதர்.

[1] ஆறு. Here the particle அம் is inserted instead of the sign of the sixth (§ 131) case: ஆறு + அம் + கரை = ஆற்றங்கரை, *the river's bank.* [Pope's II. G. 108.]

LESSON 80.

THE SEVENTH (OR LOCATIVE-ABLATIVE) CASE. [§ 21.]

§ **251**. இல், இடத்தில் are here the chief signs, but there are upwards of twenty particles denoting place or position that may occupy the place of இல். Among these are—மேல், *above*; கீழ், *below*; அகம், *inside*; புறம், *outside*; உள், *within*; முன், *before*; பின், *after*; இடம், *place* (இடத்தில்); பால், *part*; அண்டை, அருகு, அருகே, அருகில், கிட்ட, *near*; பேரில், *upon*.

☞ Some of these particles are also prefixed to verbs to form compounds, which are in constant and familiar use. [§ 225. (7).] Thus:

மேற்கொள்ளு [மேல் + கொள்ளு, § 56. (III)], *overcome* (obtain the higher place).
கீழ்ப்படி [கீழ் + படி, § 56], *submit* (sink to the lower place).
உட்பிரவேசி [உள் + பிரவேசி, § 64], *enter in*.
முன்னிடு [முன் + இடு, § 68], *put before* (give the priority to).
பின்வாங்கு [பின் + வாங்கு, § 62], *draw back* (take the place behind).
புறப்படு [புறம் + படு, § 56. (II)], *set out* (experience the outer place).

கண், meaning *place*, is also much used in books. These are essentially nouns and remain so, however compounded. [Pope's II. G. 63.]

(1) அதில் கண்ட பாம்பை எல்லாம் பிடித்தது, *it caught all the snakes that were found in it.*

(2) பொதுவிலே நாலாயிரம் வராகனைக் கொடுத்தான், *he gave* 4000 *pagodas in common.*

(3) இவன் கையில் கொடுத்தேன், *I gave it into his hand.*

(4) அவன் உடனே துலுக்கனிடத்திற்குப் போய்க் கொடுக்கிறேன் என்றான், *immediately to the Muhammadan going, 'I give,' said he.* [கு of the fourth case added to இடத்தில்.]

(5) அந்தப் பெண்ணருகில் சென்று பேசினான்.
He approached the woman and spoke.

(6) ஊரின் அருகே தனிமையாக வருகையில், *when he was coming near the village alone.*

(7) அடிமேல் அடி அடித்தால் அம்மியும்
Stroke on stroke if you strike even the grinding-stone

நகரும். (நகரு, § 60. I, *be moved.*)
will be moved.

(8) கபடியாய் இருக்கிற பிரதானி புத்திசாலி ஆனாலும் அவன் ஒருபோதும் இராசாவண்டை இருக்கல் ஆகாது, *a deceitful minister, though he be clever, must never be near a king.*

(9) அவன் காலில் விழுந்தேன், *I fell* AT *his feet.*

(10) மூங்கிலிலை மேல்   *On Bambū-leaf*
தூங்கும் பனி நீர்   *Sleeps dew-water*[1].

§ 252. **Vocabulary.**

சாதி (§ 56. III), *assert, maintain.*
செம்பு, *a brass vessel.*
முளை, *a tender shoot.*
மணம், *odour* (poet.).
எள், *rape seed.*
வறுமை (§ 131), *poverty.*
இன்னாது, *it is evil* (poet.).
திரு, *prosperity, fortune.*
கல் (§ 70), *learn.*

Exercise 79.

§ **253.** [1] ஒருவன் பத்துப்பாரம்இரும்பு வாங்கி ஒருவனிடத்திலே வைத்து மற்றொரு தேசத்திற்குப் போய்ச் சிலவருஷங்கள்கழிந்தபின்பு வந்து அவனை 'இரும்பைக்கொடு' என்று கேட்டான். [2] கொடுத்தவன் கெடுவிற் போய் அதைக் கேட்டதற்கு வாங்கினவன் நான் உன்கையிலே வாங்கினதில்லை என்று சாதித்தான். [3] நியாயாதிபதியினிடத்தில்போய் பிரியாது பண்ணிக்கொண்டான். [4] அந்தவழியாக நடந்து வந்தார்கள். [5] இரண்டு செம்புகளில் நிறைய நீர்கொண்டுவரச்சொன்னான் (two vessels full, &c.). [6] நீ அவனிடத்தில் செய்கடன் வாங்கினதற்குச் சந்தேகம் இல்லை. [7] 'மரத்தின்பழம் மரத்தண்டையே விழும்.' [8] முளையில் கிள்ளாத மரம் முற்றினால் கோடரிகொண்டு வெட்டித் தள்ளவேண்

[1] There is a story worth telling connected with these lines.

Kamban, the translator of the Rāmāyaṇam, and a great master of Tamil rhythm, passing by a tank one evening, heard a cultivator, as he watered his field, sing the line:

மூங்கிலிலை மேல்,
'On leaf of the Bambū.'

Then the man having completed his number of buckets of water, ceased at once his work and his song.

Kamban was struck with the line, and said to himself, 'What can be on the tiny leaf of the Bambū? Probably to-morrow morning the labourer will begin his work with the next line of the song. I must be there to hear it.' Accordingly, with the dawn, he stood on the border of the tank, and was rewarded by hearing the man, as he drew his first bucket of water, chaunt the second line:

தூங்கும் பனி நீர்,
'Sleeps the little drop of dew.'

Moral:—*There is plenty of poetry and sentiment in the Tamil people, if you can only get at it.*

டும். [9] மலரில் மணமும் எள்ளில் எண்ணெயும் உடலில் உயிருங்கலந் .ததுபோல. [10] ஓர்வரிக்கரைமேலே போனான். [11] மூக்குமேலே விரல் வைத்துப் பெருமூச்சுவிட்டு அப்படியா என்று விசனப்பட்டான்.

[12] 'நல்லார்கட் பட்ட வறுமையின் இன்னாதே, கல்லார் கட்
With-the-good-endured than poverty bad indeed, (is) *with-the-*
பட்ட திரு.' [ண் before ப becomes ட்.]
ignorant-enjoyed wealth.

LESSON 81.

THE AUXILIARY விடு=*leave, let, forsake, relinquish, release.* [§ 68.]

§ **254.** Many of the chief difficulties in the language are connected with the peculiar use of this and the following verbs. Each sentence is a formula. (§ 77.)

☞ It will be seen that where in English an inseparable *preposition* or *adverb* is required after a verb, the Tamil most often adds an auxiliary verb. Thus, *go* AWAY=போய் விடு. [Less. 90.]

(1) உன் இரும்பை எலி தின்றுவிட்டது.
Your iron a rat has eaten UP.

(2) அத்தருணத்திலே (அவன்) வந்துவிட்டான்.
At that juncture he came BACK.

(3) பருந்து எடுத்துக்கொண்டு போய்விட்டது.
A hawk having lifted up, has taken (*it*) AWAY.

(4) அவன் தன் வீட்டுக்குப் போய்விட்டான்.
He (*his house to*) *went* OFF *home.*

(5) அவர்களை அனுப்பிவிட்டான்.
Them he sent AWAY.

அவர்களைக் கொஞ்சத் தூரம் வழிவிட்டனுப்பினான்.
He accompanied them a little distance on their way.

(6) அவள் திகைத்து நின்றுவிட்டாள்.
She affrighted stood STILL.

(7) ஒரு செம்பு நீர் முழுதும் விட்டுக் கழுவியும் பாதிச் சேறுயினும் போகவில்லை, *a vessel-of-water whole* | *having* LET OUT | *although* (you) *washed,* | *half the mud even* | *has not gone.*

(8) தேள் கொட்டிவிட்டது, *the scorpion stung them* (redundant).

(9) ஒன்பதின் ஆயிரம் வராகனை இந்தப் பிள்ளைக்குக் கொடுத்துவிடு.
Nine-thousand pagodas to this child give UP.

(10) ஒரு நாள் இராத்திரி எல்லாம் விடாமழையாகப் பெய்து கொண்டிருந்தது. விடியற் காலத்தில் மழை விட்ட பின்பு, *for a whole night* INCESSANT *rain descended. In the morning after the rain* HAD CEASED.

(11) முதலும் வட்டியுங் கொடுத்துவிடுகிறேன், *I will pay* UP *both principal and interest.*

(12) தாரைதாரையாய்க் கண்ணீரை விட்டு அழுதான், *he wept,* SHEDDING *tears in drops.*

(13) அதை வாங்கிப் பார்க்கிறது போலப் பக்கத்திலே மூட்டம் போட்டிருக்கிற நெருப்பிலேபோட்டுவிட்டான், *taking it as though to look at it, he threw it* AWAY *into a fire which was kindled there.* [Less. 72.]

(14) அவன் வைஷ்ணவன் ஆகிவிட்டான், *he became a Vaishṇavan* (redundant).

(15) என் மேலே வருத்தத்தை வரவிட்டான், *he* CAUSED *trouble to come upon me.*

(16) அது விட்டுப் போயிற்று [போச்சு], *it has got loose.*

(17) அதை விட்டு வை, *let it alone.*

(18) இது அவன் அறுக்கவிட்ட மரம் = *this* (*is*) *the tree which he brought to be sawn* [LEFT to be].

(19) தெரியாமல் இருந்துவிட்டேன், *I lived in ignorance* (*of it*).

(20) This verb is often doubled for emphasis: என்னைவிட்டு விட்டார், *he* UTTERLY *forsook me.*

(21) தானேவந்து விடும், *it will come of itself.*

LESSON 82.

THE ROOT ஆடு [§ 62], *move, dance.* [ஆட்டு, § 160.]

§ **255.** (1) பகையாளி குடியை உறவாடிக் கெடுக்கவேண்டும்.
A hostile inhabitant feigning intimacy (you) *must destroy.*

[பகையாளியைக் குடிகெடுக்க விரும்பினால் உன்னைச் சிநேகிதன் என்று பாராட்டி அவனைக் கெடுக்கலாம்.]

(2) அவனைப் புகழ்ந்து கொண்டாடினார், *he praised him and celebrated him* (கொண்டு, ஆடு).

(3) வேட்டை ஆடுகையில், *while he was hunting* (§ 143).

(4) அவன் ஆடல் பாடல்களில் வல்லவன், *he is a very clever fellow in dancing and singing* (§§ 148, 184).

(5) வாணியர் எள்ளாடுஞ் செக்கை வளைய வரும் எருதுகள் போல் நீணிலத்தில் ஆலயங்கள் நித்தம் வலம் வந்தால் என்ன? *What will it profit though you for ever go round about temples from the right, in this wide world, like bullocks that go round the press in which oil-men grind the rape seed?*

[நீள் + நிலம் = *the wide land;* வலம் வரு, *go round from the right side* = பிரதட்சணம் பண்ணு.]

(6) அபசாரி ஆடுகிறது குலத்துக்கீனம், *the conduct of a licentious woman is a disgrace to her family.*

(7) ஆடுகிற மாட்டை ஆடிக் கறக்க வேண்டும்; பாடுகிறமாட்டைப் பாடிக்கறக்க வேண்டும், *a dancing cow you must milk dancing, and a singing cow you must milk singing.* (Adapt yourself to people's humour.)

(8) கோலாடக் குரங்காடும், *when the stick dances, the monkey dances* (§ 168).

(9) பணத்துக்காடுகிறான், *he is very urgent for money.*

(10) ஆட்டம் = *a movement, enterprise* (§ 190).

அவன் அங்கே போக ஆட்டம் ஆடுகிறான், *he keeps trying to go there.*

குரங்காட்டமாய், *like a monkey.* ஆந்தை ஆட்டமாய், *like an owl.*

LESSON 83.

THE VERB போடு, *put* [§ 68]. SEE போ, OF WHICH THIS IS A CAUSAL.

§ 256. (1) நிபம் போடுகிறாள், *she calumniates.*

என் மேல் பழி போட்டான், *on me he put guilt.*

(2) அவனுடைய கடுக்கன்களைக் கழற்றித் தன் காதிலே போட்டுக் கொண்டான், *he took off that man's ear-rings and put them in* his own *ears.*

(3) அந்தக்கிடாரி கன்று போட்டது, *that heifer has calved.*

(4) சமாசாரம் எழுதிப்போட்டான், *he wrote off the news.*

(5) வருகிறவர்களுக்கெல்லாம் சாப்பாட்டுச்செலவும் மற்றச்செலவு களும் நீங்களே போட்டுச்செய்யவேண்டும், *for all who come you yourselves must provide board and all other expenses.*

(6) கை போட்டுக்கொடு என்றான்; அப்படியே கை போட்டுக் கொடுத்தான், '*give me your hand upon it,*' *said he; so he gave his hand upon it.*

(7) இதை அந்த வீட்டில் போட்டுவிட்டு, இதோ ஒரு நொடி அளவில் வந்துவிடுகிறேன், *I will just put it into that house, and be with you in an instant.*

(8) அடிச்சட்டிக்குள்ளே கரணம் போடலாமா? *Can you make a somersault in the bottom of a pot?* [Compare also § 106. (5).]

(9) ஆற்றிலே போட்டாலும் அளந்துபோடு! *Though you throw* (money) *into the river, measure what you throw!*

(10) அதற்கு நாலஞ்சு வீடு போட்டு (vulg.), *four or five doors* OFF [perhaps for போய் விட்டு].

'போடு though so common in modern Tamil, is not found in the குறள், and is never used in old writings. It does not follow the analogy of other similar roots, ஆடு, பாடு, &c., and appears to be a corruption of போகவிடு or வோக இடு.'—STOKES.

It is not in Kan., which uses HĀKKU; nor is it in Mal. It is போகடு for போகவிடு. This latter is found in Jī. Çin.

LESSON 84.

THE VERB பிற, *be born, issue* [§ 66]. CAUSAL பிறப்பி.

§ 257. (1) நியாயாதிபதிக்குச் சந்தேகம் பிறந்து மறுநாள் வரச் சொன்னார், *the judge began to doubt and told him to come to-morrow.*

(2) ஆகாயத்திலிருந்து ஒரு வாக்குப் பிறந்தது, *a voice was heard from the sky.*

(3) ஒவ்வொரு வேளைகளிலே அருள்வாக்குப் பிறக்கும், *every now and then a gracious word proceeds forth.*

(4) ஒரு உடன்படிக்கையைப் பிறப்பிவித்துக் கொண்டார்கள், *they caused an agreement to be made* (double causal! பி and வி [§§ 160, 92]).

(5) அவன் வாயிலிருந்து பிறக்கிற வார்த்தை எல்லாம் பொய், *every word that comes out of his mouth is false.*

(6) எசமான் உத்தரவு பிறந்தால் செய்யலாம், *if the master's order be forthcoming* (you) *may do it.*

(7) எசமானுக்கு அவன் மேலே அதிக விசுவாசம் பிறந்தது, *the master took a great fancy to him.*

(8) அஜூர் உத்தரவு பிறந்தது (= சாதர் ஆச்சுது), *an order was promulgated from headquarters.*

LESSON 85.

THE VERBS போ, *go*, AND போக்கு [§§ 58, 160].

§ 258. (1) அவனுடைய அதிக ஆசை பயன்படாமற் போயிற்று, *his excessive desire was utterly unproductive.*

(2) அந்த மந்தைப்பசுக்கள் எல்லாம் இறந்து போயின, *all the cows in that herd died.*

(3) அவனுக்குச் சரிபோனபடி எல்லாம் செய், *do just as seems good to him.*

(4) மோசம் போனேம், *we have been cheated.*

(5) அவன் என்னை மோசம் போக்கினன், *he cheated me* (போக்கு [§ 56. II] is a causal transitive verb from போ).

சூதாடுவதில் பொழுது போக்கினன், *he wasted* (*his*) *time in gaming.*

(6) போக்கடிபிடித்தான், *he followed his track.* [போக்கு அடி = *the step in which* (he) *went.*]

(7) யாதொன்று போயிற்றோ அதை மறுபடி சேகரிக்க வேண்டும், *if anything has been lost it must be recovered.*

அவனுடைய பொருள் எல்லாம் அநியாயமாய்ப் போயிற்று, *all his substance has been unjustly lost.*

(8) எனக்கிருக்கிற சிநேகம் போகாது, *my friendship will not cease.*

(9) அந்தப் பேச்சுப் போகட்டும்: வேறே பேச்சுப் பேசு, *let that proposition alone: turn to something else.*

[(10) போ means *go, leave, be lost, depart, cease to be.* Added to intransitive verbs it often gives the idea of completeness:

வாடிப் போயிற்று, *it is faded.*
அழிந்து போயிற்று, *it is destroyed.*]

(11) அந்த நிலம் போக மற்ற நிலம் என்னுடையது, *setting aside that land the rest is mine.*

(12) இருட்டைப் போக்கடிக்க விளக்கு இருக்கிறது, *there is a light to scatter the darkness.*

(13) இனி நாக்கே போமோ? மூக்கே போமோ?
Shall I lose my tongue? or my nose?

(14) அவளைப்பார்த்துக்கொண்டேசெய்தேன்; அதினலே குடம் பெரிதாகப் போயிற்று என்று குசவன் சொன்னன், *'I did it while looking at her, and so the vessel became too large,' said the potter.*

(15) அவன் நித்திரை போனன், *he has gone to sleep.*

(16) அதற்கு இனி என்ன செய்யப் போகிறோம்? *What can we henceforth do for it?*

(§§ 32, 58, 124. See also போடு, § 256.)

LESSON 86.

THE AUXILIARY கொள்|ளு, *obtain, take to one's self* [§ 56. (III)].

§ **259**. Of this கொடு seems to be a causal (§ 106).

(1) விழித்துக் கொண்டேன், *I awoke.* [Answers to Greek Middle Voice.]

(2) பார்த்துக் கொள்ளச் சொன்னன், *he told me to beware, to watch, look out.*

(3) போட்டுக் கொண்டான், *he put it on* (himself).

(4) வைத்துக் கொண்டிருந்தான், *he had stored up.*

(5) சொல்லிக் கொண்டார்கள், *they kept on talking* (among themselves).

(6) அந்தக் கடாரிகள் கறந்துகொண்டிருந்தன, *those heifers were in milk.* [கற is *draw milk* and *yield milk.*]

(7) அதன்மேல் ஆசைகொண்டான், *he placed his desire upon it.*

(8) அவனைப்போலே ரூபங் கொண்டான், *he assumed a shape like him.*

(9) கோபங் கொண்டார், *he became angry.*

(10) தலை இறங்கிக் கொண்டு சும்மாஇருந்தான், *he was silent, hanging down his head.*

(11) மாங்கனியைக் கைக்கொண்டு இங்கே வந்தான், *taking in his hand the mango fruit he came here.*

(12) விடாமழையாகப் பெய்து கொண்டிருந்தது, *it* KEPT *on raining; rained incessantly.*

(13) மிகுந்த வணக்கத்துடனே கேட்டுக் கொண்டான், *he asked with much respect.*

(14) அவன் அதைச் சொன்னதுமுதல்கொண்டு இதுவரையிலும், *from the time he said that until now.* [முதல்கொண்டு, *having* (that) *for a beginning* = *from that time.*]

(15) அவர் விவாகம் பண்ணினார், *he married* (as a minister).
அவர் விவாகம் பண்ணிக்கொண்டார், *he got married.*
[Compare also § 106. (4).]

(16) அவரைச் சிநேகம் பண்ணிக்கொள்வேன், *I will cultivate his friendship.*

☞ This verb forms compounds with some nouns: thus ஆசை கொண்டார்கள் = *they* (*conceived, entertained, felt a desire*) *wished.* But ஆசையைக்கொண்டு would mean *through* (by reason of) *the desire.*

LESSON 87.

THE VERB காண், *see* [§ 70].

VERY CURIOUS AND MOST ESSENTIAL IDIOMS!

§ 260. (1) அந்த விவரங்களைக்கண்டு ஒருஉடன்படிக்கை பண்ணினார்கள், *they made an agreement in which these particulars were included.*

(2) அம்மையார் நூற்கிற நூல் கிழவனுருடைய அரைஞாணுக்குக்காணாது, *the thread which the old lady spins will not suffice for a waist-string for the old gentleman.*

(3) ஒருமந்தையினிடத்துக்குப் போய் இடையனைக்கண்டு, 'பசுவேண்டும், அகப்படுமோ' என்றார்கள்? *They went to the flock and said to the herdsman, 'We want a cow, can it be had?'*

(4) எப்படிக்கண்டு பிடிப்பேன்? *How can I find it?* ['See and take.' So கண்டடைகிறது.]

(5) அவனுக்கு ஜலதோஷமும் காய்ச்சலும் கண்டு மிகவும்வருத்தப்பட்டான், *he got a cold and fever, and was very poorly.*

(6) அவனுக்கு வியாதிகண்டு நாட்பட்டதா? *Is it long since he fell ill?*

(7) இதை அவர் கையில் கொடுத்துக் கண்டுகொண்டுவா! *Take this in your hand and go to visit him!*

(8) என்னைக் காணாமல் செய்தான், *he did it when I was not there to see.*

(9) என்ன காணும்! *What is that!* (interjection [§§ 214, 193].)

LESSON 88.

THE VERB வை, *place* [§ 64].

§ **261**. This verb often seems redundant, and sometimes almost = போடு, or causal வி (§ 160).

(1) என்னைக் கட்டிவைத்து நீ போ, *tie me up and go yourself.*

(2) பொதியோடு வைத்துக்கொண்டு பிச்சைக்குப்போனசம்பந்தமாய் இருக்கிறது, *it is like the man who stored up his wealth in sacks and yet went a begging:* =போனதுபோல்.

(3) இவர்களைச் சாப்பிட்டு வரும்படி அனுப்பிவையும், *send him to eat* [probably a corruption of அனுப்புவியும், the causal (§ 160). This is frequent].

(4) தீ மிஞ்சவைத்தாலும் பகைமிஞ்ச வைக்கலாகாது, *although you heap up fire to increase, don't allow hatred to grow.*

(5) என் பேரிலே கோபம் வைக்காதே! *Don't be angry with me!*

(6) அவன் வீட்டுக்கு அடிவைக்கிறதில்லை, (*I*) *shall not tread his threshold.*

(7) அட்டையை எடுத்துமெத்தையில் வைத்தாலும் செத்தையைச் செத்தையை நாடும், *though you take a wood-louse and put it on a bed, it will ever seek the rubbish heap* [vulg. சேற்றை].

(8) அந்தக்காரியத்தை மூடிவைத்தால் வெளிப்படாதோ? *If you cover that affair will it not come abroad?*

(9) அண்டத்தைக் கையிலேவைத்தாட்டுவோனுக்குச் சுண்டைக்காய் மெத்தப்பாரமா? *To him who bears the globe in his hand and moves it is a chundē fruit a great weight?*

(10) வைத்தால் குடுமி, சிரைத்தால் மொட்டை, *if you preserve it—a tuft; if you shave it—baldness* (=I am in your power!).

(11) அவனுக்கு வெடிவைத்திருக்கிறான், *he is lying in wait for him* (lit. he has placed a shot for him).

(12) அவளை வைத்திருக்கிறான், *he keeps her* (improperly!).

LESSON 89.

IDIOMATIC USES OF THE VERB படு, *suffer* [§ 56. (II)].

§ 262. This Lesson is supplemental to § 92. The use of படு in forming a passive voice is seen in the following (*Tiru.* xi. 5):—

உதவி வரைத்தன்றுதவி; உதவி செய்யப்பட்டார் சால்பின் வரைத்து, *assistance is not measured by itself: it is measured by the worth of those to whom it has been done.*

For வரைத்து and அன்று compare § 184.

(1) அயோத்தியாபுரி ஆளப்பட்ட திரிசங்கு குமாரனாகிய அரிச்சந்திர மகாராசன், *Harischandra, the great king, son of Trisangu who reigned over Oude.* (ஆளப்பட்ட for ஆண்ட, as in Latin.)

(2) புறப்பட்டுப் போனார்கள், *they set out.* (படு with what we should call an adverb: புறம்.)

(3) கேள்விப்பட்டேன், *I heard it.* (படு with a noun.)

(4) அவன் தலை அம்மிக்கல்லிலே பட்டு உடைந்தது, *his head struck against the grinding stone and was broken.*

(5) அதற்கு அவர்கள் உடன்பட்டார்கள், *they agreed to it.* (படு with what is equivalent to a preposition.)

(6) பன்னிரண்டு அடி நீ பட்டுக்கொள், *you shall suffer twelve stripes.*

(7) உரலில் அகப்பட்டவை உலக்கைக்குத் தப்புமா? *Can the things which have got into the mortar escape the pestle?*

(8) மனையின் வாழ்வென்னும் வலையில் விழுந்து மானைப்போல் பிடிபட்டான், *like a hart caught in the toils he has fallen into the net of domestic felicity.* படு with a verbal root = பிடிக்கப்பட்டான்.

(9) காலடி பிட்டத்தில் படும்படியாக ஓடினான், *he ran so that his heels touched his hinders.*

(10) உபாயத்தினால் எல்லாம் கைவசப்படும், *all may be accomplished by stratagem.* (கையினுடைய வசத்திலே படும்.)

(11) In phrases, thus:

படுகாயம், *a mortal wound;*
பட்டமரம், *a dead tree.*

(12) இந்நான்கும் ஒருவனிடத்தில் இருந்தால் அவன் என்ன பாடுபடான்? *If these four are in him, what will he not suffer?*

(Comp. §§ 92, 161, 171.)

(13) பலவகைப் பட்ட = *of many kinds:* ஆன.

(14) இருக்கப்பட்ட = உண்டான.

LESSON 90.

AUXILIARY VERB இடு.

§ 263. In many idiomatic expressions it is hard to say whether the verb இடு, *place, put, give* (§ 68), is இடு or விடு (§ 254).

(1) பங்கிட்டுக் கொள்ளட்டும், *let them divide it among themselves.*

[பங்கு இடுகிறது,
a part, give.

கொள்ள gives the idea of *among themselves.* § 106.]

(2) தன் பெண்சாதியை இட்டுக்கொண்டு போனான், *he took his wife away with him.*

தன் மகனை இட்டுவந்தான், *he brought his son with him.*

[Here இட்டு is used for *taking with one, giving the hand to one.*]

(3) பெருவழக்கிட்டுச் சொல்லுகிறீர்கள், *you are making a great complaint of it.* [இட்டு=*making.*]

(4) அவர் அப்படி எண்ணம் இட்டுக் கொண்டிருக்கையில், *while he was thus thinking in his mind.* [இட்டு=*turning over, giving it his thought.*]

(5) பின்னிட்டுப் போகும்படி செய்தான், *he made* (them) *turn back.*

முன்னிட்டகாலைப் பின்னிட்டுத் திரும்பினான், *withdrawing the foot that he had advanced, he turned back.*

(6) மிகுந்த கூச்சல் இட்டான், *he made a great outcry.*

(7) நேரிட்ட வழியைப் பற்றிப் போனார்கள், *he went in the way that first presented itself.* (நேர், *opposite.*)

(8) கதவைமூடிப் பூட்டிட்டு வெளியில் வந்தான்.
He shut the door, locked it, and came out.

[Here இட்டு seems = UP: *he locked it up.* This is very common.]

(9) குற்றங் குறையக் குணம் மேலிட அருளை
§ 50. § 168.
உற்றவரே! ஆவிக்குறவாம் பராபரனே!
§ 87. § 74.

O thou, who possessest grace by which my faults diminish, and good dispositions increase within me! O God, kin of my soul!

[மேல் + இடு, *increase.* உற்றவர் from உறு, *be, possess.* குணம் for நற்குணம். உறவு, *relationship,* for உறவன், *a relation.*]

(10) அதை முன்னிட்டுக்கொண்டு அவரிடத்தில் போவேன், *I will make that a pretext for going to him.*

(11) அன்னம் இட்ட வீட்டில் கன்னம் இடலாமா? *Is it right to steal from a house where they have supplied (us) with food?*

(12) என் மந்தையிலே ஒரு பசு சதைபிடித்து மேனி இட்டிருக்கிறது.
In my herd a cow has picked up flesh and increased in size. [Here பிடி also is used idiomatically.]

(13) இப்படிக் கட்டளை இட்டருளும்! (§ 68.) *Grant me this! (Thus graciously give command.)*

(14) கை நடுங்கி மெய் நடுங்கி வாய் குழறி வீரிட்டழுது கொண்டாள், *with trembling hand, and trembling body, and stammering lips, she screamed aloud and wept.* [வீர், a mere imitative word.]

LESSON 91.

USES OF THE VERB அருள், *grant, vouchsafe* [§ 62].

§ 264. (1) தன்னிருப்பிடத்திற்கு எழுந்தருளினார், *he ascended benignant to his seat.*

(2) சுவாமி! எனக்கு ஒருநல்வாக்கு அருளவேண்டும், *sir! you must grant me a favourable reply.*

(3) புத்திரசந்தானம் அருளவேண்டும் என்று தவம் பண்ணினான், *he performed penances praying for male issue.*

(4) சிம்மாசனத்தில் வீற்றிருந்தருளினான், *he arose and benignly seated himself on his throne.*

(5) சுவாமிஅவர்கள் கற்பித்தருளியபடியே நடந்துகொண்டு போதாநின்றேன், *as my Lord shall please to direct I will conduct myself.*

[Here போதா நின்றேன் = வருகிறேன். The verb is போது-கிறது = போகிறது, but the strictly poetical form, போதா நின்றேன் = போதுகிறேன், is used. Comp. § 33.]

LESSON 92.

A KIND OF PASSIVE.

§ 265. Uses of the verb உண், *eat* (§ 56. III). This is from உள், and signifies *take in, receive; eat; suffer.*

(1) வெட்டுண்டார்கள், *they were cut down.*

(2) தூணில் கட்டுண்டவள், *she who was tied to a pillar.*

(3) அமுதம் உண்கிற நாவினாலே விஷம் உண்பாரோ? *Will they eat poison with the tongue that eats ambrosia?*

(4) மை கொட்டுண்டு போயிற்று, *the ink was spilt.*

(5) முட்டிக்கொண்டு குனியாதே, *don't stoop after you've hit your head.*

(6) ஆசைகொண்டு அலையுண்டு திரிகிறான், *he goes about distracted by his desires.*

[உண்டு is either = (1) *there is*, or (2) *having eaten*—past adverb. part. of உண், *eat* [§ 56. (III)], or (3) it is used for the passive, and so equivalent to பட்டு. In this last case உண்டு is added to the root. Comp. § 133. The causal of உண் is ஊட்டு (ஊண் = *food*). Hence ஊட்டு = படுத்து: பிழைப்பூட்டு, *support*.]

LESSON 93.

THE VERB அடி, *beat* [§ 64]. THE PRIMARY IDEA IS *down*.

§ 266. (1) இம்மூன்று பேரையும் மொட்டை அடித்துத் துரத்திவிட வேண்டும், *shave these three persons bare and send them away.*

(2) அடியாத நாடு படியாது, *a country which has not suffered, will not obey.* Not படிக்காது.

(3) இன்றைக்காகட்டும் நாளைக்காகட்டும் என்று அலை அடிக்கிறான், *to-day! to-morrow! saying, he causes me to dance attendance.* [அலைய, *to wander*; அடிக்கிறான், *he knocks me about*; ய omitted.] § 140.

(4) அவன் பிரசங்கிக்கிறதற்கு முன்னே ஒருவரும் தர்க்கம் பண்ணுமல் அடித்துப் போடுவான், *by his preaching he shuts the mouths of gainsayers.*

(5) பெருமழை அடிக்கிறபோது குளிராது; சிறு தூற்றல் தூறும்போது குளிரும், *it does not grow cool when heavy rain falls, but when gentle showers fall.*

(6) குதிரையைச் சவாரி அடிக்கிறான், *he rides the horse.*

(7) ஒரு சால் அடிப்பேன் இரண்டு சால் அடிப்பேன் சும்மா மடக்கி மடக்கி அடிக்க என்னுல் ஆகாது, *I will plough the land once, or even twice; but uselessly again and again I cannot plough it.* [Here அடி may refer to the bullocks that draw the plough!]

(8) அவ்வளவு சாதமும் கறியும் இரண்டு வாயிலே பூராவாய் அடித்துப் போட்டான், *all that rice and curry in two mouthfuls he ate up.*

(9) அந்தக் கடையைக் கொள்ளை அடித்துக்கொண்டு போய்விட்டார்கள், *they robbed that bazaar and made off.*

LESSON 94.

ENLARGEMENTS OF SUBJECT OR OBJECT.

§ 267. Some idiomatic uses of relative and adverbial participles (§ 25).

(1) அவன் வருகிற குறிப்பு, *the sign of his coming.*

(2) இவன் வருகிற தேதி, *the day of his coming.*

(3) நீ இறைக்கிற ஏற்றம், *the picota with which you are drawing water.*

(4) மணி கட்டுகிற காரணம் என்ன? *Why is the bell tied?*

(5) தன்னை அடித்த அடியைக் காட்டினான், *he showed the stripes he had suffered.*

(6) பால்கறந்த பசு, *a cow in milk.* See கற in Lex.

(7) நடக்கிற வேலை எப்படியும் நடக்கும், *an affair which is predestined will happen any how.*

(8) அந்த வீடு கட்டின பணம் இன்னஞ் செல்லவில்லை, *the money expended in building that house is not yet paid.*

(9) அதை அறிகிற அறிவு, *the knowledge of that.*

So, உணருகிற உணர்வு, *the feeling of a thing.*

(10) ஆனமுதலில் அதிகஞ் செலவாகிறது சரியல்ல, *it is not right that the expenditure should be greater than the capital.* [ஆன = *which has become;* முதல் = *capital.*]

(11) பிள்ளைகள் இருந்து ஆவதென்ன? *What is the use of their existence?* [For இருக்கிறதினால்.]

(12) பால்கொடாத எருமைகளைக் காப்பாற்றிப் பலன் உண்டா? *Is there any use in keeping buffaloes that yield no milk?*

(13) இப்படிப்பட்டவன் இருந்தென்ன? போயென்ன? *What matters it whether such a creature live or die?* [இருந்து as above. போய் = போவதினால்.]

LESSON 95.

FURTHER IDIOMATIC USES OF THE VERB ஆ-கு [§ 58].

§ 268. This resembles very closely the Latin FIO. Read with Lessons 43, 44.

(1) செய்யவேண்டியதெல்லாம் செய்தாயிற்று (செய்தாச்சு), *all is done that was to be done.* [ஆயிற்று = முடிந்தது, *is finished, completed;* கெடு ஆய்விட்டது, *the time is up.*]

(2) ஒருவனுடைய குணத்தை அறிகிறதற்கு முன்னே அவனுடனே சகவாசம் பண்ணல் ஆகாது, *before knowing a man's disposition to associate with him is unfit.*

So, இருக்கலாகாது, *it ought not to be,* §§ 103, 117, 118. [Here ஆகாது = தகாது, *it is not proper, fit.*]

சொல்லலாமா?	சொல்லலாம்;	சொல்லலாகாது.
May one say?	*One may say;*	*one may not say.*

(3) கெடு ஆன உடனே ஏன் அதைத் திருப்பிக் கொள்ளவில்லை? *Why did not you redeem it as soon as the date was expired?*

(4) காற்றாய்ப் பறந்தான், *he flew like the wind.* [ஆய் + ஆகி, verb. part. See § 40.]

(5) ஆகத் தொகை, *the sum total* (§ 136).

(6) ஆகட்டும், *let be!* (§ 140.)

(7) ஆனதல்லாமல் ஆவதறிவாரோ? *What has been one may know; who knows what is to be?*

(8) ஆனவன் ஆகாதவன் எல்லாத்திலும் உண்டு, *there are good and bad everywhere.*

[(9) வேறாய் புன்மக்கள், *perverse low people.*]

LESSON 96.

IDIOMATIC USE OF THE TENSES.

§ **269**. In நன்னூல் this is called *காலவழுவமைப்பு*=*sanctioned anomaly of time.* [II. G. §§ 146–149.]

(1) அவள் குடித்தனத்திறமை இல்லாதவள் என்று அறிந்
'*She* (is) *domestic affairs' ability one who is without,' I have*
தேன்.
discovered (=*I am aware*).

கடவுள் எங்கும் இருக்கிறார், *God is everywhere.*

(2) நீ இப்படிச் செய்வாய் ஆனால் செத்தாய், *if you do so you are a dead man.* (Past for present: absolute certainty.)

(3) நீ கேட்ட வரத்தைக் கொடுத்தேன், *your request is granted.* [No delay.]

(4) எட்டு நாளையிலே பிடித்துக் கொடுக்கிறேன், *I will find it out for you in eight days.* (Present for future.)

(5) நான் செயித்து வருகிறேன் என்றான், '*I will immediately conquer and return,' said he.* [Common வாறேன் வாறேன் = *I'm coming.*]

(6) என்னைத் தன் மந்தையைப் பார்த்துக்கொள்ளச் சொல்லுவான், *he often tells me to mind his herd.* (Future to denote custom.)

(7) எப்போதும் அதிசயத்தைப் பார்த்துக் கொண்டு திரிவான், *he is always going about seeking the wonderful.*

(8) முன்னோர்கள் அப்படிச் சொல்லுவார்கள், *our ancestors said (were wont to say) so.*

(9) இப்படிச் செய்வாய், *do this!* (Future for imperative.)

☞ (*a*) The past is used for the present in some few cases idiomatically and to indicate *certainty.*

(*b*) The present is often used for the future to indicate *certainty.*

(*c*) The future is used often to express *a habit* or anything *customary.*

(*d*) The future is used, as in English, *politely for the imperative.* This is especially common in poetry. [Comp. § 140. *c.*]

LESSON 97.

SOME POETICAL FORMS AND IDIOMS.

§ **270.** The object of this work is to teach the common Tamil, as spoken by all classes of the people. There are, however, certain poetical forms which must be understood before the learner can read the little works called ஆத்திசூடி, கொன்றைவேய்ந்தன், மூதுரை and நல்வழி, by the poetess Avvaiyār[1], which must be read and re-read!

A few of these will be illustrated here. All other poetical forms and idioms must be reserved till the learner is able to read the Ist, IInd, and IIIrd Grammars, where he will find full explanations of every poetical form and idiom[2].

(1) In beginning the study of Tamil poetry, the learner must remark that the signs of the cases are *very commonly elided.* This is called வேற்றுமைத் தொகை (வேற்றுமை, *a casal termination;* தொகை, *ellipsis.* III. G. 152).

அறஞ் செய விரும்பு (for அறத்தை).
Virtue to do desire.

பருவத்தே பயிர்செய்.
Cultivate in due season.

(பருவத்து from பருவம், *a season*, is prepared according to § 18 for the reception of the casal sign, which is omitted, and ஏ emphatic inserted.)

(2) Letters are constantly omitted whenever the rhythm requires it. In the above செய is for செய்ய[3]. (II. G. 41.)

(3) Participial nouns and appellatives (§ 185) are very frequently introduced.

[1] A valuable edition of some of these was published by the Rev. J. Sugden in Bangalore. A scholarly edition of the நீதிநெறிவிளக்கம் by Mr. Stokes, M.C.S., is one of the best helps the student of high Tamil can use.

The traditions current among the Tamil people regarding the 'wonderful old woman' are very numerous.

She was one day sitting in the porch of a temple with her feet stretched out straight before her—not considered to be a very respectful position in the presence of a superior.

The officiating priest rushed out to her with the question, '*Are you not ashamed to stretch out your feet in the presence of the Swāmi?*' சாமி இருக்கிற இடத்தில்கால் நீட்டவெட் கமில்லையா?

To which she replied: மெய்தான், ஐயா! சாமி இல்லாத இடத்தைக் காண்பித்தால் அங்கேபோய்க்கால் நீட்டுகிறேன், '*very true, sir! if you will show me where the Swāmi* (Lord) *is not, I will go and stretch out my feet there.*'

[2] These can be had from the Clarendon Press, Oxford.

[3] An amusing story turns on this:

A learned man presented himself before அதிவீரராமபாண்டியன், a celebrated

ஆறுவது சினம் (ஆறு, § 56. II, *grow cool*, fut. part. noun, neut. sing., § 88), *that which will* (must) *grow cool* (is) *anger*.

ஊக்கமது கைவிடேல் (a neut. appellative for ஊக்கம், *energy*), *hide* (*neglect*) *not that which belongs to energetic action*. (Matt. xxv. 18.)

(4) A negative imperative is often found, which is not at all used in common Tamil.

காவேல் (கா, *hide* + வ் + ஏல்), விலக்கேல் (விலக்கு, *remove*), விளம்பேல் (விளம்பு, *reveal*), விடேல் (விடு, *leave*), இகழேல் (இகழ், *despise*), *do not hide*, *remove*, *&c. &c.*

ஏல் (a lengthened form of அல், *not*) is added to the root of verbs which form their present with கிறு, and those which form the present with க்கிறு insert க்க். [II. G. 92.]

(5) The root of a verb is frequently prefixed to a noun and forms with it a compound. This is called வினைத்தொகை (வினை, *verb*; தொகை, *ellipsis*, an ellipsis of the inflexion of the verb).

செய்வினை திருந்தச் செய் (செய், the root used for செய்கிற or செய்யும், § 74). [II. G. 153.] *What you do, do well.*

Sometimes a letter is introduced for the sake of euphony.

சேர்விடம் அறிந்து சேர் (சேர், வ், இடம்; here the வ் may serve to express a future idea) : = *having ascertained the fit place for you to be in, take up your abode in it.*

This is a very common idiom. Thus, வாழ்நாள் (for வாழுகிற or வாழும்நாள்), *life-time*.

(6) The (சாரியை or) particle அத்து is used instead of a casal termination. Thus,

சான்றோர் இனத்திரு, *join thyself to the assembly of the worthy*. சான்றோருடைய இனத்து (= இனத்தினிடத்திலே) இரு. [II. G. 108.]

(7) தன் is inserted euphonically before the termination of a case, and is itself 6th and 5th cases in one. Thus,

கைப் பொருடன்னின் மெய்ப் பொருள் கல்வி.
Hand-wealth (material) *than*, *true wealth* (is) *learning*.

Here, for பொருளின் = *than wealth* (§ 21), பொருள் + தன் + இன் is used (ள் and த் coalesce in ட்).

king, himself a poet of no mean ability, and when the king demanded the reason of his coming, he replied :

தங்களைப் புத்தியிலாதவன் என்று அறிந்து வந்தேன்.
'*Your Majesty* *a senseless man* —— *knowing* *I came.*'

The courtiers stood aghast. The king, however, smiled and liberally rewarded the visitor. But why? இலாதவன் = இல்லாதவன், *one who is without*; and thus புத்தியில்லாதவன் = *one who is senseless*; but also புத்தியில் = *in sense*; and ஆதவன் = *a sun*: a high poetical word!

LESSON 98.

CAUTIONS USEFUL IN TRANSLATING ENGLISH INTO TAMIL.

§ **271.** (1) *Your perishing body*—is not உன் அழிந்துபோகிற சரீரம், but அழிவுள்ளஉன்னுடைய சரீரம் or அழிவுள்ளதாகிய உன் சரீரம்.

The adj. pronoun comes immediately before its noun.

(2) Do not think you may use the passive form (படு, § 92) wherever it occurs in English. Thus,

(*a*) *He ordered it to be given to her.* Not அவளுக்கு அது கொடுக்கப்படச் சொன்னார், but அவளுக்கு அதைக் கொடுக்கச்சொன்னார்.

(*b*) சுவரில் எழுதிய சித்திரம் போலச் சற்றும் அசையாது நின்றுகல்லுங் கரைந்துருகப் பாடினாள், *like a picture painted on a wall, not moving in the least, she sang so that a stone even would melt.* (Not எழுதப்பட்ட.)

(*c*) காம்பரிந்த புஷ்பங்கள், *flowers whose stalks are cut off.* (Not அரியப்பட்ட.)

(3) Do not think it necessary always to try to find a word for '*a*,' '*an*,' or '*the*' in translating.

This is a tree, இது மரந் தான் (§ 108. *c*). Not இது ஒரு மரமாய் இருக்கிறது!

This is the man I spoke of, நான் சொன்ன மனிதன் இவன்தான்.

(4) '*His*,' &c. may often be omitted, as in Latin and Greek, when *emphasis* or *distinction* is not implied. (§ 5.)

The boy learns his lesson, பையன் பாடம் படிக்கிறான். Not அந்தப் பையன்தன் பாடம் படிக்கிறான்!

She is gone to her house, அவள் வீட்டுக்குப் போய்விட்டாள். Not தன்னுடைய வீட்டுக்கு.

(5) *I have.* Not generally நான் உடையவனாய் இருக்கிறேன், but எனக்கு உண்டு. (§ 242.)

(6) *He told me who it was that did so,* இப்படிச் செய்தவன் இன்னான் என்று எனக்கு அறிவித்தான். Not இப்படிச் செய்தவன் ஆர் என்று! CONSIDER THE DIFFERENCE BETWEEN DIRECT AND INDIRECT QUOTATION.

(7) *He said he would come,* வருவேன் என்று சொன்னான் or தான் வருவதாகச் சொன்னான். Not வருவான் என்று சொன்னான். (§ 82.)

(8) A new nominative must not come in between the adverbial participle and the finite verb that completes a sentence. Thus,

The lawyer stated their case and the judge acquitted them, வக்கீல் அவர்களுடைய சங்கதியைப்பேசி, நியாயாதிபதி இவர்கள் பேரில் குற்றமில்லை என்று தீர்த்தார்.

This is quite incorrect. Render it rather thus:

வக்கீல் அவர்களுடைய சங்கதியைப் பேச (or பேசினபின்பு or பேசினான்) நியாயாதிபதி, &c.

RULE.—Whatever number of adverbial participles may come in a sentence they have all the same nominative as the final verb. (§ 77.)

(9) Idiomatic and figurative expressions must not in general be rendered literally. '*A watery grave*' is good English; தண்ணீருள்ள பிரேதக்குழி is ridiculous: தண்ணீரில் அமிழ்ந்தி இறந்தான் is Tamil.

(10) *He told me how to act.* Not எப்படிச் செய்யவேண்டும் என்று சொன்னார், but இன்னவிதமாகச் செய்ய வேண்டும் என்று கற்பித்தார் or செய்யவேண்டிய விதத்தை எனக்குக் கட்டளை இட்டார்.

(11) It is not always sufficient to translate the English infinitive mood by the Tamil (so-called) infinitive. (§ 168.)

Thus, என்னைக் காண வந்தார்கள், *they came to see me*, is correct, implying intention; but '*it is not right to do so*' is not அப்படிச் செய்யச் சரி அல்ல, but அப்படிச் செய்வது சரி அல்ல: *to do so = the doing so.* When it is an infinitive noun-phrase translate it accordingly. (§ 87.)

These cautions might be multiplied indefinitely. I add one general piece of advice: analyse well whatever you wish to put into Tamil; break it up into shorter sentences if necessary; transfuse ideas rather than translate words; never be content till you feel that the whole meaning is fully brought out in your version. Then carefully reconsider your MS. with a view to abridgement and condensation.

LESSON 99.

§ 272. TRANSLATION FROM ENGLISH INTO TAMIL.

Beschi well says, 'Saepe dicimus Latina verba, non latine; et saepius Europeam linguam loquimur Tamulicis verbis.' We often use Latin words without the Latin idiom, and still more frequently do we clothe European idiom in Tamil words.

The mind must be to a great extent imbued with Tamil habits of thought before a man can speak idiomatically. When the learner has with great labour and study acquired the habit of THINKING (and even of FEELING) in Tamil, he may hope to speak the language well; but not till then. Extensive reading and constant, thoughtful, sympathetic intercourse with Tamilians are essentially necessary to him who would excel.

A few examples may perhaps serve to aid the learner in translating. It is worth while to try these and similar sentences again and again, till you get a version not altogether unsatisfactory!

(I) 'Heaven is that fold of the great Shepherd into which no enemy enters, and from which no friend departs.'

And, first, as to the words: *Heaven*—is best rendered here by பரமண்டலம் (*the other sphere*); for this indicates *a place*, which the sense requires; and not *a state*, which மோட்சம் (*liberation*) signifies[1].

Fold,—மந்தை, தொழுவம். The former means the *herd* or *flock* rather; the latter *that in which they are enclosed.*

Great,—பெரிய means this; but மகா, பரம, சிரேட்ட, உன்னத, பிரதான are all words not inapplicable.

Shepherd,—மேய்ப்பர், *one who feeds.* Not இடையன், *a name for the caste.*

Enemy,—சத்துரு or பகைவன் (விரோதி, *an opponent*; எதிராளி, *an adversary*), பகைக்கிறவன்.

Enter,—உட்பிரவேசி (§ 56. III); புகு (§ 56. II), நுழை (§ 56. I), *creep in*; சேரு (§ 56. I), *draw near.*

Friend,—சிநேகிதன் (மித்துரு opposed to சத்துரு; அன்புள்ளவன் to பகைவன்), நேசிக்கிறவன்.

Depart,—விட்டுவிடு, போய்விடு, பிரிந்துபோ, விட்டுப்போ, விட்டுநீங்கு (§ 56. II).

Then the construction, if exact, will require the relative participle, and may run thus:

'*Heaven . . . no enemy entering, and no friend departing . . . of the great Shepherd . . . the fold . . . is.*' Otherwise, '*Heaven is the fold of the great Shepherd. No enemy enters it; no friend departs from it.*'

1. பரமண்டலமானது சத்துரு ஒருவனும் உட் பிரவேசியாததும் சிநேகிதன ஒருவனும் விட்டுப் போகாததுமான பிரதான மேய்ப்பருடைய மந்தை (or தொழுவம்) ஆய் இருக்கிறது.

2. பரமண்டலமானது பெரிய மேய்ப்பருடைய மந்தை. அதில்பகைக்கிறவன் நுழைவதும் இல்லை. நேசிக்கிறவன் பிரிந்து போவதும் இல்லை.

3. மோட்சம் பரம மேய்ப்பரின் மந்தையாம்; அங்கே பகைவன் ஒருவனுஞ் சேர்வதும் இல்லை, சிநேகிதன் ஒருவனும் விட்டு நீங்குவதும் இல்லை.

[1] The number of pairs of words for *this world* and *the world to come* is surprising. These are a few: இம்மை, மறுமை; இகம், பரம்; மண், விண்; பூமி, வானம்; பூலோகம், பரலோகம்; இம்பர், உம்பர்; வையகம், வானகம்; பூமண்டலம், பரமண்டலம்.

4. மோட்சமானது எதற்கு ஒப்பனையாம் என்றால், பெரிய மேய்ப்பருடைய தொழுவத்துக்கு ஒப்பாகும். எப்படியெனில், அத்தொழுவத்திலே பகைக்கிறவர்கள் வந்துசேரவும் மாட்டார்கள்; நேசிக்கிறவர்கள் அதை விட்டு பிரிந்துபோகவும் மாட்டார்கள்.

(II) 'He is the freeman whom the Truth makes free,
And all are slaves besides.'

WORDS.—*Freeman*, சுயாதீனன் = *one who rests on his own foundation.*
விடுதலையானவன், விடுதலை அடைந்தவன் = *one who has obtained release.*
விடுவிக்கப்பட்டவன் = *one who has been released.*
தன்னிச்சைக்காரன் = *one who lives as he likes.*

Truth, சத்தியம், மெய், உண்மை.

Slave, அடிமை = *a bond slave.*
கட்டுண்டவன் = *one who is bound.*
சிறை = *a captive.*

CONSTRUCTION.

By truth—a freeman made—freeman is; all else slaves are.

1. சத்தியத்தால் விடுவிக்கப்படவனே விடுதலையானவன்; மற்றெல்லாரும் கட்டுண்டவர்கள்.

2. சத்தியம் எவனை விடுதலை ஆக்கினதோ அவனே விடுதலை பெற்றவன்; மற்றயாவரும் சிறைகள்தான்.

3. சத்தியத்தால் சிறை நீங்கினவன், சிறை நீங்கினான்; மற்றயாவரும் சிறைப்பட்டவர்களே.

4. உண்மை அறிவினால் விடுதலை அடைந்தவனே விடுதலை அடைந்தவன்; மற்றெல்லாரும் அடிமைகளாய் இருக்கிறார்கள்.

(III) 'Vanitas est longam vitam optare, et de bonâ vitâ parum curare,' *it is vanity to desire to live long, and to care too little about living well.*

WORDS.—*Vanity*, மாய்கை; அவத்தம், *falsehood*; வீண், *vain*; வீண்காரியம், *a vain thing.*

Life, சீவன், ஆயுசு. The former, *life itself*; the other, *life-time.*
சீவகாலம், *life-time* (not pure Tamil); வாழ்நாள், *happy days.*

Long, நீளமான, நீண்ட, நீட்டமான, நெடிய, நெடு.
சிரக்காயிசு, Sanskrit = *long life.* பூரண ஆயிசு = *full age.*

Desire, விரும்பு (§ 62), ஆசி (§ 64), வேண்டு (§ 62), கோரு (§ 62), வாஞ்சி (§ 64); *care*, கவலைப்படு (§ 56).

Well, நன்றாய், செம்மையாய் (நல்லவனாய் = *as a good man*), நல்வழியில், *in a good way*. Here you will have to paraphrase.

To live, நட (§ 66), ஒழுகு (§ 64).

CONSTRUCTION.

About a good life, or living well—not caring—a long life (to live long)—*to desire is vanity*.

1. நல்லவனாய் வாழ்வதைக் குறித்துக் கவலைப்படாமல், தீர்க்காயுசுள்ளவனாய் வாழ வேண்டும் என்று

விரும்புவது	வீண்.
விரும்புகிறது	வீண்காரியம்.
ஆசிக்கிறது	விருதாவாம்.
ஆசிப்பது	மாய்கையாம்.

2. நெடுநாளாய்ப் பிழைக்கவேண்டி, நன்றாய்ப் பிழைக்க நாடாமல் இருப்பது மாய்கை. Here நன்றாய்ப் பிழைக்க is too literal, and almost unmeaning.

3. பூரண ஆயுசு விரும்பித் தேவபத்தியுள்ள ஆயுசு மறந்து விடுவது விருதாவாம்.

4. நன்மை நிறைந்த நாளாய் வாழவிரும்பாமல் நீண்டநாளாய்வாழ விரும்புவது அபத்தம்; or நீண்டநாளாய் வாழவிரும்பி, நன்மை நிறைந்த நாளாய் வாழவிரும்பாமல் இருப்பது வீண்.

[நன்மை நிறைந்த is ambiguous (as in the English *well*), and may refer only to *material prosperity*. The '*fruits of good living*' is a parallel case.]

The learner will find that this may be varied and amplified almost at pleasure, but the first expresses something of the meaning. The following verse embodies nearly the idea.

It is a *Kuṛṛaḷ veṇbā*.

பலநாள் பெரிதோ அறஞ்செய் திலனேல்?
நலஞ்செய் தொருநாள் பெரிது.

'*Are many days great if a man does not virtuous deeds? One day spent in doing good is great.*'

அறம், *virtue*; இலன் = இல்லாதவன், *one who is not*; செய்திலன், *one who has not done*; எல், *if*; நலம், *goodness*.

LESSON 100.

§ **273**. Imitative words like the following are in very frequent use in Tamil. Their use varies considerably in different localities.

(1) உலை தளதள என்று கொதிக்கிறது, *the rice-pot boils with a bubbling sound*.

(2) திடீல் என்று (திடீர் என்று) கீழே விழுந்தான், *he fell down with a thump.*

(3) அந்த நாய் வாள்வாளென்று கத்துகிறது, *that dog keeps up a howl.*

(4) சக்கரத்தைக் கிறுகிறென்று சுழற்றினான், *he turned round the wheel with a whirl.*

(5) கோ என்று புலம்பினான், *he wept aloud.*

(6) தண்ணீர் குளுகுளென்றிருக்கிறது, *the water is icy cold.*

(7) அடுக்குப் பானையைப் பூனை மடமடென்று உருட்டிவிட்டது, *the cat rolled over the pile of pots with a crash.*

(8) அவன் மளமளென்று பேசினான், *he spoke very loud.*

(9) வாய்க்காலிலே தண்ணீர் சிலு சிலு என்று ஓடுகிறது, *the water runs in the channel with a gurgling sound.*

(10) நடுநடுங்கிப் பயந்து கூவினான், *he cried out fearing and trembling greatly.*

(11) அவளிடத்தில் வாய் கொடுத்தால் மொலு மொலென்று சண்டைப் பிடிப்பாள், *if you let her talk she will get up a terrible quarrel.*

(12) கோழி பிலு பிலென்று புறப்பட்டது, *the fowls came forth with a rushing noise.*

(13) மழை சொளசொளென்று பெய்தது, *the rain came down in torrents.*

(14) உடம்பு கணகணென்று காய்கிறது, *the body is hot with fever.*

(15) இருந்தாற்போலே இருந்து படபடென்று மழை வந்துவிட்டது, *the rain came pattering down suddenly (other things continuing as they were).*

(16) பார்த்தும் பாராமல் படபடென்று பேசிவிட்டான், *he seeing saw not, but spoke rashly.*

(17) திருடன் திடுதிடென்று ஓடினான், *the thief scampered off sharp.*

(18) முறுக்கு மொறுமொறென்றிருக்கிறது, *the thin biscuit is very crisp.*

(19) உடம்பெல்லாம் வறவறென்றிருக்கிறது, *the whole body is parched up.*

(20) உடம்பு கொதுகொதென்று காய்கிறது, *the body is dry with fever.*

(21) வயிற்றிலே கொதுகொதென்று போகிறது, *the bowels are violently disturbed.*

(22) விளாம்பழம் குடுகுடென்று ஆடுகிறது, *the viḷām fruit rattles in its shell.*

(23) அந்தப் பட்டு வழவழென்றிருக்கிறது, *that silk is very soft.*

(24) அந்தத் துணி பொசுபொசென்று கிழிந்துபோச்சுது, *that cloth has torn* (being rotten before).

(25) சந்தனங் கமகமென்று மணக்கிறது, *the sandal yields a fragrant odour.*

(26) எனக்குக் கிறுகிறென்று வருகிறது, *I am quite bewildered,—my head whirls round.*

(27) அவனுக்கு உடம்பு என்னமோ விறுவிறென்றிருக்கிறது, *his body is somehow rather fat* (he wants a thrashing—is insolent).

(28) தூங்குகையிலே பல்லைநெறுநெறென்றுகடிக்கிறான், *he grinds his teeth in his sleep.*

(29) என்னமோ, முணுமுணென்று ரகசியமாய்ப் பேசினார்கள், *they talked about something or other in a low mysterious way.*

(30) என்னமோ, முகம் மினுமினென்றிருக்கிறது, *the face is somehow glistening.*

(31) அதைத் தொட்டால் கொளகொளென்றிருக்கிறது, *if you touch it, it is soft.*

(32) நகைகள் பளபளென்று மின்னுகிறது, *the jewels glisten very brightly.*

(33) அந்த வீட்டிலே நெருப்பு சுருசுரென்று பிடித்து, பகபகென்றுபற்றி, மடமடென்று எரிந்துபோச்சுது, *the fire seized that house briskly, burned brightly, and the house is burnt up.*

(34) எந்நேரமும் வெடுவெடென்று பேசுகிறான், *he is always speaking sharply.*

(35) ஆற்றிலே வெள்ளம் மொகுமொகென்று வருகிறது, *the water comes down in the river.*

(36) உடம்பு பசபசென்றரிக்கிறது, *the body is itching all over.*

(37) சுவரெல்லாம் உப்படித்து பொலபொலவென்று உதிருகிறது, *the whole wall is crumbling away with the salt air.*

(38) அவன் நன்றாய்த் தடதடென்று வாசிக்கிறான், *he reads fluently.*

(39) மழை பெய்தபின் புல்லு பசபசென்று முளைத்திருக்கிறது, *after the rain the fields are green with grass.*

Many nouns are formed in this way:

சுறுசுறுப்பு, *diligence;* பசபசப்பு, *an itching sensation;* கடுகடுப்பு, *severity;* விறுவிறுப்பு, *a numbness of the limbs;* துடிதுடிப்பு, *palpitation;* கிறுகிறுப்பு, *giddiness.*

LESSON 101.

IDIOMATIC SENTENCES.

§ 274. Each of these is a formula.

(1) பழிபாவத்துக்கஞ்சாததுஷ்டன், *a wretch who fears neither guilt nor sin.* (பழிக்கும் பாவத்துக்கும் அஞ்சாத துஷ்டன்.) [Here உம் is omitted.]

(2) தங்களிடத்தில் இப்படி விண்ணப்பஞ் செய்யலானேன், *I have thus made my petition to your worship.* [செய்யல், *the doing;* ஆனேன், *I have become.*]

(3) In the conclusion of a letter இப்படிக்கு stands for '*thus writes,*' &c., = the old form '*this from your*' (loving friend, &c.).

(4) இவ்விரண்டு பேருக்கும் பேர்பாதியாகக் கொடுத்துவிடுவோம், *we will give half to each of these two persons.* [பேர்பாதியாக = ஒவ்வொருவனுக்கும் பாதியாக; or பெயர்.]

(5) என் உடைமையை இப்படியாக விலைமதிக்கவும் நேரிட்டதா? *Has it come to this that my goods should be so estimated?* [நேர், *right in the way, direct;* இடு, *give, be;* நேரிடு = *come to pass, happen.*]

(6) சாட்சிகளைக் கொண்டு வாதிநிசப்படுத்தினால் தண்டனைக்குள்ளாவேன், *if the complainant prove it by witnesses, I will be subjected to punishment.* [உள், *within, under;* ஆவேன், *I shall become.*]

(7) தங்கள் வித்தையினுடைய அருமை பெருமைகளைக் காண்பித்தார்கள், *they showed off the rareness and greatness of their learning.* [அருமை and பெருமை joined together, and the plural termination added to the latter.]

Thus, சுகதுக்கங்கள், *joys and sorrows.*

(8) இந்தக்குதிரைகள் என்ன விலை? *What is the price of these horses?* [An ellipsis of the 4th case.] இந்தக் குதிரைகளுக்கு . . .

(9) அதைச் சொல்ல வாய்வராமல் மரம்போல் நின்றான், *he stood like a tree, unable to say it* [lit. *the mouth not coming*].

(10) மேலுக்குச் சம்மதித்தவனைப்போலச் சொன்னான், *he spoke as though he approved of it.* [மேலுக்கு, *outwardly.*]

(11) காற்றுவிசேஷமாகக் கேள்விப்பட்டார், *he heard it reported.* [காற்று விசேஷமாய், *as a thing borne by the winds.*]

(12) முறை முறையாக, *respectively, in order.* [Repetitions of this kind are frequent: thus, அன்றன்று (அன்று, அன்று), *day by day.*]

(13) செல்வம் யாவரிடத்திலும் நிலையாது; தேர்க்கால் போல் கீழ்மேலாய்வரும், *prosperity abides not with any one, but like a chariot wheel turns upside down.*

(14) In சிதற அடி, *put to rout* (§ 56. III); பறக்கடி, *put to flight;* and similar forms, there is a contraction:

சிதற அடித்தான் = சிதறும்படி அடித்தான், §§ 168, 157.
பறக்க அடித்தான் = பறக்கும்படி அடித்தான், §§ 168, 157.

(15) பார்க்கப் பார்க்க மனோரம்மியமாய் வேடிக்கையாய் இருக்கும், *the more one looks the more the spectacle satisfies the mind* (the infinitive doubled, § 168. Thus, வர வர = *by degrees*).

(16) அந்த மகா பாதகன் இன்னான் என்று உனக்கு முன்னே
['*That great sinner such an one' saying to thee before*
அறிவித்தேன் அல்லவா?
I told, did I not?] *I told you before, did I not, who was the great sinner?*

புருஷன் இன்னான் என்று குறிப்புக் காணமாட்டாமல் திகைத்தாள், *she feared, not being able to recognize her husband.* [இன்னான் = *such an one.*]

(17) இந்தநான்கும் ஒருவனிடத்தில் இருந்தால் அவன் என்ன
If all these four be with a man what will he
பாடுபடான்?
not suffer?

(உம் = *all.*) ☞ The idiom here is English.

(18) அந்தப்பிள்ளைகளைத் தன்வீட்டுக்கு அழைத்துக்கொண்டுபோனான், *he took the children home with him.* (Observe the use of அழை.)

(19) யாவரும் மேலான காரியத்தையே ஆலோசிக்க வேண்டும், அது கைகூடாவிட்டாலும் பெருமைவரும், *all must meditate great things; if they are unattainable, still greatness will be the result.*

(20) நீர் சொன்னபடியே கேட்பேன், *I will obey you strictly.* [கேட்பேன், *I will hear.* To hear is to obey, in Tamil.]

(21) அதுகாரியம் (for அந்தக் காரியம்), *that affair.* [Here அது and காரியம் are put in apposition.]

(22) அவனுக்கு ஏக்கம் பிடித்து விசனத்துடனே படுத்துக் கொண்டான், *deep distress seized him and he lay down with grief.* [Both பிடி (§ 56. I) and எடு (§ 56. I) are used idiomatically. எனக்குப் பசி எடுக்கிறது, *I am hungry.*]

(23) அதற்கவர்கள் சொன்னது: எங்களுக்குத் தெரியாது, *they said, 'We don't know.'*

(24) வலதுகாது, *the right ear;* இடதுகாது, *the left ear.*

வலதுகை, *the right hand;* very commonly சோற்றுக்கை, *the rice hand.*

இடதுகை, *the left hand;* very commonly பீச்சக்கை, *the hand used for baser purposes.*

(25) கொழுப்பேறியிருக்கிறது, *it is grown fat.* [கொழுப்பு ஏறி இருக்கிறது, *fat—having ascended—is.*]

காரியம் நடந்தேறி வருகிறது, *the affair is prospering.* [நடந்து ஏறிவருகிறது, *going on—ascending—it comes.*]

(26) அவனை அழைத்தனுப்பினேன், *I sent for him.* [Here the adverb. part. அழைத்து seems to be used for the infin. அழைக்க = *I sent to call him.*]

So, கேட்டனுப்பு, *send to inquire* = கேட்கும்படி அனுப்பு.

(27) குரு உபதேசித்தானவுடனே.

[உபதேசித்து (§ 77. (*b*)) ஆன (§ 130) உடனே (§ 106. (2)).]

As soon as the Guru had finished teaching.

So, அவன் பெரியவன் ஆன பிறகு, *after he was grown up.*

(28) அட்டாலும் | பால்சுவையிற் | குன்றா | தளவல்ல
100 245 110
நட்டாலு | நண்பல்லார் | நண்பல்லர்;
கெட்டாலும்
மேன்மக்கண் | மேன்மக்க | ளே; சங்கு | சுட்டாலுந்
தான்மிக்க | வெண்மை | தரும். [மூதுரை, 4.]

அளவு + அல்ல = *abundantly*. அல்லார், அல்லர் = *persons destitute of*. (§§ 43, 121.)

Tho' (you) boil (it), milk's taste is not deteriorated;
Tho' without measure (you) cultivate (their) friendship, (the) unfriendly ones are unfriendly (still);
Tho' ruined, the lofty-souled are lofty-minded (still);
Tho' (you) burn conch-shells, they yield abundant whiteness.

(29) கற்க கசடற கற்பவை; கற்றபின்,
140 168 88, 50 85
நிற்க அதற்குத் தக! [*Kurraḷ*, 391.]
242 168

So learn that thou mayst faultless learning gain;
To lesson learnt obedient aye remain!

END OF THE LESSONS.

GENERAL INDEX

[The numbers refer to the sections, unless otherwise marked.]